S0-ALL-404

Poiret, Dior and Schiaparelli

Poiret, Dior and Schiaparelli

Fashion, Femininity and Modernity

Ilya Parkins

London · New York

English edition
First published in 2012 by
Berg
Editorial offices:
50 Bedford Square, London WC1B 3DP, UK
175 Fifth Avenue, New York, NY 10010, USA

© Ilya Parkins 2012

All rights reserved.
No part of this publication may be reproduced in any form
or by any means without the written permission of Berg.

Berg is an imprint of Bloomsbury Publishing Plc.

Library of Congress Cataloging-in-Publication Data

Parkins, Ilya.
Poiret, Dior and Schiaparelli : fashion, femininity and modernity / Ilya Parkins.
p. cm.
Includes bibliographical references and index.
ISBN 978-0-85785-326-4 (alk. paper)
ISBN 978-0-85785-327-1 (alk. paper)
ISBN 978-0-85785-329-5 (alk. paper)
ISBN 978-0-85785-328-8 (alk. paper)
1. Women's clothing—Social aspects. 2. Clothing and dress—Social aspects.
3. Fashion—Social aspects. 4. Feminism—Social aspects.
5. Dior, Christian. 6. Schiaparelli, Elsa, 1890–1973. 7. Poiret, Paul.
8. Fashion designers—France. 9. Women fashion designers—France. I. Title.
GT1720.P37   2012
391'.2—dc232012012690

British Library Cataloguing-in-Publication Data

A catalogue record for this book is available from the British Library.

ISBN   978 0 85785 326 4 (Cloth)
           978 0 85785 327 1 (Paper)
e-ISBN 978 0 85785 328 8 (institutional)
           978 0 85785 329 5 (individual)

Typeset by Apex CoVantage, LLC, Madison, WI, USA.
Printed in the UK by the MPG Books Group

www.bergpublishers.com

Dedicated to Lorraine Code

Contents

List of Figures

Acknowledgements

The research for this book was supported by the Social Sciences and Humanities Research Council of Canada. Additional financial resources were gratefully received from the University of British Columbia Okanagan's Internal Grants program.

As with any project involving historical sources, librarians, archivists and museum curators have been an invaluable source of support and help. Dominique Revellino of the Musée Galliera's library, Dilys Blum of the Philadelphia Museum of Art, and especially Caroline Pinon of the fashion library at the Musée des Arts Décoratifs have given generously of their time and knowledge. I also thank librarians at the Bibliothèque Nationale de France and various City of Paris libraries, and Maria Montas of the CBS News Archives, for their provision of key texts.

I was fortunate to have the assistance of many people as I gathered the images for this book: Sherri Savage of the UBC Okanagan library was extremely helpful. Tricia Smith and Michael Slade of Art Resource went above and beyond in their assistance. Giema Tsakuginow of the Philadelphia Museum of Art and staff at the University of Washington Libraries' Special Collections and CSS Photography also came through with important illustrations.

Lara Haworth was an exceptional research assistant. I relied on her wisdom, discernment, and sleuthing ability and I am thankful both for her help and her friendship; she and Nicole Cormaci were bright lights in my life as I worked on this book. I am also grateful to Johanna Olson, who came through with last-minute help when the manuscript was being finalized.

I am deeply indebted to several wonderful friends who read key pieces of the text and asked questions that helped me to strengthen it: Elizabeth Sheehan, Rob Heynen and Marlo Edwards. My father, Bob Parkins, provided his keen editorial eye at an important point. All the members of my online writing group, and most especially Susan Gaylard, have helped me to situate a fulfilling writing practice in the context of a whole life. Other friends and colleagues have been equally generous and encouraging: I thank T. L. Cowan, Lois Cucullu, Jane Garrity and Celia Marshik for both facilitating the dissemination of earlier versions of this work in a number of presentations, and providing much-needed intellectual community.

At the University of British Columbia Okanagan, I have been lucky to work with Diana French and Cynthia Mathieson, who were especially kind and accommodating during this process. I am grateful to all of my colleagues in Community, Culture, and Global Studies for providing such a supportive and collegial interdisciplinary environment over the course of my research and writing. I wish to thank Shelley Pacholok for her friendship as we navigated the vagaries of our academic lives.

Ainsley Kling saw me through the last half of writing this book, enriching my life immeasurably and bringing much-needed balance, perspective and levity to the process. She also provided meals, escapes and cheering that sustained me. I know that this book is better for her presence and her love.

An earlier version of chapter 1 appeared as 'Fashion as Methodology: Rewriting the Time of Women's Modernity', *Time & Society* 19, no. 1 (2010): 98–119. Minor portions of chapter 3 were published in 'Elsa Schiaparelli and the Epistemology of Glamorous Silence', *Topia: Canadian Journal of Cultural Studies* 25 (2011): 90–5.

Introduction: Fashion, Femininity and Modernity in Designer Self-fashioning

This is a book about the ways that femininity and modernity were related to one another through fashion, symbolically and actually, in the first half of the twentieth century. By examining the ways that couturiers Paul Poiret, Elsa Schiaparelli and Christian Dior represented themselves in their memoirs and other writings, it traces the complexities and contradictions embedded in the modern as a relatively new way of understanding and relating to time. The concept of the modern began to have some significance for Western cultures around the time of the Renaissance, in what is conventionally known as the early modern period. It was deeply enmeshed with the rejection of authority—of both the church and monarchical structures of governance. As a counter to received authority, the modern first raised the idea of the human as a powerful, rational and self-governing being. The ideological heritage of the early modern era coalesced in the late eighteenth century, at the close of the Age of Enlightenment. Toward the end of this century, we can trace the rise of a concept of the human being as a 'sovereign subject of all possible knowledge'.[1] That is, the (male) human came to be seen as immensely powerful, having the capacity to know everything through reason. The modern concept of the self stabilized in this era: aside from reason and knowledge, that model of human selfhood included the ability to reflect on the self, the capacity for progressive development, a deep interiority that belied the surface presentation of the self, and a sense of apartness and individuality. It must be noted that white men with some wealth were seen to be the essence of the human; people of colour, working-class people and women of all races were imagined not to possess this same capacity for reflexivity, reason, depth or positive development.

In the nineteenth century, we can begin to identify the elements of modernity that influenced the structure of the modern fashion industry. This is a period distinguished, as Marshall Berman notes, by an ethos of experiment and revolution in the arts on one hand (modernism), and industrialization and urbanization (modernization) on the other.[2] Both of these processes involve conceptions of movement, speed and change. Modernity has long been associated with the thrilling violence of dynamic self-fashioning. As heirs of modernity, Western subjects were and are conditioned by concepts of renewal, temporal and spatial change, perpetual movement and fragmentation. As Harvie Ferguson puts it, '[m]odernity comes to itself in perpetual inner motion, as a continual process of restless self-production.'[3] Here is the connection to fashion: it is fashion's relationship to time that makes it such a quintessentially modern form.

Fashion is also modern because it embodies within itself the two poles of modernity: aesthetic modernism and industrial modernization. This is unusual, for although both of these elements are indispensable to any definition of modernity, they were—and often still are—imagined as distinct from one another, even opposed to one another. In fact, many critics argue that this ideological opposition, which essentially translates into a dichotomy between art and commerce, is a structuring principle of modernity. Thus, fashion calls attention to the foundations of the modern, revealing these two poles to be uneasily shifting toward one another. Fashion, we could say, performs the important task of revealing the cracks in modernity's façade. More specifically to this book, Poiret, Schiaparelli and Dior had an important role to play in the shaping of ideas about what was modern in the first half of the twentieth century.

WOMEN AND THE TIME OF MODERN FASHION

In an article about the mysterious state of being *à la mode*, which appeared in the April 1930 issue of Paris *Vogue*, the anonymous author characterizes fashion in these terms: 'Fashion is indifferent, like forgetfulness. She ignores what she no longer loves, she only appears fickle because she is so loyal— loyal to her own desire to please.'[4] Fashion here is personified—as a woman. Not only is she a woman, but she is a fickle woman, too. These, of course, are familiar metaphors to the contemporary reader, and would already have been equally banal to *Vogue*'s readers almost a century ago. The equation of women with fashion, and fashion with inconstancy, was by then long-established. And it rested upon a linking of women, adornment and artifice, only to denigrate each one.[5] Notions of naturalness and artifice have long and gendered histories in Western cultures, being closely connected to images of clothing or veiling. In the biblical story of Adam and Eve and their fall, the state of paradise is a state of nakedness, and therefore is authentic and free from deceit in the form of artifice. As Efrat Tseëlon observes, 'since the Fall is blamed on the woman, the links between sin, body, woman and clothes are easily forged.'[6] This association is a tenacious one, and it is part of the reason why feminists have had such a conflicted relationship to fashion as a concept and a practice.

Invoking the relationship of fashion with women and with changeability also speaks to a particularly modern *time signature*, as it were.[7] As Elizabeth Wilson puts it, '[f]ashion is dress in which the key feature is rapid and continual changing of styles. Fashion, in a sense *is* change.'[8] Indeed, that change is popularly figured in the fashion world as a constant orientation to the *new*, as if fashion were relentlessly innovative. That promise of novelty and innovation is certainly what has sold fashion for centuries—and by the time this *Vogue* commentary on the changeability of fashion was published in 1930, it was being borne out in the capacities of industrial production, which promised more new things, faster. But it is surely more complex than that, the temporality of fashion. For instance, fashion historians point out that periodic, cyclical temporal rhythms were part of what defined the advent of fashion—usually considered to have emerged and taken its distinct form in the cities of fourteenth-century Italy. This cyclical character accelerated in the nineteenth century, and it was reflected in everything from the standardizing of industrial production of dress, to the clockwork regularity of designer collections and the periodic revivals of historical dress styles that brought the past into the present. The 'fickle' quality of fashion, then, has a contradictory character: is it the logic of novelty or a grim reminder of the impossibility of true change?

If we foreground the peculiar *time signature* or *temporality* that is at the root of modern fashion's changeability, then we also need to consider what that temporality might mean for femininity, which is so readily associated with fashion and its rhythms. In the early decades of the twentieth century, the constant invocation of 'the new' in the realm of fashion actually contained, as some feminist historians and fashion analysts have recognized, the potential to situate women firmly in the modern.[9] In fact, when cultural commentators and theorists such as Charles Baudelaire, Georg Simmel and Walter Benjamin pointed to fashion's unique tempo as exemplary of Western industrial modernity, they were unwittingly placing women at the very heart of this era characterized by discourses of novelty, dynamism and fragmentation.[10]

If it is true that the feminization of fashion aligned women with the accelerated tempo of modernity, then this was a significant intervention. Rita Felski and others have traced the persistent longing for the impossible ideal of a 'prehistoric' woman, a foil against the uncertainties of modernity.[11] This conservative concept of femininity was characterized by its inflexibility; women apparently embodied a core or essence, a quiet, placid quality, that was impervious to cultural change: 'woman … stands for the behind and the beyond, for the sublime mystery of temporal otherness; she is the token of a far-distant past as well as a future that exceeds our grasp.'[12] The concept of women as static beings who stand unchanging outside or beyond history, of course, neatly removes them from the landscape of the modern, since the modern is about relentless change. Fashion's tempo intervenes, though: as a reflection of a frantically paced modern condition, it offered a very different account of femininity. It seemed to admit women into modern time, into the fabric of social and cultural action.

Thus we must not consider the unjustly trivialized realm of fashion and dress peripheral to accounts of modernity. Rather, fashion fuelled or animated pervasive understandings of modernity as characterized by a 'crucial shift in time consciousness', one in which the social world could be seen 'in a state of flux or motion'.[13] What is most significant about fashion's peculiarly modern temporality is that it functions as a kind of double category, relating the abstraction of time consciousness to the bodies of its models, wearers and consumers. Thus fashion knots together the macro and the micro, the grand and the mundane, in intriguing ways. It relates women's everyday lives to the broad sweeps of history, clearly juxtaposing those lives with the intricacies of production, consumption and other areas of public culture. In this sense, studies of fashion take seriously everyday lives and experiences of moderns, honouring people's intimate investments in the clothing they wore and the symbolic systems in which they participated through that wearing. Fashion is a key mode of accessing the rhythms of public culture and modern history—and for women consumers in the early twentieth century, it was a key mode of participating in modernity.

A focus on the meanings that surround the consumption of fashion, though, is not enough to explain how the tempo of the fashion industry was modern—and how it was gendered. Perhaps more than other consumer items, fashion's consumption is dependent on and bound up with its marketing, with the way it is constructed and represented by the industry itself. Fashion's production cannot neatly be hived off from its consumption. Any cultural analysis of fashion and its operations must include the conditions of its production and marketing, and any understanding of the modern industry and its peculiar relationships with time demands an analysis of both production and consumption.[14]

TIMING WOMEN AND FEMININITY IN FICTIONS OF THE DESIGNER SELF

Attention to the industry itself does not necessarily entail turning the critical gaze away from personal, consumptive mediations of fashion. Attention to the couturier is a useful complement to studies of fashion that ask what kinds of selves are enabled through dress and what is involved in self-fashioning. Particularly remarkable in assessing the body of written work related to a couturier is the degree to which designers were consciously engaged in their own image creation and manipulation. Beginning in the 1860s with Charles Frederick Worth, Western fashion designers became high-profile public personae, and designers themselves were instrumental in facilitating this shift. They played upon social class as they successfully cultivated links with cultural elites and artistic avant-gardes to increase their cultural capital, while their fashion houses benefited financially from the so-called 'democratization' of fashion (the ever-increasing production, accessibility and visibility of fashionable clothes). Various designers accrued individual mystiques, which allowed them to profit from the fashion industry's emphasis on novelty and originality.[15] In the twentieth century, in the wake of modernist experimentation across the visual and performance arts to which fashion was linked, designers projected images of themselves by establishing relationships to such categories as the 'new', the 'classic', and the 'timeless'. The self-representational labour done by designers is above all an exercise in mediating *time*.

A careful reading of fashion-designer writings reveals that figures of women and femininity *in time* were absolutely central to the creation of many fashion designers' public personae by the early twentieth century. It is for this reason that Poiret, Schiaparelli and Dior are at the centre of this work: unique temporal rhetorics inform their self-representations. These three very different designers are linked through their complex articulations of the relationship between past, present and future, which connect with the temporal status of fashion more generally across the first half of the twentieth century. One of the remarkable features of these fashion designers' representations of themselves and their work is the constant invocation of and femininity as either modern or prehistoric. Women figured concretely as muses, models and clients; and femininity figured as an abstraction that helped to drive the myth-making efforts of designers. Figures of women and femininity are invoked throughout the life writing of these three couturiers, and appear in notably complex and often seemingly paradoxical ways.

These texts thus complicate the picture, often advanced by fashion historians and feminist critics, of an early twentieth-century femininity whose modern status was unproblematically guaranteed by fashion's constant appeals to the 'new'. Though designer life writing has received virtually no critical attention—presumably because these texts are dismissed as mass-market fluff—these are highly complex texts. In them, fashion-consuming women appear as unstable, vastly contradictory categories, and ultimately women's ardent relationship to fashion aligns them with irrationality and works to position them in opposition to the modern. This is a far cry from the image of the 'new' woman that dominates much of the feminist historical and critical literature on early twentieth-century fashion. Attention to the life writing of designers is critical because it complicates the narrative we tell ourselves about the positioning of women in relation to fashion—and, ultimately, in relation to the modern itself.

This is not to say that the images found in these texts are straightforward. At their heart, like the women portrayed in them, these are highly unstable, deeply changeable representations of women and of femininity. The books slip with breathtaking ease from portraits of liberated, chic and thoroughly modern women to depictions of femininity as an inconstant, unreasonable and mysteriously ancient mode of being in need of modern mastery by the designer. The way that these couturiers' masterful self-assertions give way to descriptions of relationships with women suggests a fluctuating rhetoric of self that mirrors the changeable tempo of the fashion industry. As an exercise in self-fashioning, the life writing of designers has a unique time signature that seems to bear the burden of the specific, temporal pressures imposed by fashion design. Just as fashion does, the representation of self in these texts moves between an allegiance to industry and to art, the former with its almost frantic, historically contingent tempo, the latter with its gestures toward the eternal. The result is a collective portrait of the designer at the intersection of two ways of knowing the world: through art and through industry. Their memoirs are an important forum for the construction of coherent and masterful selves, which are necessary for coherent and successful business strategies and design houses. That the works fail to register such coherence points to the pressures experienced by both the industry and its major figures. This study takes as its point of departure the complicated relationship between aesthetics and commerce, which were meant, according to dominant understandings of art, to be opposed to one another. The analysis is indebted to and follows from the work of Nancy J. Troy, whose *Couture Culture* established that the art/industry tension shaped the face of modern fashion. As the studies of individual designers make clear, this was a contradiction that they attended to in their own fashioning of public personae.

Such contradictions are not incidental or innocent (though they may well have been unconscious), but are a crucial component of the work of consolidating designer identity. Projecting an identity was itself key to the larger project of self-promotion and to the marketing of a fashion house, and it mattered to the business that these texts were unstable and ambiguous. As Penelope Deutscher puts it, 'ambiguity can be constitutive.'[16] It can *produce* states of being, ideas, ideologies; it does not merely reflect them. That is, instability does not necessarily *destabilize* destructive cultural constructions of gender: 'there is no reason to think that exposing gender as founded in incoherence contributes to the dissolving of gender.'[17] Rather, 'the masculine connotations of reason are mobilized by their instability.'[18] It is this kind of mobilization that interests me: what effects did the complex, internally contradictory self-representations of designers have on the structure of gender in modernity? It is often real women or a figural femininity—in Elsa Schiaparelli's case, her own femininity—along with conceptions of time, that provide the ground for the fractures of identity. The concept of femininity as temporal thus underlies the industry's persistent ambiguities: between art and commerce, between past and present, between spectacular and intimate. What does it mean that femininity—metaphorically, if sometimes in extremely sub-tle ways—is invoked as the ground on which the industry's contradictions lie?

Eva Feder Kittay notes that '[w]omen's activities and women's relation to man persistently are used as metaphors for man's activities and projects. In these metaphors, man mediates his engagement with the world through a representation of it as Woman and metaphorically transposes his relation to Woman on to his relation to the world.'[19] This underscores the nature of the self-portrayals of designers (although the suggestion that it is always *men* using women as others is challenged by the case of Schiaparelli, a woman who uses women as others). The use of women as mediators expresses precisely what is at stake in the fashion designers' self-representations in their relation to time. Kittay suggests that the mediating function moves 'be-tween an assimilated … conceptual domain and a distinct and separate do-main which needs to be newly assimilated or reconceptualised', so that it can be made 'intelligible'.[20] Women, in other words, help men work through new ideas. In temporal terms, the woman-as-metaphor thus facilitates the de-signer's movement from the knowable domains of the past and present into the imagined future: a time that is unknowable but still crucially important to the success of any designer. The woman is highly changeable, and takes on a number of different roles as a mediator. Sometimes, she emerges as a kind of balm for the stresses of modern life; she is the guarantor of the possibil-ity of escape. In this sense, the woman mediates between present and fu-ture as sites of fear, and the past as a site of certainty and comfort; but she ultimately steps outside of this duality altogether to become timeless. Other times, she appears as a vector of the future and thus becomes the figure which the designer uses to mediate her or his relationship to that future. Can it be mastered, penetrated, pressed into service? The ambivalent movement between times is a source of anxiety in the fashion designer's domain: the industry's demands upon designers to speak simultaneously for the present, the past, the future and the timeless leads to angst. These women become metaphors for the unease produced by this complex time. Femininity emerges as a key symbol not only of time but of *anxious* time.[21] As Robert Smith ar-gues, '[m]odernism is anxious about the loss of a solid objective, the loss of something behind temporal sequence.'[22] Modernism, with its strident belief in the capacity for newness, is nevertheless insecure about that newness. For novelty relates to knowledge or the lack of knowledge; it points to the decline of certainty. If something is new, it is unknown.

Attention to these figures helps us see that the temporal negotiations of fashion were also negotiations of *knowledge* in a Western cultural land-scape characterized by increasing fragmentation and disorientation on mul-tiple fronts. The self-representations of designers reveal them to be navigating fashion as an important symptom of a broader unease about modernity.

Fashion stood as a primary vector of an emergent way of knowing that was contingent, shifting and uncertain. Fashion's spectacles, as the twentieth century wore on, became increasingly abstract and extra-rational. Elements of abstraction, minimalism and surrealism in the visual language of fashion—window displays, magazine illustrations, and photography—were visible beginning in the late 1910s in France and the late 1920s in the United States. From early in the century, fashion was a form that embodied the kinds of questions and dilemmas about knowledge that were being worked through in social life more broadly. In this sense, it was paradoxical. Fashion traded in both the abstract (the unknowable, the imaginary) and the material (tangible clothing).

The role that women play in the self-representations of designers reflects this odd doubleness. They are mobile images, figuring either as abstract and symbolic, or as concrete and material. They are used by the designers to oscillate between registers of abstraction and solidity. In a commentary on the roles of women in Enlightenment philosophy, Natania Meeker calls this spectral quality of femininity 'dematerialized matter'.[23] The concept of dematerialized matter is useful in thinking about the appearances of women in fashion-designer life writing. Their shift from material bodies into an ephemeral and abstract substance is never complete. Rather, these representations reconstitute endlessly, resurrecting women's solidity when it is needed for some purpose—as models or clients—and seeming to liquefy it when a more malleable and abstract femininity is called for, from which the designer will gain inspiration.

NAVIGATING THE ART/COMMERCE DIVIDE

Of course, these movements correspond to the foundational tension in fashion—between art and industry. Women's physical bodies were the vehicles upon which fashion traded. A designer needed models to show clothing, and clients to try it on, buy it and wear it. Embodied femininity was directly linked to commerce in this sense. Ethereal femininity was disconnected from living women's bodies and invoked by designers as a source of inspiration for their work. This ethereal femininity appeared to be linked to understandings of beauty as a timeless value; it was, on the surface at least, more concretely related to aesthetic concerns than commercial ones. But of course, foundational to my reading of these texts is that art and commerce were linked—one could not be hived off from the other, in fashion particularly. Aesthetics were the key to successful business. This meant that the signs of women and femininity, too, could not remain *either* material *or* abstract. Their appearances fluctuated as they helped to mediate designers' access to these competing, but ultimately entwined, realms. As Kathy Psomiades has shown in the context of Victorian aestheticism, the doubleness of representations of femininity was a powerful way for artists to deflect but remain connected to the mucky business of economic capital.[24] Part of the doubleness Psomiades traces, in fact, is the movement of de- and re-materialization that is intrinsic to the rhetoric of femininity among the fashion designers in this study. Reading Dante Gabriel Rossetti's poem, 'Jenny', she notes that as a beautiful woman selling sexuality, 'Jenny brings together the realms of art and economics in a single beautiful body ... As woman, Jenny is the prostitute who sells her body, but she is also the mysterious soul that cannot be compromised ... Jenny is thus always both that which can be possessed and that which is unpossessable, and she lends that double nature to everything her body figures.'[25] She is embodied and time-bound, but alternately ethereal and timeless. As Psomiades's account shows, this dual state is a *productive* one.

Indeed, the instability of representations, instead of undermining coherence, in fact helps to *produce* coherent narratives of selfhood for designers. Feminists have asked how representations of women in philosophical texts, for example, facilitate the creation of a masterful, transcendent male subject with the exclusive authority to know and to act in the public sphere.[26] That question becomes: how did the unstable logic of fashionable femininity—as both modern and not modern—underwrite the creation of designers' public images? How did it contribute to the production of stable, public personae for designers, even retrospectively (as two of the three I will treat here wrote their memoirs at the end of their careers)? And how did these representations contribute to the accumulation of capital and the expansion of the fashion industry? How do these texts expose femininity as the motor of the industry, even as they portray women's antimodernism as anathema to the business of design?

In pursuing this approach, the question of artistic modernism and its relationship to commerce necessarily comes into view. For modern fashion design was propelled by its claims of *avant-garde* innovation. The fetishization and even the institutionalization of the new among modernists were explicitly shared by most haute couturiers in the period of this study.[27] Indeed, in a more visible way than artists or writers, fashion designers were vitally dependent on the new, since newness was the quality by which fashion was sold and by which fashion designers secured and maintained their livelihoods. In the cases of two of the three designers I examine, Poiret and Schiaparelli, the connection to modernist innovation was overt; both consorted and collaborated with the preeminent experimenters of their day—there is Poiret's work with the Ballets Russes, for example, or Schiaparelli's collaborations with major surrealist artists, which solidified her reputation as a vanguardist.[28] With Dior, the connection is not so straightforward; he explicitly repudiated modernist abstraction, and his designs were more obviously a return to an older tradition. But as I shall discuss, his relationship with modernist newness was more complex than it seems at first glance. A look beyond the dominant narrative of Dior as a conservative show that he did indeed engage directly with discourses of the new in order to build his brand.

Of course, artistic and literary modernisms were built on their overt repudiations of markets and commerce. But the growing literature on the marketing of modernism has shown, contrary to this assumption, that modernists were deeply invested in the marketing of their work and of modernism more generally.[29] Nancy J. Troy, in *Couture Culture*, has extended this insight to account for modernist fashion's dual rhetorics of *avant-garde* revolution and commercialization. The fashion industry, no matter how heavily cloaked it was in the rhetoric of aesthetic transcendence of commerce, was marked by commerce even in its most rarefied spaces. Troy's work foregrounds the centrality of the designer in the marketing of the work, and highlights the importance of building a public persona. Often, this involved the careful cultivation of the image of designer as artist and art connoisseur; couturiers such as Jacques Doucet and Paul Poiret built impressive art collections to shore up this image.[30] The life writing of fashion designers should be considered a highly important site for the expression of an apparently revolutionary sensibility in the service of commercial success. Representations of both designers and women as having a particular place in or outside of modern time were central to that expression. What I trace here is the *early* discourse of fashion designer as celebrity, a figure, as Tiziana Ferrero-Regis notes, 'who capitalises on media attention and on close relationships with other fabricated celebrities, such as actresses, media and political personalities'.[31] What this makes clear is that *relationships with others, including women as models, muses, and clients*, were central to the designer's cultivation of reputation.

REPUTATION, CELEBRITY AND THE 'PROFESSIONAL' DESIGNER

Aaron Jaffe analyses the cultivation of reputations as a speculative activity in literary modernism. He writes, 'modernist value capitalizes … through the systematic devaluation and effacement of a host of other literary labours first by modernist others and later in multiple scenes of reading and assorted cultural encounters.'[32] If we apply to fashion this understanding of the development of the modernist reputation, it becomes clear that it is women who are devalued and effaced—*even as* they constitute the conditions of possibility for a successful design career. Femininity provided a ground for the development of the rhetoric of identity among designers, be they men or women, in an industry whose foundations were shifting and which thus put the personae of its celebrity couturiers into question. Was the designer in essence an artist, or a businessperson? Were they ultimately a conduit for or an executor of consumer desire—the desire of women, in this case—or were they the force that dictated that desire?

These are questions of control. Who shaped the aesthetic and commercial field of fashion? Was it women, as consumers, or designers, as producers of desires and styles? What becomes clear in reading designers' self-representational efforts is that this question mattered a great deal: given the industry's increasing responsiveness to consumer desire, there was a need for the designer to display their mastery of the client. In 1914, the designer Jean Worth (son and heir of the pioneer of *haute couture*, Charles Frederick Worth) lamented the way that the rapid diffusion of fashion was threatening the authority of the couturier as the final arbiter in matters of style. He writes nostalgically of his father's day—the 1860s and 70s—as one in which

> everything was arranged by M. Worth; for, whether France were imperial or republic, he at least remained Uncrowned King of Fashion. His practised eye discerned the color and style of robe that would most completely enhance a woman's charm, and with complete serenity she might leave the matter to him and give her mind to the contemplation of home affairs, her children, and philanthropies.[33]

Jean Worth implicitly stages himself here—unlike his father, *he* has to contend with modern women who do not leave it all up to him and go off to enjoy their feminine pursuits. Along these lines, the works I analyze here can thus be read as studies in the production not only of a coherent persona, but of a supremely and somehow innately knowledgeable one, whose position would not be threatened by the competing, intimate knowledges of women in a rapidly industrializing field. In this sense, the genre of life writing is crucial. As a site for the projection of fictions of a coherent and masterful self, it is an ideal forum for the establishment of superiority over clients.

For this reason, the autobiographical work might be understood as a reflection of the establishment of the designer as a professional. Discourses of professionalism emerged in the latter half of the nineteenth century and primarily involved the institutionalization of careers based on academic knowledge. In that sense, professionalism on the surface does not precisely describe the work of fashion design. And yet, the claim to something resembling professionalism as the gatekeeper of knowledge emerges in fashion during this period. Consider Thomas Strychacz's discussion of professionalism in the context of literary modernism, another field supposedly far removed from professional structures and interests. As he notes, '[t]he key to this institutionalization of professional power is the ability to employ *expert* knowledge.'[34]

The hallmark of the professional is access to a body of obscure knowledge that only a special class of professionals has access to; 'a key characteristic of professional knowledge is its inaccessibility to a mass public.'[35] In other words, the maintenance of a knowledge divide—the upkeep of trade secrets—is crucial to the continued mystique of the professional. Agnès Rocamora, tracing representations of designers in the contemporary context, indicates the importance of knowledge to the sense of the designer as legitimate: 'in the French newspaper, not only is fashion a high art, but it is also a métier informed by the artful and intelligent mastery of traditional knowledge, a knowledge that can only be acquired with experience.'[36]

POSITIONING THE DESIGNER IN LIFE WRITING

The portrayal of professional mastery points to the autobiographical narrative form—the life writing—that is at the centre of my analysis. Conventional autobiographical writing participates in a logic of coherent selfhood alongside which all instances of failure or instability appear stark. A generation of life writing scholars has made clear that the autobiographical form rests upon the unquestioned dominance of the singular, disconnected 'I'.[37] According to Martin Danahay, '[t]he genre that came to be called "autobiography" in the late eighteenth and early nineteenth centuries depends upon ... the ideals of individualism.'[38] As Sidonie Smith and Julia Watson explain, at the heart of the form in its traditional guise is a narrative: '[t]his Enlightenment "self," ... identical to other "I"s, enshrine[s] the "individual" and "his" uniqueness.'[39] The life writing of couturiers on one level confirms this model of self. As will become clear, they used this medium to portray themselves as artists in a milieu marked by mass reproduction. That is, they wrote to preserve some conception of the self's integrity, besieged as that self was in a fashion system beset by cultural anxieties about the relationship between art and industrial production.

Designers' writings thus needed to reflect their uniqueness. Pierre Bourdieu's analysis of the field of fashion affords some insights here. Bourdieu suggests that the value of fashion objects does not reside in the objects themselves, but in the 'rarity' of the couturier:

> the magical power of the figure of the 'creator' is the authoritative capital attached to a position that has no power unless it is mobilized by an authorized person, or, better, if it identified directly with this person, with their charisma, and guaranteed by their imprimatur. What makes Dior is not the biological individual Dior, nor the House of Dior, but the capital of the House of Dior operating under the auspices of a singular persona who could be nobody but Dior.[40]

Bourdieu's analysis makes clear what is at stake in the designer's culti-vation of reputation: nothing short of the health of his or her design house. The couturier, perversely, must cultivate a financially disinterested artistry, a sense of their originality and genius, in order to make money and preserve their status or legacy. The memoir offered a forum to advance that perception of the designer as individual genius.

Yet though designers wrote in part to uphold the understanding of them-selves as artists, even retrospectively, this too was a minefield because their memoirs were mass-marketed works. The very form of the commercial mem-oir potentially compromised the designer's carefully cultivated position as an artist and connoisseur of high culture. As Julie Rak writes in an analysis of the autobiographical representation of disgraced media magnate Conrad Black, '[i]n order to sell his autobiography, Conrad Black has had to become a com-modity himself, a commodity who must act as if he is not a member of the elite in order to be marketable.'[41] For all their anxiety about commerce and investment in connections to a cultural elite, the memoir form threatened to expose them as ordinary dressmakers and merchants. It required a *per-formance* of ordinariness, as twentieth-century celebrity culture demanded a point of access for fans, and was increasingly invested in presenting celebri-ties as 'just like us'. There was a contradiction between the apparently elite ties of the couturier and the mundane nature of the form. Rak further asks, '[w]hat happens ideologically to the writer of memoir for a mass market, or more to the point, what kind of subject must s/he turn into when identity be-comes a commodity that can be bought and sold?'[42] Here is yet another chink in the armour of the couturier-as-artist: to secure a reputation using memoir, she or he must step uncomfortably out of the myth of singular genius.

Given designers' vested interest in coherently portraying themselves as masterful geniuses, the instabilities in these texts become all the more intriguing. In particular, the presence of women in the accounts challenges the individualist model of identity built into traditional life writing. The texts, though written in order to secure a legacy for their authors as singular ge-niuses, move between the register of the distinct and unfettered self and that of the self-in-relation. The nexus between these two models of selfhood is the heart of this subgenre of fashion writing. Life writing theorists Sidonie Smith and Julia Watson write, '[t]he autobiographical occasion (whether per-formance or text) becomes a site on which cultural ideologies intersect or dissect one another, in contradiction, consonance, and adjacency. Thus the site is rife with diverse potentials.'[43] One of these potentials is the recogni-tion that men and masculinity are dependent on femininity for their coherent existence.

In a classic essay, Nancy K. Miller puts it thus: 'representing the other—the one who is not us, even the one against whom we understand who we might be—*also* allows us to perform that which is most us: being an artist, for instance, a son, or a daughter.'[44] Miller's articulation underscores how the relational self that seems on one level to issue such a strong challenge to the Enlightenment ideal of the singular individual can in fact at the same time *confirm* the narrator's individuality. It is one thing to acknowledge that the self is constructed in relation to various others. But the structure of that relationship is of the utmost importance. If otherness is engaged and then cast aside, or if the relationship to the other is suppressed or denied, then what emerges is a picture of the triumphant, singular self. We must be careful, then, in applying the very useful frameworks of the relational self that have been developed in the last two decades by feminist and other critical scholars; we must not conflate relationality with a necessarily critical effect. If a sustained, symbolic violence is done to the other in a self-fashioning effort, then the presence of this other does not necessarily undermine ideas about the masterful and singular self at the centre of the account. If we recognize, as contemporary social theories of gender do, that 'gender hegemony is produced through the relationship between masculinity and femininity,'[45] we see that *relationships* are also critical in the reproduction of existing ideological configurations. The existence of a relational dimension in a self-narration must thus be seen as either of two things: a structural necessity and a *possible* or *potential* opening into new understandings of selfhood, or, in this case, particularly the gender of the self. In reading these fashion memoirs, we are in the realm of a largely *unrealized* possibility to disturb conventional gender. These texts do, nonetheless, reveal through their contradictions a more nuanced and less polarized view of femininity in its relation to fashion, sidestepping the unhelpful caricatures of the industry as unswervingly oppressive or liberating.

RETHINKING MODERN FEMININITY

Indeed, these texts allow us to rethink some fundamental feminist assumptions about the nature of femininity's relationship to the modern. For when we are writing about the first half of the twentieth century and the marketing of fashion, we are also in the realm of the spectacularization of images of women's bodies. As Abigail Solomon-Godeau and others have argued, the development of new means of reproducing images, beginning in the mid-nineteenth century with photography, was an extended moment of 'the ideological naturalization of the feminine-as-spectacle ... that is the precondition for the apparently self-evident [link] between the seductive, possessable feminine and the seductive, possessable commodity'.[46] But as the works by designers show, the saturation of Western culture in imagery of women was an uneven process. The status of modern femininity as spectacle was undeniable—especially in the fashion industry—but it was not constant and all-consuming. Instances of erasure were as prevalent, as the autobiographical texts make clear. A curious effect of the presence of intermittently 'irrational' consuming women in these texts is their ability to render femininity spoken for, mute and mastered even as it is spectacularly visible, effecting a quasi-*in*visibility. Visibility and invisibility are so closely articulated in these works that they become almost inseparable. And so, it might be more accurate to point to the *variable* visibility of femininity in modernity, and most relevant to think critically about the operation of invisibility in an industry so dependent on the visible.

Christine Buci-Glucksmann argues that ambiguity signalled by the feminine is a key to understanding the overall tenor of modernity: '[t]he feminine could delineate certain scenes of modernity, certain of its negative or positive utopias, which appear close to the spaces of the baroque with their multiple entrances and doubled, ambiguous aspects.'[47] Though Buci-Glucksmann's articulation of the feminine is often tied to female-bodied persons, such ties are not essential to her argument; rather, she sees femininity as a principle or structure that traverses all of the scenes of modernity, in *variously visible* ways. The doubleness and ambiguity she speaks of here describe what I have located in the designer autobiographies: a simultaneous absence and hyper-presence of femininity. What is significant about this formulation is that it sees femininity in *all* of its articulations as a key to modernity, and so does not discount as ineffective or unimportant those instances in which femininity is silenced, repressed, absent. For those very instances of invisibility are what help to constitute both moments of feminine hyper-visibility and the relationship of masculinity to modernity. Feminist critics must not merely rail against disavowals and silences—though that can be an important task. We must also ask how they structure the *presence* of gender.

As newer approaches to the study of women suggest, femininity is not a singular entity; broad claims about femininity fail to account for the differences which produce vastly dissimilar experiences and social positions for women (and feminine men) of various races and ethnicities, classes, nations, sexual orientations and abilities.[48] This study is reflective of the sense that there are multiple femininities at play in the self-representational efforts of designers; indeed, they are built upon the oscillations between different characters of femininity. Thus feminine multiplicity does a kind of ideological work when it is invoked relationally, even as it is papered over by the myth of a singular, timeless feminine.

Of course, even though there are multiple femininities evident within the texts I am analysing here, each milieu I treat is distinguished by its whiteness and its class-specificity. The range of femininities invoked is, in that sense, quite narrow. It is also inaccessible to large numbers of women. When we are speaking of the others through whom designers construct the self, we are of course often in the realm of feminine *ideals.* These would have been un-achievable for those without access to the expensive clothing and lifestyles that fashionable elegance demanded, and even more out of reach for women who were not white—women who remained almost entirely invisible in the system of *haute couture* throughout this period. Further, each designer self-represents intermittently through *colonial* tropes, invoking the self as some-thing akin to a colonial master. This underscores the whiteness not only of the feminine ideal, but of the couturier self who is calling on this feminine ideal in order to represent the self.

METHODOLOGIES

As these are such well-known designers, there is quite a vast literature on each of them, and most notably on Dior. The majority of the literature in these areas is not scholarly, but consists of popular biographies or exhibi-tion catalogues—although some exhibition catalogues, such as the one from the Metropolitan Museum of Art's 2007 Poiret exhibition, do feature short scholarly essays.[49] There is also a smattering of scholarly attention to Dior, especially his role vis-à-vis the profound cultural change in postwar France, and on the significance of his designs for concepts of women's emancipation or oppression.[50] Much of this work, however, is contained as asides in other works of history or cultural theory. Alexandra Palmer, however, has recently written an authoritative, scholarly analysis of Dior that is richly illustrated and popularly accessible.[51] Aside from Palmer, my approach is inspired in partic-ular by Caroline Evans's work on Schiaparelli (noted above) and on Poiret's wife Denise, and by Nancy Troy's groundbreaking book, *Couture Culture*, which includes detailed analysis of Poiret.[52] These scholars' work considers the relationship between celebrity designers and the cultural, ideological and in-stitutional conditions that produced them as celebrities.

Unlike many studies of fashion, in many ways the primary object of this inquiry is not precisely fashion itself; rather, fashion is a rich and compelling *mediator* of larger questions concerning the relationship of women and femi-ninity to modernity. Fashion makes visible some overlooked aspects of gen-dered modernity, precisely because of the ways that it juxtaposes ephemeral time with the dominant appearance of femininity. But appearance need not imply only visual presence. Conducting neither a study of fashion objects nor of the visual culture of fashion, instead I engage in a textual excavation. In the spectacularly visual culture of fashion, this approach is rare.[53] A couturier is conventionally remembered by her or his material and iconic traces—the gar-ments and images left behind—and not by her or his words. But attention to the words of designers reveals fashion as a field that matters to our analyses of gendered modernity in a host of ways that have been overlooked. After all, in *The Fashion System*, Roland Barthes recognized the profound relationship between what he called 'image-clothing' and 'written clothing', which was reconciled and embodied in the material garment.[54] For Barthes, fashion writing essentially produces the larger fashion system: clothing only actualized an 'instituting discourse'.[55] In the period since he wrote that major work in 1967, it has been largely overlooked. I propose, in the spirit of Barthes's work on clothing, that the written element of fashion is just as important as the visual field, and indeed can illuminate the context of that visual field.

For one thing, designer life writing makes the designer visible as an engaged agent within the fashion system. However, this personage becomes visible at the centre of an otherwise consumption-oriented analysis, since these memoirs describe and are marketed to clients, and are published in order to illuminate the figures behind the consumerist visual and material cultures of fashion. This kind of fashion writing—whether done by the designers themselves or by the press—is necessarily relational, putting producer and consumer, 'master' and 'servant' (to use the language of much modern fashion writing), into dialogue and revealing their mutual dependence. Such relationality would not be captured in an analysis which overlooked the written texts of fashion. As well, fashion writings help to add texture to accounts of women in urban, Western modernity. If we looked only to the spectacular visuality of fashion, so heavily weighted with women's images, we would not be so easily able to discern the ways that women simultaneously appear and are, or are made, *invisible* in the cultures of modernity. Finally, Laird O'Shea Borelli makes the point that 'fashion is perpetuated by the [written] fictions created about it.'[56] The narrative structures of written fashion are more intelligible than those of fashion visual images, they are more continuous, less fragmented and isolated. The conventions of fashion writing are easily connected—more easily than visual conventions, which are often deliberately opaque—to broader cultural narratives about women in the first half of the twentieth century.

For this primarily textual analysis, I have centred the life writings of these three designers, but I have also read outward from them, hoping to understand their places within a network of representations. Close examination of other press has helped me to establish the tenor of the discourses that surrounded the designers, against or alongside of which they worked to position themselves in their own books. I read these texts in conversation with a range of cultural and feminist theory that takes fashion, femininity or modern time as its object, revealing the consonance of these theories with each other. In contextualizing the primary documents, I examine the pressured appearances of both 'real' women and a figural, abstract femininity: where do they appear, and in what relation to the designer? What does it mean when femininity is invoked, and what is its relation to the living women who are also described in the text? I also, of course, foreground time in my analysis of women and femininity, asking what temporal category they are relegated to, and how that changes according to context. Using time as the lens through which to approach femininity opens onto a range of other issues, from secrecy to glamour to spirituality to aesthetic philosophy, which allows us to bring these disparate issues into view as sites for the formation of ideas about modernity.

But this is a project centrally concerned with the *relational* qualities of women and femininity as images, including their relationships with masculinity. Femininities are foregrounded in relation to one another—to designer femininity, in the case of Schiaparelli's public persona—and in relation to the ambivalent masculinities of both Poiret and Dior. As Kittay's above-noted discussion of women as metaphors makes clear, invocations of feminine metaphors contribute to the *labour* of selfhood; they do the work, in essence, of helping designers mediate between the multiple, distinct and sometimes oppositional temporal domains that they must navigate in order to remain both commercially and aesthetically viable. These close readings, then, are not only oriented to understanding how the figures constitute femininity, but how they equally and powerfully constitute masculinity.

In its attention to the relational and networked quality of the couturier, the analysis is inspired by Bourdieu's sociology of culture. He writes, 'the sociology of cultural products must take as its object the whole set of relationships (objective ones and also those effected in the form of interactions) between the artist and other artists, and beyond them, the whole set of agents engaged in the production of the work, or, at least, of the social value of the work.'[57] Bourdieu recognizes that the symbolic value attached to the field of fashion extends far beyond the designer, a situation which most studies of individual fashion figures do not explore. His is a framework that allows us to take seriously the roles of clients and even of imagined femininities in the production of value in fashion and foreground the relational establishment of the major couturier as a way of securing or maintaining a reputation.

To engage in this way with the memoirs of couture designers is unusual. Critics of fashion appear to have a conflicted relationship with these works. Notably, the books are often called upon as primary evidence in popular accounts of these designers; authors quote from them liberally, using the episodes and mindsets they narrate as the foundations of claims about the designers. However, they do not consider the broader contours of the genre, nor usually examine the implications of using texts written for a mass audience—which presumably have been crafted with the demands and interests of that audience in mind—as 'true' representations of their subjects. An important exception is Caroline Evans's 1999 article on Elsa Schiaparelli, which reads the complexity of Schiaparelli's memoir alongside the clothes she designed, making a case for the relationship between them as art forms.[58] In this book, the memoir is also viewed as an art form; it is a fundamental pillar in the designer's fashioning and strategic presentation of the self, and not necessarily an accurate representation of that self.

TRUTH AND AUTHENTICITY IN DESIGNER SELF-FASHIONING

To engage in an analysis like this one, with texts that are so inextricably linked to the commercial enterprise of fashion, and which so transparently straddle the line between memoir and advertisement, is to wade into the murky waters of credibility. How can we read these documents as the narrative 'truth' of each designer's life? The answer is that the 'truth' that counts, here, is the social truth of the functioning and management of a public persona. This shifts the terms of engagement. It does not matter whether these designer accounts are 'accurate' representations of the circumstances of designers' lives, because this study already assumes that the only traces left to us are of the *public management* of self. As Andrew Tolson frames it in another context, 'if this is not simply a revelation of an essential "real person," it is nevertheless a disclosure of a way of being a celebrity, a way of coping with its pressures, by mapping out and following through a self-conscious personal project.'[59] The question becomes, then: what choices did designers make in narrating these presentable selves, and what is the meaning of those choices?

It must be recognized, however, that these memoirs were published in a context that valued authenticity. What is their relationship, then, to the category of authenticity, which was growing ever more resonant as industrial modernity advanced? As scholars of celebrity have pointed out, since the 1930s—the period when the first of these texts was published—celebrity culture depended on the perception that publics could reach stars' authentic voices through the press.[60] This means that aside from a general performance of a couturier self, the texts must be understood as performances of authenticity. As Richard Dyer notes in a now-classic essay on what he terms 'the construction of authenticity,' indications 'that the star is *not* like he or she appears to be on screen serve to reinforce the authenticity of the star image as a whole'.[61] The couturier memoirs trade on this split between the public self and the private self, employing a host of devices to impress upon the reader the fact that the designer's fame is, in some sense, unwanted, that it flies in the face of their 'true' personality. Kirk Curnutt explores the celebrity's common assertion that fame is a restriction of their freedom, which underlines a sense of the celebrity's besieged, authentic selfhood.[62] The cultivation of such a split between publicly available surface and interior depth has value.

He writes, 'insisting that the public identity does not accurately represent the inner "I" is an act of artistic self-possession.'[63] That is, it suggests that the celebrity's *artistic* integrity has not been compromised by what the public understands as the sullying effects of fame. For the fashion designer, this is a particularly important perception to uphold, owing to the precarious position that fashion occupies between art and commerce. The narration of an authentic self has an important function in this industry in particular, as it provides a barrier against the denigration of fashion as a mere commercial enterprise.

Thus authenticity was an important concept for the designer, specifically because of fashion's historically charged relationship with this category. Fashion is aligned with the idea of lying or deceit as a feminine trait, in a linked chain of binaries that includes the gendered opposition of authenticity and artifice. Fashion designers were potentially suspect as shallow beings themselves, occupying yet another tense position in this respect. They were required to simultaneously celebrate the performances of self (artifice) that fashion enables *and* make clear that they, themselves, were genuine, reliable figures. The stakes of the performance of authenticity were raised for them, lest they become tainted by the ambiguous artifice of fashionable clothing that they were so invested in.

This raises again the question of the feminine, an 'artificial' construct in the symbolic economy that promoted such dualisms. If the designer needed to shore up her or his own authenticity, the artifice of fashion needed to be displaced, and yet kept intact. Who was better suited to take on that artifice than the women with whom such deceit was already associated? This proves to be another key to the relational invocation of femininity by designers. Women carried the weight of this category that was necessary to the fashion industry's health but could not be borne by the designer, lest the designer accrue to herself or himself the negative connotations of artifice. Here, then, we have another clue to the ambivalent positioning of women throughout this body of life writing. Positioned at once as celebrated style icons and muses, they are at the same time the bearers of falsity against which the designer can elevate his or her own status as an authentic artist.

Yet an array of motivating factors seems to underpin the memoirs of each designer. Notably, each book is relatively poorly written, its narrative strangely organized and sometimes book-ended by clumsy, experimental strategies, as in the case of Schiaparelli and Dior, suggesting that an expertly written, finished product was not necessarily the goal. While these are undoubtedly texts that cannot be divorced from their commercial contexts, none can be read as necessary to the life of the author's design house. Indeed, the texts by Poiret and Schiaparelli were written shortly after the closing of their businesses; they could not, in this sense, be understood as attempts to shore up their commercial success. What interests motivated each designer to write these texts?

I suggest that these memoirs are clearly attempts to engage in a sort of retrospective branding, to secure a lasting legacy for each designer. Poiret is particularly striking in this regard—his publication of three autobiographical works within five years suggests a curious drive toward his own memorialization (if not a breathtaking narcissism). Schiaparelli, for her part, failed to give the audience what it surely wanted—a wealth of in-depth detail about the fashion industry and her clientele—and concentrated on what were perhaps less obviously engaging questions. Dior's text was published ten years after his debut, while he still reigned over the fashion world. His memoir thus was not motivated by profit alone, and more likely was conceived as a beginning step in his own memorialization. The drive to create distance between authentic couturier and inauthentic fashion is undoubtedly part of this legacy creation; the preservation of a positive legacy requires that the designer be positioned as candid and honest, for these are the only ways to accede to timelessness and instil a sense of that which is so rhetorically important to both the fashion industry and the creation of a lasting legacy: transcendent fame. In his history of the changing cultural profile of fame, Leo Braudy notes that for the famous, '[t]he "aspiration to immortality" ... [is] a way out of the shackles of the present moment.'[64] Here, then, we have an intimation of the intersecting concerns of temporality and the tense relationship of art and commerce in the designer's self-fashioning. The designer knows her or himself to be ineluctably bound to daily time—dependent on its rhythms for her or his livelihood—and yet is intermittently in search of an escape from this tedium into the cultural safety of a purely artistic career.

This confluence of factors suggests that the books were not principally documents with a dollar value to the design house, but more complex texts with manifold potential motives and uses. The texts represent a *compulsion to narrate* even as they stand out as poorly executed. Beyond the question of securing a legacy, the works have something to tell us about the discursive positioning of the designer. In their instabilities, the texts, read together, suggest that the designer inhabited an anxious space. Even if these books had a primarily memorializing function, a designer needing to appeal to a conventionally cultured audience (as each of these did) would ordinarily strive to present a less fractured narrative, one that revealed their supposed 'character' in a more coherent way. The texts' failure to cohere thus functions as testimony not to some truth of each couturier, but to the condition of the designer more generally, in the context of their industry's tense convergence between art and commerce in the wake of modernism, and of concerns about the dualism of artifice and authenticity.[65] While the works do not necessarily capture the designers' *actual*, lived relationship with women, they suggest something more broadly about the *reasons* for the mediations that women and femininity represent in the self-narrations of designers. The 'truth' represented by this textual assemblage is the inescapable and disturbing knowledge that the designer is pinned between industry and aesthetics. The narrative force behind these works is the struggle to find a territory ungoverned by the tension between them. This is what accounts for the saturating presence of women and femininity as mediators.

The forum of life writing is particularly well suited to fashion. Fashion is a complicated and ambiguous site for the projection and management of individual and collective identity. It offers opportunities for the individual to mask and project various aspects of identity, and it does the same for collectives. As with fashion, life writing is a form that can be used to both express and hide aspects of identity and that thus reveals the inner multiplicity of selfhood. In the case of fashion designers, the conflicted self-representation may not be a complete or entirely 'true' account of the subjective life, but it is an account of the social and cultural pressures on these figures, which push them to identify in particular ways and to establish links with other people. Life writing has a kind of formal affinity with fashion in this respect, which makes it an ideal forum in which to locate the expression of identity in a way that is specific to the *haute couturier.*

As well, the oscillations and contradictions of fashion-designer personae are revealed in the very *structure* of the memoir form. Life writing as a genre is well positioned to bear the particular temporal tensions of fashion. This is because life writing also brings together the present and the past in a way very similar to fashion. The memoir or autobiography is a form that complicates the dominant modern model of linear time, because it cannot portray a pure past. Rather, the autobiographical model narrates the past in light of the present. As Jens Brockmeier writes, '[w]henever I tell my life, I unavoidably see it in the light of the end or the present in which I present my story.'[66] Rockwell Gray suggests that autobiography reflects the subject's profound anxiety about the juxtaposition of time in a self-narration. Gray argues that life writing is the product of a struggle to reconcile multiple time signatures, and that it emerges as part of 'an impulse to stay the flight of time', thereby 'gaining a ground for the self'.[67] He sees the form as 'dramatiz[ing] our ambivalent attitude toward the past' and its incursions into the present.[68] Fashion might productively be understood in the same light—its cyclical structure illuminates the visitation of the past upon the present, annihilating the possibility of linear narrative.

What follows is not a history in any traditional sense. Rather, it is a close reading of these texts and the ephemera that surround them. Where most studies of historical fashion design turn outward in a move to contextualize garments in broader cultural trends, this analysis reaches inward to fashion texts as a kind of rhetoric, using this rhetoric to *complement* the rich and nuanced fashion histories that surround all of these designers. Yet, this approach does not abstract the texts from their contexts, no matter how close the reading. Indeed, these works are emblematic, in many cases, of the rhetoric of fashion more generally in the period in which they were published. What is compelling is the way that broader cultural constructions of fashion are internalized and personalized in designer life writing, and what this sort of mediation can tell us about the status of the fashion designer as an eminently *modern* figure. For if we understand the pressures that were brought to bear on the designer as a modern icon, we can get a good deal of the way toward understanding how those other modern icons, women, figured in the landscape of modernity.

In addition, in hewing closely to the texts, it is clear that these works effect a remarkable conversation with several currents of criticism and theory in contemporary modernist studies. Each body of work helps to illuminate the other. Fashion life writing, in a sense, tests the hypotheses of the criticism, offering a sense of how the relative abstractions of theory in this area can be applied to case studies, narratives and lives. These designers' articulations bring to life the helpful theoretical language we have developed for talking about modernity and about modernism.

Bringing this loosely defined body of theory to the constellation of fashion moments described here shows us that fashion has resonance and implications far beyond its relatively narrow field. It can illuminate for us a host of broader questions about the temporal structure of modernity and the relationship of femininity and feminine bodies to the modern. It connects women and femininity to questions which have recently become central to the evolving field of modernist studies: questions of modernist celebrity, along with representations of the close but ideologically contested relationship between art and commerce in modernist cultural circles. What fashion makes possible is a simultaneous attention to local, materialized phenomena, to people, to broader structures of knowing in this period and to the implications of all of this for positioning ourselves as critics in the present moment. By excavating the heretofore largely ignored life writing of designers, this book hopes to enrich this critical conversation in modernist studies. And by bringing fashion into this conversation, it ensures that we take seriously this feminized and trivialized form as central to modernity.

–1–

Fashion and the Time of Modern Femininity

The fetishization of the new is a commonplace phenomenon in studies of late-nineteenth and early-twentieth-century modernity. The period was governed by a cult of progress that was colloquially rendered as a fascination with newness. It was evident in the arts, which often embraced experiment for its own sake, as an expression of the yearning for new horizons of experience. It was also discernible in industry, where it was driven by the productive capacities afforded by new technologies of production and consumption. Yet, as feminist theorists have shown, the tendency to exclude women from, and even to oppose them to, the category of the new was endemic in the arts, politics and social and cultural theory.[1] The consolidation of a dominant time consciousness around the middle of the nineteenth century has been said to have taken place by way of a rejection of the feminine.[2] In this period, the very *time* of modernity was highly gendered.

Of course, countercurrents to the cult of newness existed. Some of them were visible in the simultaneous fascinations with categories such as degeneration, especially in the final decades of the nineteenth century. Following the logic which excluded women from the new, these deathly or degenerate conceptual models themselves were often figured in terms of femininity.[3] To date, most intellectual and cultural historians have tended to treat the interest in newness and in degeneration as two quite separate traditions. There is, however, a significant body of theoretical writing on time which avoids this tendency to hive off the two understandings of temporality—as linear and progress-oriented, and as stalled, cyclical or degenerative. Instead, such research understands them as utterly dependent upon each other. For feminist theorists interested in challenging the masculinism which persists in accounts of modernity, this move to counter the opposition of new and old would seem to hold some promise to redress the exclusion of women from these accounts.

In *The Politics of Time: Modernity and Avant-Garde*, Peter Osborne writes, '[m]odernity is a form of historical time which valorizes the new as the product of a constantly self-negating historical dynamic ... In producing the old as remorselessly as it produces the new, it provokes forms of traditionalism the logic of which is quite different from that of tradition as conventionally told.'[4]

Here Osborne refers obliquely to a familiar binary between new and old, a belief that past and present are completely unrelated. This is the opposition upon which, with what Tony Meyers calls its 'epochal self-consciousness',[5] modernity was defined. But though the 'new' that Osborne refers to is founded upon the idea of a definitive break from the past, it can never be entirely free of the old; that is, it is never completely new. Rather, it is compromised from within by an unshakeable relationship with the old, with its past.[6] This violation of the binary construction of new and old is a subject of intense scrutiny for scholars such as Walter Benjamin, who challenge the conception that modernity only narrative of time was progress-oriented. The variety of relationships between past and present in modernity, such literature insists, contain within them the seeds of political change.[7] But this work is strikingly inattentive to gender, disappointing those of us who might have looked to it as an aid in theorizing the relationship between women and the time of the modern.

What does emerge that might be of interest to feminist theory, though, is that constellations of past and present are often understood to be embodied in fashion. Certainly, historians have shown that sartorial fashion, as we know it today, is a distinctly modern phenomenon, its rise enabled by the development of the capitalism that became a hallmark of the modern era.[8] One might say, then, that the early modern period gave rise to the very possibility of modern fashion. Or, as Gilles Lipovetsky puts it,

> [a]n unprecedented social value was beginning to radiate, that of *novelty*. Fashion could not have existed without this reversal of the relation to historical evolution and to ephemera. In order for fashion to come into being, the 'modern' had to be accepted and desired; the present had to be deemed more prestigious than the past; in an unprecedented move, what was novel had to be invested with dignity.[9]

But the relationship between fashion and modernity goes deeper than that, as Walter Benjamin and several of his commentators have recognized.[10] Indeed, fashion possesses the same temporal structure as modernity itself—or, at least, as modern modes of time consciousness. Andrew Benjamin observes that fashion is 'inextricably linked to a certain conception of historical time', and suggests that, for this reason, the peculiar temporal rhythms of fashion must be seen as 'part of the construction of culture'.[11] Hence it might be fair to say that the form shares similar political stakes or even, surprisingly enough, revolutionary capacities with modernity itself. Do the questions that critics ask about modern qualities of time—about the secret romance of the new with the old, about the failure of 'progress' in the face of eternal cycles, regression and deterioration—make sense in relation to sartorial fashion, that undeniably material phenomenon? Can fashion materialize theories of modern time?

If we take seriously these questions about the temporal status of fashion in modernity, we are returned to the gendered character of modernity. For fashion itself is highly gendered, its development increasingly bound up both with representations of femininity and with actual women as consumers from the early nineteenth century onward.[12] In a sense this history is useful for those of us who are interested in rethinking the figuration of femininity and modernity. By intervening in the dichotomous or oppositional positioning of past and present that characterized temporal consciousness from the Revolutionary Period, fashion thus also allows us to begin to think of other possibilities for women's modernity. It allows us to see our way out of the positioning of women as outside of the modern. By opening up the debates on modern time to a distinct but related set of concerns in feminist theory, fashion can indeed contribute to the forging of a politics of the time of modernity. Indeed, fashion, a medium that is highly feminized, allows us to view the time consciousness of the period from about 1860 to 1940 as gendered. It does so in four ways. First, it allows us to consider how ideologies that emphasized newness and an affinity with the present and the future functioned to disenfranchise women by excluding the symbolic realm of the feminine from the possibilities for *becoming* that were seen to define the modern. Second, rather than simply admit women to the realm of the new, fashion challenges the conceptual opposition of new and traditional, present and past, upon which the exclusion of women rests. Third, fashion complicates a major feminist theoretical narrative, which tends to favour an account of women's absolute exclusion from conceptions of the modern, by giving us a host of examples in which women were represented as quintessentially modern. Finally, fashion can show us not only that modern time was gendered, but that it was lived, felt and materially experienced in everyday life. This chapter examines these potentials of fashion in order to delineate where and how feminist theories of modernity and of time might be brought into a broader conversation about the structures of time in the modern age—a conversation which has largely excluded them. In this sense, it contributes to what Emily Apter terms a 'becoming-feminist' of time theory itself.[13]

EXPOSING MODERNITY

Peter Osborne asks, 'What kind of time does modernity inscribe?'[14] His book-length answer is foundational in a small but crucial body of literature about the temporal character of modernity. This literature establishes that the basic challenge of modern temporal consciousness is its reflexivity: modernity becomes the first era equipped to recognize itself as an era, and to distinguish itself from earlier eras—the past—while opening toward the future.[15] The intellectual historian, Reinhart Koselleck, has traced the shift in time consciousness to the early modern period and the crumbling hold of religious worldviews. In the fifteenth century, he explains, '[t]he end of Church supremacy gave way to politics: politicians were concerned about the temporal, not the eternal.'[16] In the second half of the seventeenth century, it became possible 'to look back upon the past as medieval … Since then, one has lived in modernity and been conscious of so doing.'[17] Epochal self-awareness ushered in the Age of Revolution, which was ever-oriented toward the possibility of things to come. Thus a key result of the transformation of faith was a changing sense of the future, which was now no longer governed by prophesy of the inevitable end-time and the promise of the eternal, but was instead opened up as a new 'horizon of expectation' that might contain any number of outcomes shaped by human concerns. The future, in short, signified possibility, choices.

What Koselleck outlines is the establishment of the concepts of the past and the future as distinct, opposed times, and the privileging of what I would term a 'politics of the present' in opposition to them. It is this politics of the present—the new, or the now, as many would have it—that concerns most present-day commentators. The establishment of a coherent sense of the present, founded on a notion of linear, historical progress, sometimes takes on the quality of a disavowal or even a repression of the past. The relationship to the future, of course, is not so grim in a progress narrative. It is in fact this relationship to the future which is the guarantor of movement, of the sense that time changes, and that the present is not just present, but new. As Jürgen Habermas puts it, '[b]ecause the new, the modern world is distinguished from the old by the fact that it opens itself to the future, the epochal new beginning is rendered constant with each moment that gives birth to the new.'[18] Movement toward the future becomes the utopian end or purpose of the present.

As Tony Meyers notes, however, the fetishization of the present and the related longing for the future betray a certain anxiety: 'The old merely persists as yesterday's newness, and therefore the oldness of previous epochs, against which modernity measures its newness, disappears. In such a situation modernity can no longer index its qualitative transcendence of all other epochs. Modernity, on this reading, is perpetually ill at ease with itself.'[19] Modernity represses or at least anxiously covers over the ways that past touches present and issues a challenge to its own discourse of distinct times. The temporal structure of modernity, then, is plagued by a troubled relationship to the past—even to memory—which challenges the narrative of progress.[20] The close relationship between present and past has been the subject of intense scrutiny and re-theorization for historical materialists descended from Walter Benjamin. Benjamin's redrawing of the critical map in relation to time has enabled critics to explore and even embrace the political stakes of revolution, which is itself an oppositional time category, as it is premised on the complete overthrow of the past in service of renewal.

Most relevant to a discussion of Benjamin's views of temporality and of fashion is his conception of the dialectical image, a visual-political flash that lays bare various truths about the social world. The dialectical image materializes most fully in *The Arcades Project*, where Benjamin explains that such an image emerges from a particular way of looking that was engendered by various features of nineteenth-century Paris, including shopping arcades, iron decoration, Art Nouveau and fashion (though the concept of the dialectical image is also found in other contexts across his body of work). Dialectical images, for Benjamin, contain the potential to destroy accepted historical consciousness. They are constellations of past and present. They also act to interrupt the unexamined reproduction of the social world. Interruptions destabilize the narration of history as continuous and progressive. Of course, the idea of interruption is central to any understanding of the modern; it aptly describes the frenetic tempo of everyday life that dominates in descriptions of modernity. Benjamin's conception of interruption diverges from this one; in Peter Osborne's words, his 'aim was to refigure the interruptive tempo of modernity as redemption' by 'shifting from story to image'.[21] The dialectical image refuses modernity's binary distinction between the new and the old, the modern and the traditional, in favour of a sense of lightning-flash fusion of past and present times that interrupts by startling and awakening the masses, prompting revolution. Importantly, these images allow for the breaking of a deadening cycle—they prepare an exit from the endless, cyclical repetition that characterizes industrial capitalism.

It is here that we find the relevant connections to both the issue of fashion and the questions of feminist theory and representations of women. A conception of time as eternally recurrent and a conception of time as an interrupting force both prompt reconsiderations of the relationship between past and present. This is a critical question that intervenes in a discourse of modern time that largely refuses a meaningful role for the past in the present—a discourse that also anchors the conceptual exclusion of women from the modern.

WOMEN, FEMINIST THEORY, AND THE TIME OF THE MODERN

In *The Ends of History*, Christina Crosby offers a clear sense of the stakes of a discussion of time for women in the cultures of the modern. Though she works through the problematic of time via nineteenth-century literary and historical texts, the themes she locates can be seen as broadly applicable to the emergent culture of modernity and its time consciousness. What happens, she asks, when *history* comes to be seen as the repository of 'order and meaning', replacing theology as the site of truth?[22] A long quotation from her book underscores the stakes of the time consciousness she traces. In the Victorian era,

> women live most intimately with the white men of the English bourgeoisie ... thus the Victorian obsession with 'women,' with their nature, their functions, their aptitudes, their desires, with, above all, their difference from men. The nineteenth century is the time both of history and of 'the woman question,' the time of Hegel and the angel in the House, of the progress of history and the fallen woman. Men are considered as historical subjects and find 'man' in history by virtue of locating women elsewhere.[23]

What is important about Crosby's study is the attention she devotes to tracing this 'elsewhere' as broadly *constitutive* of the central figures of man and history that dominate Victorian historical consciousness; that is, men come into being, are produced as masculine, *through* women, through *not being women.* Her understanding of women's banishment from history implicitly relies on a concept akin to disavowal, or even abjection. Both of these concepts describe the way that individuals or institutions (such as nations) emphatically push away something they recognize as an element of themselves, something close to the core, but which might throw the self into question. The man, for instance, must reject evidence of femininity in himself in order to become masculine. In this account, then, women are central to the picture, even in their absence—because rendering them absent, pushing them out of the picture, takes *work.* Women, in their relegation to the outside of history, in fact *structure* that history. What is more, Crosby shows that the dominance of a concept of history as truth is confirmed by the presence of women as that which is not knowable, which is 'unhistorical'.[24] Women remain central, then, to the development of modern historical consciousness. Much as in the visual culture of the period—with its spectacular images of women's bodies—women were abundantly present in historical consciousness, but as spectral subjects, seemingly silent.

Crosby's discussion of representations of women and time makes clear the political stakes of temporality. As political theorist Valerie Bryson observes, 'in treating time as a given, common-sense fact of life, [white, middle-class, Western men who hold social power] have generally failed to recognise either that many people experience and understand it in other ways, or that these differences may be politically significant.'[25] The question of different lived practices of time has been significant to the feminist theories of time. It is only in attending to differences in the experience of time that we can understand how power operates in and through ideologies of time, and how these ostensibly abstract concepts have excluded and marginalized various groups.

Crosby's intervention is important; the feminist literature on the time of the modern is relatively limited. But what the existing literature does show is that the ideologies of historical consciousness and conceptions of the new and the *avant-garde* created categories of persons with different relationships to the social world and public life. Gendered conceptions of 'fitness' for public life have functioned to exclude women and other Others from participation as full agents in it. Feminist and postcolonial theories of time make it clear that a persistent trope across ways of knowing, as these were consolidated in the era of industrial modernity, was a dualistic conception of time.[26] This was an understanding of past, present and future that understood white, middle-class men in the West, alone, to possess the power and capacity to make and remake themselves and their social world: the capacity for *becoming*. Aligned with conceptions of a somehow energetic or even virile sense of the now and a glorious future toward which they were progressing, these privileged social actors depended upon a strict differentiation from the past, variously figured as archaic, bucolic and degenerate: woman as static *being* to man's progressive, changeable *becoming*.

Applying a feminist theoretical lens to the debates on time in modernity, then, makes clear that this is a conversation about the politics of *knowledge*, about who can know well, and thus who can participate in modern life. For designations of categories of persons as archaic and hence unfit for full participation in the modern social order were also designations of certain categories of knowers as irrational in a world that valued rationality above all. In the consolidating temporal order of the early nineteenth century, the emphasis on progress presumed a kind of triumph over a past defined by faith-based, and hence irrational, knowledge of the world. If science and industry together constituted the pinnacle of progress, then the knowledges and knowers they presumed to leave behind were the antithesis of progress. It was this concept of knowledge into which all women, working-class men and people of colour, in a move which makes visible the stakes of knowledge and time, were fit.[27] Here, it becomes clear that seemingly abstract debates about the nature of modern time have real consequences. They are in fact discussions of which groups had meaningful access to the social world. This demands that we consider the material effects of denying that access, based on conceptions of irrationality and archaism. Analysing time gives us an important key to the social exclusions of modern life.

But a dualistic understanding of time—visions of the past as irrational, mysterious and irretrievably lost—is, as I note above, marked by anxiety. Modernity is shot through with anxiety related to the recognition that there *is* in fact a relationship between past and present. The concept of anxiety provides a crucial key to understanding the positioning of women and femininity vis-à-vis the time of the modern. Is it not after all anxiety which propels the constant relegation of women and femininity—as prehistoric relics—outside the modern imaginary? When women enter concepts of history, they gain status as agents, as people related to the public sphere. Their subjugation is called into question. To prevent this, women must remain *outside of time.* Masculine mastery over women—as with white, colonial mastery of racialized subjects—can be seen to rest upon a temporal order. Ideologies of time have consequences for the conception and representation of human beings, and thus for their access to the modern imaginary. A feminist analysis of modern temporality reminds us that time is intimately tied to the possibility of freedom for women, racialized people and other Others who are understood not to 'fit' modernity.

FASHION, FEMINIST THEORY, AND MODERN TEMPORALITY

Fashion intersects with this feminist analysis of the material consequences of temporal consciousness in modernity. The existing literature on the temporality of fashion is not, in the main, written from a feminist theoretical perspective, yet it has such clear consequences for conceptions of gender. Feminist work on time *grounds* theories of temporality—it shows that ideologies of time *matter* in profound ways. So, too, does fashion allow us to see how temporal consciousness is materialized in objects and lived social relations.

   As well, fashion implicitly proposes that knowledge is made not by individuals, but by communities of knowers, together. In working with fashion, I broaden the claim of feminist philosophers that knowledge is a communal production, asking that we consider the *things* we encounter—and not just the people—as important in the production of knowledge. For the presumption that knowledge is made by wholly autonomous knowers, rather than communities of knowers, has been identified by feminist philosophers as intrinsic to the construction of the ideal knower as masculine. Women have not, in modernity, been understood to satisfy the criteria designating an autonomous individual. But while fashion is a social practice, it is *also* an intimate, individual one. It thus challenges the inaccurate yet dominant conception of the autonomous individual as completely distinct from others. Analysing fashion's temporal status, then, allows us to think about the ways that individual wearers and consumers mediated broader ideologies of time, and internalized the development of time consciousness. Of course, any discussion of fashion must surely recognize the medium's limitations; fashion does not offer a utopian playground. Its relationship to narrowly defined, corporeal ideals is certainly questionable. And, as fashion theorists have long understood, fashion is a primary field for the reproduction of social class; regimes of taste that govern fashionability function on the basis of class-based exclusions. But its peculiar temporal rhythms, at least, are suggestive of ways of organizing social life that do not rely on rigid social distinctions.

On the face of it, what is most notable about fashion for feminist theorists is simply its dynamic, change-oriented character, which accelerated aggressively with the development of new technologies from the middle of the nineteenth century.[28] As Joanne Entwistle notes, '[f]ashion thrives in a world of social mobility, a dynamic world characterized by class and political conflict, urbanization and aesthetic innovation, so it is not surprising that fashion flourished in the nineteenth century, when social upheaval reached a new zenith with the French and the Industrial Revolutions.'[29] It is precisely this changeable character of fashion that made it so suggestive to social theorists of the late nineteenth and early twentieth centuries, who saw it as an embodiment of the fragmentary character of modernity.[30] But this equation deserves unpacking; the rhetoric of newness that change implies is, in fact, more complex than it would at first seem.

Consider the constant interplay of past and present that is evident in fashion's tendency to reference the past. The modern period gave us several important examples of this tendency, but one of the most influential and complex in the era of fashion's modernity is the revival of a modified *Directoire* silhouette by Paul Poiret in 1906. Poiret borrowed the silhouette from the simple, muslin, 'Empire' waisted chemise dress style that was popular in the *Directoire* years immediately following the French Revolution.[31] In their original incarnation, *Directoire* dresses were associated with classical Greek column dresses—this early modern fashion had itself been an imitation of an earlier style. The style, then, marked the inevitability of repetition in fashion, and complicated associations of fashion with newness. Indeed, Poiret's own understanding of his *Directoire* dresses was that it was their *historical quality* that guaranteed their *novelty*: by appropriating French Revolutionary styles, he was able to fashion himself and the dress line as crusaders for 'Liberty'.[32] The introduction, disappearance and return of the bustle between about 1870 and 1890 offers a slightly different take on the phenomenon of historical revival—and the initial appearance of the bustle in the early 1870s was itself inspired by dress styles of the previous century.[33]

And so, Elizabeth Wilson is surely correct to declare that 'fashion *is* change'. But the *kinds* of change that modern fashion instituted—always cyclical, and so often oriented to the past—compromised associations between change and progress.[34] The nineteenth-century preoccupation with progress that characterized modern science, history, politics and economics was countered by a

Figure 1.1   This French evening dress, from 1804–05, offers an excellent example of the *Directoire* style. The Metropolitan Museum of Art, Purchase, Gifts in Memory of Elizabeth H. Lawrence, 1983 (1983.6.1). Image © The Metropolitan Museum of Art. Image source: Art Resource, NY.

secondary philosophical interest in 'eternal return' or 'eternal recurrence' as the condition of modern life. Fashion materially reflected that orientation to recurrence, and its widespread diffusion made it a powerful counter to the philosophy of progress. Thus it was a tangible and visible intervention in those philosophies of time that would disavow the relationship between past and present.[35] In Caroline Evans's elegant formulation, '[t]he traces of the past surface in the present like the return of the repressed. Fashion designers call up these ghosts of modernity and offer us a paradigm that is different from the historian's paradigm, remixing fragments of the past into something new and contemporary that will continue to resonate into the future.'[36]

Fashion's tendency to underscore the close relationship between the past and the present should engender feminist interest in this question, since

Figure 1.2   This rendering of two evening dresses from Poiret's 1908 collection highlights the similarities to the original *Directoire* dresses. Paul Iribe (1883–1935), evening dress design from *Les Robes de Paul Poiret,* 1908. The Art Archive at Art Resource, NY.

fashion was so deeply feminized in the popular imagination. Recall that women were commonly figured as anterior to the modern—either as mired in the past or as altogether outside of time. This figuration was a kind of determination of their identities. Women's time was seen to relegate them to static *being*, and exclude them from the possibilities of becoming and creation, which were the qualities valued in modernity. But fashion's constellation of past and present implies movement and change. First, if the past refuses fixity, and instead visits itself upon the present, then femininity itself can be seen to visit the time of the now, to refuse imprisonment in an inaccessible past. Second, the movement must not be seen as unidirectional, characterized by the constant thrust of the past into the present. In a cyclical structure, the present also gives way to the past; the modern gives itself over to femininity. A cleanly delineated modernity, defined against that feminized, pre-modern past, is compromised. In either case, repetition is a clear alternative to a linear temporality which presumes a definitive break with the feminized past. More importantly, in challenging the association of women with a distant past, a repetitive temporality refuses to affix women to any single time or space, or any one identity. Instead, it presumes that femininity is not singular, not knowable or masterable.[37]

This refusal of feminized fixity can also be seen in the everyday life of fashion and its wearing. The wearing of dress underscores the difficulty of identifying the wearing subject. As sociological studies of dress make clear, different outfits are, at the very least, suggestive of different modes of being, different identities. In an early-twentieth-century context, for instance, there is evidence that the ephemeral character of fashion issued a material challenge to conceptions of feminine identity and, as such, threatened the social control of women, and their legibility as feminine. In France, Mary Louise Roberts details the change in the fashionable silhouette that occurred over just twenty years—from the introduction of Poiret's less structured silhouette in 1906 to the brief dominance of severe, 'boyish' straight lines and shorter skirts by 1925—and how that change was met with anxiety on the part of cultural conservatives and celebration on the part of feminists. The popular press and literature were filled with images of French women reimagining their lives as a result of changes in sartorial fashion. Both cultural conservatives and feminists read the change in feminine fashion as, to use Roberts's word, a 'maker' of concrete, material change in women's lives.[38] The power of fashion to effect shifts in both representations of women, and perceptions of women's *being*, is directly related to its fluctuating temporal logic.

Repetition is also—contrary to the assertions of those, like Benjamin, who would see it as singularly deadening—a modality of change. As Rita Felski writes, 'the task for feminist theory is surely to connect repetition and change rather than to sever them. Cyclical time and linear time are not opposed but intertwined; the innovations of modernity are made real in the routines of everyday life.'[39] Felski's formulation underscores two important things for a feminist analysis of time and fashion: it reminds us that the repetition of fashion is—quite apart from its spectacular display—an *everyday* modality, and it also reminds us that repetition does not necessarily mean sameness. Repetition can denote micrological change that is visible in everyday life. In at least these two senses, then, a feminist analysis of repetition interrogates the insistence that repetition is necessarily a politics of the same.

The first question, that of the everyday, is addressed by Rita Felski in her article 'The Invention of Everyday Life'. Here, she argues that the association of repetition with everyday drudgery, such as household tasks, has long been a part of its feminization and trivialization. And the identification of repetition as deadening coincides with the identification of femininity as prehistoric, static and distinctly unmodern. Felski responds by recuperating repetition in a way that resonates productively with descriptions of fashion's time. She writes, '[r]epetition … situates the individual in an imagined community that spans historical time. It is thus not opposed to transcendence, but the means of transcending one's historically limited existence.'[40] Arguing against the modernist romance with the new, and the related dismissal of the past as static and deadening, Felski proposes that repetition be embraced as a modality of the everyday life of modernity—one that is 'internally complex' and that 'combines repetition and linearity, recurrence with forward movement'.[41]

Felski's antidualistic move with respect to modernity's pasts and presents is an apt metaphor for fashion. As Caroline Evans notes, '[f]ashion is a paradigm in the way that it can carry a contradiction—this is very modern—the whole thing is a kind of "dialectical image" or "critical constellation" not just of past and present but of differing modernities, and its "now-time" can hold them together in suspension.'[42] Evans's concept of fashion as a modality of ambivalence, one that is suggestive of 'multiple modernities', is crucial in excavating the positions of women and femininity in the modern. The hidden narratives of modernity challenge the heroic romance with the new. They are also the location of femininity, key to the project of 'seeing' women in the modern.[43] But of course, those narratives cannot be isolated from the narratives of public, heroic modernity against which they are defined. And fashion—experienced both intimately and publicly, hiding secrets and revealing them—allows us uniquely to hold these elements against each other, to trace their relations. To read a hidden and feminized narrative against the progress narrative is to push at a power-saturated tension. The hidden narratives of the modern show us that women and femininity can be seen as a *structuring* Other of modernity. These narratives call attention to a kind of double-time of modern feminine representation, in which images of women are both visible and invisible, present and absent from the scenes of history.

This presence—even hyper-visible presence—is crucial, though it is not always sharply in focus in accounts of the relationship between women and modernity. Often these read simply as tales of the alienated relationship between feminine representation and the modern. It is less common to consider the ways in which femininity is *synonymous* with industrial modernity. What interests me is the simultaneity of this relationship, the *unevenness* of the temporal figuration of women: depending on the context, they were seen as both modern and unmodern. And fashion, with its undeniably spectacular dimension of display, balanced by its intimate relationship to the wearer, can illuminate this paradox.

In part, fashion sheds light on the presence and absence of women from the modern imaginary by enacting, only to problematize, the split between public and private. This is because the thoroughly inaccurate perception of a division between public and private—between civic life and home life—can be seen to mirror the temporal split between modernity and its Others. Whereas time and space have tended to be treated separately in social theory, an attention to both asks us to reconsider the way in which time maps gendered spaces and spheres. Home life was alternately figured as having one of two temporal dimensions in industrial modernity: it was either outside of time altogether, or it was a relic of past time. In both cases, the private can be seen to function as a kind of nostalgic playground—as a balm for the weary, masculine subjects of a frenetically paced modern world. When the feminine is relegated to the private sphere, then, it is also relegated to another time.

Counter to this identification of women with the private sphere, modern fashion was very much a public endeavour, a thoroughly social forging of the norms and practices of femininity. It was so from its most rarefied realms— the spaces of couture houses, for example, and the mannequin parades that developed early in the twentieth century—through its increasing presence in the print media and informal public practices of fashion such as window-shopping. All of these manifestations of fashion in public involved the spectacle of women's bodies, of femininity, in ways that seemed to privilege associations of women with modern time. For instance, Caroline Evans notes that 'by 1925 mannequins [live fashion models] did have a social and symbolic presence: they were eloquent icons of modernity, even in their silence. From the beginning of the century, journalists had identified the mannequin as a new kind of career girl, distinct from the *demi-mondaine* or the actress.'[44] In the French context, Roberts has closely detailed the ways that popular mediations of dress and personal style effectively transformed women into representations of modern life. And as Martin Pumphrey explains for the American situation in the 1920s, '[f]ashion ... encouraged women to become involved in modernity not in abstract theoretical ways but in terms of image and lifestyle.'[45] Liz Conor traces how fashion's spaces and rituals allowed for the development of a new, peculiarly modern form of being for women in Australia in the 1920s.[46] Fashion was one important arena where women were represented—and experienced themselves, as Roberts's and Pumphrey's work shows—as agents of modernity and its public life, and not its outsiders. Fashion's sheer visibility worked to establish the women who were its primary consumers as icons of the modern age. Indeed, fashion *depended* on the intermittent modernization of femininity; this temporal realignment of femininity with progress would be the engine of the fashion economy.

But, after all, the task is to complicate the neat dichotomy between new and old, and so we must not satisfy ourselves that public, spectacular dimensions of fashion simply inserted women into the narrative of modernity. One must also consider the intimate dimensions of fashion, the ones which are not so readily understood as public practices: the acts of admiring, desiring, touching and wearing that are also key to women's relationship with clothing in this period. Certainly, the consumption of fashionable clothing takes place in public, but it too has an emotive dimension that complicates the opposition between public and private and the temporal split that is written into this. Importantly, garments as material things have a singular power to evoke memory, to bring the past into the present. In this way dress and fashion once again have the capacity to destabilize the carefully guarded boundary between past, present and future that defines modernity.

Consider, for example, the episode described by Peter Stallybrass in his essay 'Worn Worlds: Clothes, Mourning, and the Life of Things'. It begins with a personal account of Stallybrass delivering a conference paper while wearing the jacket of his recently deceased friend and collaborator, Allon White. As Stallybrass describes it, 'I was giving a paper on the concept of the individual when I was quite literally overcome. I could not read, and an embarrassing silence ensued. I cried . . . Later, when I tried to understand what had happened, I realized that for the first time since his death, Allon White had returned to me.'[47] Stallybrass writes that his paper on the individual was an attempt to

> invoke Allon. But at no time in the writing of it was my invocation answered. Like the paper, Allon was dead. And then, as I began to read, I was inhabited by his presence, taken over. If I wore the jacket, Allon wore me. He was there in the wrinkles of the elbows, wrinkles which in the technical jargon of sewing are called 'memory'; he was there in the stains at the very bottom of the jacket; he was there in the smell of the armpits.[48]

Here, Stallybrass locates memory—and mourning—in the very stuff of clothing. He describes the garment's ability to shock the subject by intervening in a carefully ordered temporality that separates 'now' from 'then'. His is only one particularly elegant meditation among a large number of works that show clothing's powerful ability to bear the past into the present.[49] Writ large, and considered in light of modern time consciousness, this is a major intervention—and one that has gendered consequences. Remember that clothing is associated with the feminine, with women, in the modern period. If it is the case that clothing, as a feminine article, begets memory, then we have another example of the gendered encounter of past and present. Once again, a figural feminine finds its way into the present, into the new, but only by bearing traces of the past. The repression of the past, as Stallybrass's anecdote makes clear, is impossible. Through his wearing, his past creeps into his present life in unanticipated, uncontrollable ways. This is a useful way of conceiving of the feminized past in modernity: as a repressed temporal register whose presence makes itself known in any number of ways, in that sense complicating the narrative of the ever-new that functions to exclude women from the modern.[50]

FASHION'S EPHEMERALITY AS
FEMINIST CONCEPTUAL TOOL

All of the examples outlined above provide an outline of the *ephemeral*, or changeable, in the modern age. It must be noted that the ephemeral has historically been equated with superficiality, which signals a danger in appropriating this concept in thinking about women and fashion in the modern era. Gilles Lipovetsky, for example, in his book *The Empire of Fashion*, suggests that the most important characteristic of fashion in modernity is its 'logic of inconstancy, its great organizational and aesthetic mutations ... Fashion is a trifling, fleeting, contradictory object par excellence.'[51] Indeed, he argues that '[t]he fashion economy has engendered a social agent in its own image: the *fashion person* who has no deep attachments, a mobile individual with a fluctuating personality and tastes.'[52] Of course, the tight association of fashion with women means that this attachment-lacking '*fashion person*' of Lipovetsky's is by default a woman—although gender is conspicuously absent from his book-length account. In linking the ephemeral with superficiality, then, Lipovetsky inadvertently points us to the potential danger in using ephemerality as a theoretical vehicle to problematize the exclusion of women from modernity. It can fall into the trap of incessantly reproducing concepts of women and femininity as irrational, inconstant and 'trifling'. Longstanding cultural associations between substance and permanence associate fashion with 'mere' artifice; it is often dismissed as simply a means of masking the authentic. This unwritten connection between women and artifice that Lipovetsky indulges in, which opposes femininity to authenticity and depth, thus places at the centre of modernity a vision of the human which feminists might wish to interrogate.

But there are other possibilities for thinking about ephemeral time, possibilities which contradict rather than support the history of ideas about women's superficiality. In *Esthétique de l'éphémère*, Christine Buci-Glucksmann proposes that the ephemeral is a kind of in-between time: 'It captures time in ... intervals.'[53] The ephemeral time that she theorizes refuses the kinds of dichotomies that have operated to exclude women from the scenes of the modern. For instance, a thread running through her short monograph is that 'ephemerality both *is* and *is not*'[54]; neither wholly existent nor non-existent, it is imperceptible but still potent. This in-between state must not be dualistically opposed, she warns, to weight, solidity and perceptible, material being. Rather, Buci-Glucksmann suggests that the ephemeral represents a 'novel temporal paradigm that brings together the fragile, the transitory, the perishable and the hollow ... From this commotion comes a true *cogito* of ephemerality, which will slowly extinguish the old relationship between being and becoming that characterizes western metaphysics and Renaissance humanism.'[55] Using the figure of glass to represent the ephemeral—as both fragile and solid—she advances a new kind of materialism, one that she terms 'crystalline'.[56]

Buci-Glucksmann's framing of the ephemeral is useful in conceptualizing the feminized medium of fashion. In industrial modernity, fashion's ephemerality lay in its changeability; it had the potential to undermine the profound stasis of images of women as prehistoric or otherwise antimodern. Those static images encased women in narrowly defined identities, pitting them against the ideal of movement and change that was aligned with men. But rather than settle on one image of femininity, the ephemeral logic of fashion depends upon the proliferation of *multiple* images. While feminists might surely, like Walter Benjamin, fault fashion for privileging only an illusion of change, and not authentic change or diversity, fashion nevertheless inaugurates and indeed makes socially available a temporality characterized by change: the ephemeral. For, though it is not fixed, fashion does not turn femininity into nothing more than a mobile image. It is, by its very nature, a constellation of image and matter, sitting at the crossroads of the two. Its abstract cultural meaning is undeniable, but it depends upon the tangible acts of touching and wearing. In this sense, foregrounding a notion of ephemeral time allows us to animate ideas about the feminine, but without losing sight of the actual bodies of women.

In moving us away from static feminine identities, Buci-Glucksmann's more fluctuating order of temporality foregrounds instead the ways modern women were *known*. This allows us to think about how women came to be visible, and identified as antimodern or modern through their constantly shifting relationships with fashionable clothing. Foregrounding fashion as ephemeral makes it possible to think about modern women as subjects and objects of knowledge, whose location relative to modernity was neither fixed nor stable. Rather, it was the result of negotiations with a social world that was constantly changing. When we understand time as a question related to knowledge, we are able to start bringing individual gendered subjects into view, asking how they accessed and mediated modernity. Rather than give us straw figures of modernity—the quintessential, active bourgeois man pitted against the static, antimodern woman—a framework of ephemerality gives us the conceptual tools to *animate* the gendered representations that we attach to the modern. Foregrounding the ephemeral shows that thinking about time might revitalize our understandings of the historical dimensions of everyday life in the modern period. Fashion, as an ephemeral practice that links the self to the social, is a productive ally in linking theoretical frameworks of time to social and cultural histories of the modern, histories that have been useful in centring women as agents of modernity.

Clothing and fashion thus show that women's figural relationship to modern time operates in several different, overlapping and sometimes conflicting registers. It is not simply about being relegated to the outside of modernity. Certainly, such representations of femininity as antimodern are powerful and common, but they are not the only way that women's relationship with modernity has been figured. The seeds of other kinds of relationships between women and the time of the modern exist. For, on one level, early-twentieth-century fashion depended on the positioning of women as central to the modern, thus providing an important contrast to representations of women as antimodern. On another level, fashion's peculiar, cyclical temporal rhythm contributed to an interrogation, even a deconstruction, of the dualistic understanding of femininity as premodern. Fashion's tempo, because it was materially embodied in the feminized world of garments themselves, suggested a kind of spectral visitation of femininity upon the masculinized world of the modern. Altogether, fashion helps brings into focus the ambiguity and contradictory character of representations of femininity in the modern era. Underscoring ambiguity in the relationship between women and modernity is not as straightforward as reclaiming women from historical invisibility, but it may allow us to ask questions about whether what appears to be invisibility is, in fact, a compromised, variable visibility—and to inquire into the conditions that shape such a relationship to visibility.

EPHEMERAL FASHION AND THE IDENTITIES OF COUTURIERS AND CLIENTS

The question for this project, of course, is what relationship couturiers had to ephemerality as a feminized construct that undergirded their industry. Did their handling of the question of the ephemeral accord with or challenge the potentially positive interventions made by a theory of ephemeral feminine identities that I discuss above? Pierre Bourdieu's work on cultural fields, and specifically his work on fashion and the persona of the fashion designer, proves helpful in contextualizing the relationship of the designer to this fundamental condition of fashion. He foregrounds the manipulation of time, including ephemeral time, that was necessary for the viability of the couturier's house, tied as it was to the necessarily charismatic persona of the designer.

There is no question that designers recognized the ephemeral character of their industry. But where the ephemeral was invoked, it was usually with a tinge of melancholy or at least negative judgment—as in Schiaparelli's formulation that dressmaking is 'a most difficult and unsatisfying art, because as soon as a dress is born it becomes a thing of the past'.[57] Poiret, for his part, associates ephemerality with women's irrationality, and constructs himself as helping to save women from this handicap. And *Dior by Dior* contains a number of despairing pronouncements about the ephemeral; Dior clearly presents himself as longing for certainty, for a stillness impossible to achieve in his industry.[58] All of this shall be discussed in more detail in subsequent chapters. For now, the important point is that the couturier revealed their discomfort with the governing temporal logic of their field.

Bourdieu's work helps us see that this distancing from the ephemeral is closely related to the precariousness of the designer's position in a highly changeable industry. He notes the disadvantage that attends the couture designer who hopes to be accepted as an artist: 'the *couturier* is involved in an art of inferior rank in the hierarchy of artistic legitimacy and cannot avoid accounting, in his work, for the future social image of his product.'[59] There is an anxiety related to time built into the designer's work, then; she or he is aware of success's dependence on time, aware that the future might do one of two things: it will either date their work in the moment it appeared, or suggest that it will persist into the future, becoming 'timeless'. For a charismatic major couturier, one who personifies the design house and whose image is wedded to the label (like all three of the designers in this book), the question becomes: 'how can the unique irruption which brings discontinuity into a universe be turned into a durable institution? How can the continuous be made of the discontinuous?'[60] In other words, one of the couturier's primary tasks was to *manage* perceptions of time, in order to reconcile the demands for material changeability of dress and image with the need for a figurehead who would embody not only charisma, but stability. This was the management, then, of two very different registers of time: the ephemeral and the timeless.

The manipulability of time was made possible, for Bourdieu, by 'one of the most important properties of all fields of production, namely the permanent presence of the past of the field, which is endlessly recalled'.[61] The presence of the past allows it to become an index against which designers can register the relevance and aesthetic importance of their own creations—and, crucially, the relevance or irrelevance of consuming women's knowledges. In both his work on fashion and on cultural fields more generally, Bourdieu points to the ways that creators 'discredited older principles of production and judgment by making a style that owed much of its authority and its prestige to its age ("classic couture house," "house founded in ... ," etc.) appear outmoded, irrelevant, old-fashioned'.[62] Thus the activity involved in producing the couturier persona is principally one of establishing *authority* through the manipulation of time. Power is achieved through the displacement to past time—or archaic time—of aesthetic forces that might threaten the supremacy of one's own aesthetic vision. This includes other designers, of course, but—as I shall show in Chapter Two with respect to the case of Poiret—it could conceivably include other actors in the field of fashion, including the women whose apparently 'innate' and 'frivolous' knowledge of fashion and style contained the potential to unseat the couturier by challenging his or her style supremacy. In an exemplary instance of the popular argument that it was women who held authority in matters of style, a 1936 editorial in the first issue of *New York Woman* asked:

After all, who really makes the fashion? The dressmaker? The great Paris couturier? The fabric manufacturer? Or, the mighty fashion designer? *No!* They all make what they *hope* will be the fashion. It's you who make the fashion. If you like a thing and wear it, it is the fashion. All the dressmakers in creation can't put over one single new thing unless you accept it.[63]

Thus the structure of the modern fashion industry *potentially* situates the woman in modernity by aligning her fashionable changeability with the undeniably presentist tempo of the industry. But the designer's struggle to preserve legitimacy in a precarious field by denying women's knowledge of fashion and style could be seen to re-relegate women to the premodern, the archaic.

Bourdieu defines the field of culture as 'the battle between those who have made their names (*fait date*) and are struggling to stay in view and those who cannot make their own names without relegating to the past the established figures, whose interest lies in freezing the moment of time, fixing the present state of the field for ever'.[64] There is a telling contradiction here that is crucial to understanding designers' relationships to the ephemeral: they must shore up their own newness through denying others' threatening newness by suggesting that the others are stuck in the past. They thereby maintain the appearance but neutralize the effects of the ephemeral. After all, the *appearance* of the ephemeral is necessary to their continued aesthetic and commercial success: they must be seen to constantly introduce new styles, in order to generate desire and thus sales.

Management of time perception thus means harnessing the ephemeral in order to adapt it to the needs of a commercial market, for the market is what drives both the development of the couture house and the charismatic persona of the couturier. If the ephemeral has the potential to free women from the tyranny of femininity as a fixed and static identity, this potential is threatened by the *management* of the ephemeral in the service of a static and publicly available, profit-dependent identity of another. The ephemeral thus must not be imagined to stand outside of the structures in which it is implicated. As it materializes in this field, it is subjected to the structural rules of *haute couture*, which, as Bourdieu makes clear, are arranged around the designer as a singular, iconoclastic entity. He writes, '[t]he creator's signature is a mark that changes not the material nature but the social nature of the object.'[65] He is arguing that the designer's signature makes a difference in more than simply the material, object-based field of fashion. In the manipulations of time that the couturier's situation demands, the social nature of the changeable object is closely tied to femininity, to living women. When these manipulations involve subtle adjustments to the perception of fashion as a living, ephemeral field, they necessarily implicate femininity. They threaten to reinstall a static, fixed idea of femininity as the primary object of the fashion industry.

This is not to say, of course, that the potential of the ephemeral was completely overlooked by designers. On the contrary, Bourdieu reminds us that '[p]eople too often think in simple dichotomies. "Either it changes, or it doesn't change." "Static or dynamic".'[66] Ephemerality can be mobilized in any number of different ways, as the example of fashion shows. In this instance, it circulated in the spectacular and linguistic structures of fashion in ways that could not be controlled by designers. After all, designers did not ultimately direct the representation of the ephemeral by the fashion press, mass-produced fashion or the reception of these domains by consumers. But the ephemeral was also mobilized in a domain that couturiers could control to a large extent: their own self-representations. And so, designer manipulations of ephemeral time did not completely define the figuration of women in the field, but they constituted a strong counterbalance to the circulation of images of dynamic femininities.

Just as the ephemeral both frees femininity from stasis and potentially re-affixes it to an antimodern past, so can women's positioning in the fashion field in the early twentieth century not be finally defined as 'good' or 'bad', liberating or oppressive. Like fashion itself, with its temporal complexity, women's place in modernity is a site of contradiction. Norbert Hillaire writes, 'fashion and modernity echo one another in the affirmation of the same principle of contradiction, that makes a crisis a positive value, and time passing a threat and a promise at the same time.'[67] Hillaire reminds us—recalling Bourdieu's broader reminder that we are unnecessarily wedded to dichotomies in our understanding of social phenomena—that one of the most important characteristics of fashion for the feminist critic working on this period is its ability to complicate the binary frameworks that too often inform our work. Consider Caroline Evans and Minna Thornton's formulation: 'fashion has always existed as a challenge to meaning where meaning is understood to involve some notion of coherence, a demonstrable consistency.'[68] The meaning of the ephemeral, in this case, shifts according to context and according to the actors involved; the meaning is as ephemeral as the phenomena it describes. What becomes important, then, is to locate *tendencies*. The complex and ironic rendering of the ephemeral as archaic—which implicates women as supposedly ephemeral beings in designer self-representations—constitutes one such important tendency. It complicates our inclination to imagine modern fashion as a straightforwardly liberating site for women and femininity, and instead brings into focus the contradictions at the heart of the industry's uses of women. The following chapters, examining in close detail the figurations of time that buttress the self-representations of these three designers, reveal fashion as a site of contradiction that staged an implicit encounter between different visions of women's relationship to modern time.

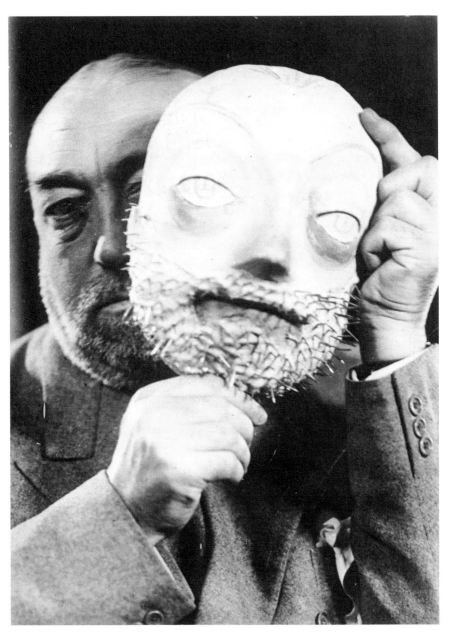

Figure 2.1 Photograph of Paul Poiret with portrait mask of himself, by the artist Goursat. Around 1935. Photo by Imagno/Getty Images. Hulton Archive. © Getty Images.

Paul Poiret: Classic and New in the Struggle for Designer Mastery

Paul Poiret (1879–1944) attests in his major memoir, *King of Fashion*, that he was attracted to aesthetic work, and especially to women's fashion, from a young age. He designed for the great couturiers Jacques Doucet (from 1898 to 1900) and the House of Worth (from 1900 to 1903) before opening his own couture house in 1903. He achieved renown around 1906, through his introduction of the *Directoire* collection, which is said to have 'liberated' women from the need to wear corsets. This line, which dominated his work into the next decade, featured a high waistline that fell just below the bust—what is best known as an Empire waist—and was notable for what appeared to be a radical re- or even de-structuring of the feminine silhouette through its softly flowing lines, in comparison to the highly structured and flagrantly corseted Edwardian silhouette. Notwithstanding the hyperbole attached to claims that it ended the reign of the corset,[1] Cheryl Buckley and Hilary Fawcett describe the *Directoire* style in this way: 'Poiret's fashions were worn looser around the body, and designs such as the kimono coat from 1908 wrapped, rather than structured, the body ... The overall outline was rectilinear, although occasionally the gown would be drawn tight under the breasts, but the natural waistline was almost completely disguised.'[2] Other designers, such as Lucile (Lady Duff Gordon), worked with similar visions of uncorseted bodies, but it is Poiret whose work was and continues to be overwhelmingly singled out as revolutionary in its reform of dress. His work with the *Directoire* silhouette is often remembered through its iconic rendering in original, hand-drawn *pochoir* illustrations by Paul Iribe (published in the book *Les Robes de Paul Poiret*, 1908) and Georges Lepape (*Les choses de Paul Poiret vues de Georges Lepape*, 1911).

Poiret continued to design into the mid-1930s, with several breaks (to briefly serve France in the First World War, for example, and after his company was sold in the late 1920s). His downfall in the 1920s was well documented, including by Poiret himself. His company was sold in 1929, after several financially precarious years, though Poiret briefly designed under its name in the 1930s. Famously positioning himself in opposition to what he saw as the unoriginal styling of newer designers, such as Chanel, he railed against changed ideals of femininity and new aesthetic regimes that seemed to exclude him.

Figure 2.2   A Poiret dinner dress from 1910. Brooklyn Museum Costume Collection at The Metropolitan Museum of Art, Gift of the Brooklyn Museum, 2009. Gift of Ogden Goelet, Peter Goelet and Madison Clews in memory of Mrs. Henry Clews, 1961 (2009.300.1289). Image © The Metropolitan Museum of Art. Image source: Art Resource, NY.

Poiret's ambivalent legacy—which he thought was tarnished by the turbulence of those later years—did not include fashion alone, however. He also established a perfume company and an interior design/decorative arts business, named after his daughters Rosine and Martine, respectively. As Harold Koda and Andrew Bolton note, 'he was the first couturier to align fashion with interior design and promote the concept of a "total lifestyle."'[3] Further diversifying his work, he also undertook some costume design for theatre and dance, including most famously his work with the Ballets Russes.[4] Poiret also painted, wrote a recipe book and hosted a dinner club in the 1920s; he fashioned himself as a kind of Renaissance man.

Chequered later history aside, reports of Paul Poiret from the period of his dominance of *haute couture* are singularly reverential. Called the King of Fashion—a title borrowed for one edition of the English translation of his first

Figure 2.3   This Poiret opera coat from 1911 emphasizes the 'rectilinear', 'wrapped' line of the body that distinguished Poiret's early work. The Metropolitan Museum of Art, New York. Alfred Z. Solomon-Janet A. Sloane Endowment Fund, 2008 (2008.288). Image © The Metropolitan Museum of Art. Image source: Art Resource, NY.

memoir—Poiret was also, for example, held up in 1912 as a 'Prophet' working in a kind of holy sanctuary.[5] A brief *Vogue* homage from 1920 tells us that 'the Parisienne cannot *not* love Poiret; she sees in him one of the most inspired priests of the cult of her body.'[6] In 1921, a profile renders him as akin to an oil or steel baron—those most powerful of figures, in that prosperous decade—and, mixing metaphors, characterizes his workplace as a temple.[7] In 1925, the effects of this power are revealed: women are (contentedly) enslaved by the King of Fashion, states a brief newspaper profile and interview.[8] Even several years after his demise, the preamble to a *Harper's Bazaar* article by him declares, 'the Poiret of the fabulous era before the war was a dictator to whom the beauties of the world paid awed tribute.' 'He ruled despotically,' wrote Jean Cocteau. 'Women who dared question his edicts ended by begging him not to order them out, to continue dressing them.'[9] Indeed, as the market for his ideas and his fashions, women are woven into all of the worshipful representations of this most revered couturier. Most often, they are revealed as this king's *subjects.*

This tendency is reflected in his own self-representations; Poiret was a prolific writer who published three autobiographical books, dozens of articles on fashion, feminine beauty and French culture in the popular press, as well as an unusual diversity of other titles ranging from *Deauville*—an irreverent portrait of high society life in the Norman resort town, illustrated by Kees Van Dongen—to *Popolôrepô*, an experimental wordplay that was marketed by its publisher as 'Dadaist'. His publication of the three autobiographical volumes within five years, from 1930 to 1935, suggests an intriguing drive toward his own memorialization as a designer. This is not surprising, considering that by 1930, when the first volume was published, Poiret had fallen far from the heights he occupied early in his career. The memoirs offered him a chance to rehabilitate his name, and confronting the unfortunate (and, to Poiret, shameful) dissolution of his career, we begin to understand why he felt so compelled to narrate his life. They are thus curious documents, for the tone he strikes is defensive and insecure, in contrast to the confident and masterful persona by which he clearly hopes readers will remember him. This contradictory character is evident throughout the works, structuring his readings of everything from the aesthetic quality of his designs—were they traditional or modern, timeless or historical?—to the women who worked for him and, above all, those who bought and wore his clothes and were thus instrumental in his success. These representations of the women and the designs—the two integral components of his professional life—must not, however, be considered apart from Poiret's sketches of himself: indeed, they are all related to the work of narrating a *professional* life, making a claim to professional authority. The conflicted representations of self, of work, of clients all point to a foundational instability that ultimately authorizes Poiret's claims to greatness. If this is the case—if this instability ultimately translates into the maintenance of reputational capital by Poiret—then what becomes of the women upon whom it is built? How does the limited, but still thoroughly conflicted, range of femininities in his work sustain the masterful figure that Poiret is so deeply invested in recuperating and preserving for the future?

In his first and best-known memoir, *En habillant l'époque* or *King of Fashion*, Paul Poiret unwittingly establishes the stakes of his profession for his readers:

> A creative dressmaker is accustomed to foresee, and must be able to divine the trends that will inspire the day after to-morrow. He is prepared long before women themselves to accept the accidents and incidents that occur on the trajectory of evolution, and that is why we cannot believe in a resistance by women, in their

clubs, or through tracts, lectures, meetings and protests of any sort, against that which to him seems logical, ineluctable, and already certain.[10]

This statement succinctly encapsulates the relationship between himself and women that Poiret unfolds across his autobiographical work and indeed in many of his other self-representational efforts. It is a relationship that, for him, is determined by temporal categories. His success ultimately derives from his ability to occupy, or at least access, multiple times—including, crucially, the future. On the other hand, his clients, who often stand in for femininity as a general category, are disabled by their inability to transgress boundaries of time: they are aligned *either* with the past or with the now. In any case, the ability to inhabit multiple times might be seen as one element of the capacity for magic that Pierre Bourdieu sees as essential to what he calls the 'field' of cultural production. For Bourdieu, the creator's signature functions as a 'quasi-magical' symbol, conferring authority on the individual creator by 'mobiliz[ing] the symbolic energy produced by the functioning of the whole field', in this case, the field of *haute couture* fashion.[11] Such magic constitutes the foundation of Poiret's apparent mastery, and Poiret's above quotation reveals that the mastery of his field is simultaneously a mastery of femininity in general.

Certainly, such descriptions of women are a dominant theme in Poiret's work, but they are not the only ones that he engages. The designer's understandings of femininity are complex and contradictory, and match his descriptions of himself as a master of fashion while being simultaneously undermined by his defensive tone. Indeed, the defensiveness must follow from his own sense that his credibility is imperilled. This leads to a parallel figure in his representations of women, which might be understood to proceed from a sense of professional diminishment and insecurity. There is a persistent sense, across his writing, but especially in *King of Fashion*, of women as holders of secrets, secrets to which his work potentially—but never completely—allows access. The anxiety that cuts across Poiret's self-representations, then, can be traced to this sense of his mastery being short-circuited by women's withholdings of themselves, of their knowledge, of their worship of him. After all, their acquiescence and even enslavement to him was the basis for Poiret's commercial success, and it was a withholding of such worship and deference, he believes, that precipitated his downfall.

In this chapter, I begin from the unstable *relationships* that characterize Poiret's extensive self-representations. An individualist and iconoclast, Poiret would be scandalized by an attempt to understand his persona primarily in relation to others. But if his autobiographical writing reveals anything, it is that this was a figure whose sense of himself was deeply inflected by a history of gendered concepts. Poiret's self-perception was as heavily dependent

Figure 2.4 Advertisement for Paul Poiret Couture, *Harper's Bazaar*, June 1926. University of Washington Libraries, Special Collections, UW29993z.

upon his distant but masterful relationship to an imagined femininity as his commercial success and failure were dependent upon the preferences, social status and capital of living women. And so, here I explore how the intricate registers of time in Poiret's self-representational strategies, as integral as they were to his self-concept, at the same time contributed to the forging of relationships. These relationships are characterized by a deep ambivalence, confusion and anxiety about the designer's status, which is projected onto the women upon whom he depends. This is key to understanding not only the gendered condition of the designer in early twentieth-century modernity, but the centrality of fashion in the creation of ideological landscapes of femininity in this period—and, of course, vice versa.

WOMEN AND THE DEFINITION OF FASHION
AS A CULTURAL FIELD

In a meditation on the accumulation of symbolic capital in the fields of cultural production, Bourdieu, who views fashion as one among many such fields, explains that the production of time is central to the work of distinguishing the artists: 'To "make one's name" (*faire date*) means making one's *mark*, achieving recognition (in both senses) of one's *difference* from other producers; at the same time, it means *creating a new position* beyond the positions presently occupied, *ahead* of them, in the *avant-garde*.'[12] For this reason, he theorizes,

> the agents and institutions involved in the game are at once contemporaries and out of phase. The *field of the present* is just another name for the field of struggles (as shown by the fact that an author of the past is an author of the present insofar as he is at stake) and contemporaneity in the sense of presence in the same present exists, in practice, only in the struggle which synchronizes discordant times ... But the struggle which produces contemporaneity in the form of the confrontation of different times can only take place because the agents and groups it brings together are not present in the same present.[13]

Bourdieu's conception of the field tends to concentrate exclusively on the producers of fashion (or art or literature or any other art form), and he does not include the consumer when he specifies the players in the field.[14] But if we consider the shaping influence of consumer desire and demand on the fashion industry, as more recent theories of fashion allow us to do, then we must take seriously the consumer as a player in the field of fashion.[15] Of course, in fashion—especially the field of fashion as it was configured in the era of Poiret's dominance—the category 'consumer' designates women. By reconfiguring Bourdieu's field, we begin to see the prominence of women as players in fashion's field of struggles.

Taking seriously women consumers allows us to reframe the question of the fashion designer's production of time through her or his willed differentiation from other artists. As Bourdieu notes, the designer secures a reputation through his or her references to past, present and future and through the relegation of other players to the past. Bourdieu means that the designer relegates other *designers* to that past. In that sense, women as consumers do not qualify as that past against which the designer's originality is defined. But, as we shall see, an integral, if unconscious, theme in Poiret's self-representational efforts is that women *are* artists of a kind: that they innately possess the secrets of feminine beauty and aesthetic self-fashioning.

They thus become competitors. Indeed, the tenor of Poiret's rhetoric changes over the course of his career, until finally he suggests that it was women, with their insistence on making their own stylistic choices, with their turning toward uniform sportswear and away from originality and opulence, who were his downfall.[16] Poiret's written work reveals a kind of obsession with the threat posed by women; they figure much more prominently than do any other designers in his otherwise individualist self-concept. For this reason, Bourdieu's analysis of the artist's production of time provides a useful framework for understanding the temporal relationship established between Poiret and women. It is women—or, alternately, a figural femininity—which Poiret must relegate to the past in order to justify his preeminence, and even his work. Poiret's originality depends upon the maintenance of a temporal dichotomy between himself and his potential clients, his female employees and indeed women in general. As Bourdieu writes, 'setting fashion is more than declaring unfashionable the products of those who were in fashion last year, it is declaring unfashionable the products of those who *set* fashion the year before, thereby stripping them of their authority on fashion. The strategies of newcomers aim to push the older designers back into the past.'[17] Those outdated types who are relegated to the past but who possess a threatening authority, nonetheless, are women.

Bourdieu's schema stresses the ability of the designer to produce time. To do so, she or he must be actively invested in the work of denying or disavowing others' relationships to the work of design. Indeed, Poiret's work can be read as the product of an anxious labour of rejection, an elaborate edifice of representations erected as a kind of psychic *and* commercial defence against his failure. The stress on the designer's agency allows us to foreground the anxieties that underpinned modern time in this field. In the case of Poiret, these tensions which were so instrumental in the production of time revolved around the charged concepts of secrets, rationality and originality.

WOMEN'S SECRETS

Women's fashion and personal style have long been understood to constitute a domain of secrets, lies, masks, disguises, dissemblance.[18] This is where much of fashion's philosophical interest lies, of course: in its drawing of truth into question. Fashion tells us something about the individuals who wear it, but does it tell us the 'truth' of who the wearer is, or does the wearer use fashion to 'hide' herself? What are we seeing when we see fashion—the self or a strategic performance of the self? Of course, this confusion is also where much of fashion's apparently threatening status derives from. Since fashion is so closely associated with femininity, of course, this question of fashion's masking of truth has been linked to women. Unfortunately, a longstanding cultural suspicion of artifice means that this relationship between femininity and fashion as artificial has been cast in a negative light.

From a feminist theoretical perspective, it might be said that fashion has not been negative, but that it has conflated femininity with a principle of *uncertainty*. When we read someone's clothing, we do not know *exactly* who we are seeing. Moreover, such uncertainty runs counter to empiricism, the dominant understanding of knowledge since the early modern period that legitimate knowledge is accessible only through the senses and that it is certain, absolute, transparent. Fashion thus problematizes the assumption that we can know things and people absolutely and with certainty and finality. In this sense, it has the potential to challenge rigid determinations about women's lives, about who women *are*. Susan Kaiser argues that managing identities through fashion and style 'can be an epistemology of ambiguity. It acknowledges that self-truths are necessarily contingent.'[19] That is, fashion helps us see that truths about the self shift and change according to context. One puts on clothing and emphasizes one aspect of a complex self, which reminds us that the self is fluid and flexible, as is any person's life. This emphasis on changeable and flexible representations of self is of particular interest for many feminist theorists, who are interested in the provisional and contested nature of truth and of identity.

A paradigm like this, which acknowledges the way that clothing allows us to flexibly present and withhold various aspects of identity, brings up the question of secrets. Does fashion turn us into secret-keepers? Secretiveness is suggestive for feminist theorists interested in fashion (among many other domains) because it is about *possibility*. Secrets reveal the more hopeful side of the generally threatening notion of unknowability, which is that if something is withheld, if it is uncertain, it cannot be controlled or mastered and thus it is open to change. If a text contained no secret dimension, as Jacques Derrida puts it, 'there would be no way to have a future'.[20] This possibility of a future seems critical for feminist theory, particularly in the context of the modernist era, in which women were painted as outside of the possibility that modernity represented. Secrets thus have a temporal dimension. Though they might at first appear to be vestiges of history—certainly, secrets are often represented as knowledge that is handed down from the past—secrets also open onto the future. Their capacity to disturb certainties about feminine identities is, I suggest, the chief source of their interest to Poiret, and of his anxiety about them. As John Jervis puts it, '[t]he "secret of woman"—that is, both the solution to the mystery of woman and to the mystery of the otherness that woman serves to symbolize—is thus a source of both desire and fear.'[21]

The secrets that thread through Poiret's writings and interviews are of a particular kind: they are 'beauty secrets', 'fashion secrets', which are linked to women's seductive capacities, hence to their relationships with men. This brings us to an important characteristic of the secret: its relationality. The secret is not offered up; indeed, it depends on the keeper's refusal to offer it. There is a folding-in on oneself implied in the construction of a secret—it is a withholding. This would seem in one sense to imply an individual withholding—one person keeps a secret. But when we are referring to understandings of 'beauty secrets' or 'fashion secrets', we are more usually speaking about the shared secrets that make up a group identity—in this case, the identity 'women' can be seen to consolidate in the guarding of secret knowledge against others. Secrets are as often, or more often, held in common as they are held entirely individually. They weave a kind of fabric of relation between secret-sharers.

What is less obvious is that secrets inaugurate a relationship between secret-keepers and those who are *not* let in on the secret. As Jeremy Gilbert asks in an essay on 'public secrets': is 'a secret … really a secret as-such at all before it has been told?'[22] He continues, 'What if it is only the act of disclosure, surveillance, or confession which constitutes any particular piece of the continuum of experience as "a secret"?' Gilbert stresses the importance of the audience for the secret, and thus the relationship between the keeper of secrets and those who do not know the secrets. Luise White writes, '[k]eeping a secret requires negotiating a social world.'[23] Whereas the word 'secret' tends to denote a belief in its privacy, its fundamental 'apartness', Gilbert and White remind us that secrets are relationships that do not suppress as much as they *order* knowledge. As White puts it, secrets 'give a charged status to information'.[24] The secret glitters, beckons in a kind of spectacular way, when others are aware of its existence but not privy to its content.[25]

What is more, the secret is at the centre of an *epistemological* relationship: that is, it calls into question the status of knowledge, of access to knowledge. In fact, what the secret does, especially when secretive knowledge is linked specifically to women, is suggest the *limits* of knowledge. With its refusal of transparency, its attachment to opacity, this kind of secret hints at the possibility of partial knowledge. Ultimately, the secret rejects mastery and omniscience—the sense that all can be seen and known—as values attached to knowledge. It thus claims some kinship to a refiguration of terms that has been central to the feminist intervention in the theory of knowledge. In her classic essay, 'Situated Knowledges', Donna Haraway describes this re-description of the knowledge relation: 'feminist objectivity is about limited location and situated knowledge, not about transcendence and splitting of subject and object.'[26] This is exactly the terrain occupied by the secret, because it is a relationship in which one party is denied full knowledge. Not only is complete knowledge impossible, but by withholding, by refusing to proffer certain kinds of knowledge, the secret-keeper takes an active role: she emerges as an agent.

The beauty or fashion secrets presumed to be held by women also traditionally depend upon women's relationships with each other. Thus they constitute another kind of challenge to conventional understandings of knowledge which privilege the individual knower: 'For each knower, the Cartesian route to knowledge is through private, abstract thought, through the effort of reason unaided either by the senses or by consultation with other knowers.'[27] But beauty secrets are imagined to be passed among groups of women, sometimes cross-generationally, sometimes in the context of a single generation or gendered social milieu. Indeed, Ellen Rosenman finds that it is precisely this sense of expert knowledge circulated *among women* that emerged as threatening in the Victorian period; not only did this knowledge appear to be unavailable to men, but it was thought to constitute the basis for an entire homosocial and even homoerotic world that excluded men.[28] An analogy might be made between women's secrets and gossip as a knowledge form. The latter is explored in an essay by Lorraine Code. Here, she examines a case taken from literature, one in which women gain knowledge of the circumstances of an abusive situation through what is usually dismissed as trivia: 'There is no doubt that it is knowledge that the women construct out of their activities—knowledge that neither one of them could have produced alone.' Further, 'the gossip accompanies, grows out of, and embellishes (cognitively) their practical preoccupations.'[29] Beauty secrets, too, can be understood as seemingly trivial, but are actually pieces of materially significant knowledge that emerge from the 'practical preoccupations' of adornment and everyday self-representation. These are secrets that gain their currency in their circulation, and not in being zealously guarded from other women.

PENETRATING SECRETS

What does this relational status of secrecy, its interrogation of the possibility of transparent knowledge, mean for fashion design? More specifically, what does it mean for the designer? The professional domain of the designer necessarily overlaps with the world of women's 'secrets'. Given that the designer is, at least in part, motivated by profit, these secrets potentially become threatening. They constitute an obstacle to both the designer's development of a professional identity based on a sense of complete knowledge and mastery, *and* the potential of commercial success. Poiret's work bears out this sense of secrets as a threat, but that representation of secrecy is ambiguous. An unstable depiction of secrecy emerges, achieved through the simultaneous celebration and repudiation of women's secret-keeping capacities. Poiret manages to both praise and supplant his female clientele by using the relational power of secrecy to consolidate his own public persona.

Indeed, Poiret is very clever. He uses the figure of the secret to flatter women, as in this question from the very first pages of his *King of Fashion*: 'Cannot women wear anything and everything and do they not possess the secret of making beautiful and acceptable the most improbable and audacious things?' But Poiret ends this very same paragraph, which begins with adulation, by substituting designer expertise for the seemingly innate skill of women: 'so skilled are those artists who devote themselves to the embellishment of women.'[30] His discourse on the gendered character of knowledge, secrecy and expertise is never straightforward. In fact, the autobiographical work is characterized by intriguing slippages between the figures of the secret-keeping woman as expert, and the male designer as expert. This is only one of countless illustrations of this oscillation; the text moves continually between, on one hand, women's self-mastery as they trade in feminine secrets, and on the other, their submission to the will of the male expert as diviner of those same secrets.

The early pages of *King of Fashion* nicely establish this theme of knowledge and expertise, but the secret is most persuasively used as an accolade in the lectures he gave to American and Canadian women upon his tours of North America. The lectures are reproduced in the book, and are notable as the best-developed and most coherent statement of an aesthetic philosophy in Poiret's vast body of work.[31] Here, he tells the gathered women that their knowledge and skill in matters of style and fashion is an innate privilege, something that should, by rights, exclude him: 'When hundreds of lovely women are gathered in the same hall because of an interest in fashion, one may well ask oneself what role can a man play in such a matter? Do you really believe that men can teach you anything in matters of elegance?'[32] In this way, Poiret appears to humble himself, to defer to the superior—and secret—knowledge of women in these matters. We begin to divine the relational character of secrets: they constitute privileged knowledge for women, and it has dangerous consequences for others, for men like Poiret.

The veneration of secret-keepers continues, making more and more apparent its relational vein. A full sketch of Poiret the professional designer emerges, and it positions him as responding to women's secrets, indeed deriving his professional purpose from them. His self-characterizations are telling. He writes, for instance, 'I present myself before you armed with a pair of antennae, and not a rod, and I do not speak to you as a master, but a slave desirous of divining your secret thoughts.'[33] Along the same lines, he flatters women and appears to undermine his own position: 'Perhaps it would be better to let you believe that I command and that you have only to obey ... The truth is that I respond by anticipation to your secret intentions.'[34] Here, Poiret appears to deflect the issue of his own role and establish his humility. He is only the *servant* of fashion and women, he suggests numerous times throughout his lectures. It is women who have the upper hand in matters of fashion, a view that was popularly circulated with regard to designers in general, in the fashion press at the time.

It is useful to consider the way that secrets are associated with power for Poiret. By positioning himself as a 'slave' who is merely responsive to women's fashion and style secrets, he suggests that fashion is a domain in which women exercise power. But, given the way that Poiret develops this representation throughout his work, it is necessary to consider its negative implications. As I note above, the perception that women circulated fashion and beauty secrets among themselves was a locus of anxieties over women's access to knowledge and, indeed, expertise. Poiret was certainly someone who negotiated with some anxiety the meaning of women's apparent beauty secretiveness. This is not surprising: Poiret's continued securing of a privileged position on the commercial fashion market depended on his ability to cultivate an expert image, which might be threatened by the incursion of knowledgeable women.

In the early twentieth century, when the creation of fashionable clothing was becoming the domain of male 'experts', this had a special significance. It threatened Poiret on the terrain he was staking out as a self-styled revolutionary. And so, in his memoir he inserts himself into the economy of women's secrets that he appears to venerate. Representing women as secret-keepers makes it possible for Poiret to *colonize* the imagined domain of the secret and to claim fashion design for himself, an eminently modern subject.

This is the key, this move to colonize, to access. It brings us to the analytical centre of the feminist work on secrets, most of which treats the early modern period. This work traces the shift to conceptualizing women's bodies (or nature, figured as a woman) as the domain of secrets.[35] The response was to harness newly available scientific tools to penetrate them. In an article on changing medical discourses of women's bodies, Monica Green notes that the new notion of '*secrets of women* did not enshroud women's bodies with a protective barrier to the male gaze; rather, it rendered women's bodies open for intellectual scrutiny.'[36] This was a key element in the transformation of medical culture, the roots of its modern professionalization. An irony, then: representations of secrecy justified and guaranteed access in this period. Clare Birchall asks in another context, '[w]hat happens when secrets are presented as fully revealable?'[37] This is, again, a question of knowledge: what happens when we presume we can know all? As she is writing in the context of the early twenty-first century's 'War on Terror', offering a critique of its ideological underpinnings and violent interrogation techniques, her question suggests the grim results of the presumption of full and complete knowledge. And the literature on the late medieval and early modern periods suggests that the answer to Birchall's question—what happens when secrets are presented as fully revealable?—is that institutional or at least professional knowledges trump local knowledges, 'secret' knowledges, to the great detriment of women's autonomy. Secrets are not only social relations, then, but sites of *opening* to professional power, rather than a closing off or restriction of access.

MASTERY AND THE DESIGN PROFESSIONAL

Such an understanding of secrets as enabling access and contributing to the accrual of professional power helps to clarify what is at stake in Poiret's representations. It must be remembered that Poiret's field was mainly a visual one, and that this was the era of what is sometimes called the 'spectacularization' of fashion. The 'secret' stands in opposition to this visual spectacle. Evelyn Keller suggests that the early modern development of the scientific method was the inauguration of a 'drama between visibility and invisibility'. 'In this interpretation,' she says, 'the task of scientific enlightenment—the illumination of the reality behind appearances—is an inversion of surface and interior, an interchange between visible and invisible, that effectively routs the last vestiges of archaic, subterranean female power.'[38] Now, of course, early-twentieth-century fashion discourses are a very different context from the scientific method. Still, Keller suggests something more broadly about knowledge that might be usefully applied to the context of fashion, since the modern fashion system is so undeniably a domain of spectacle. By representing women as entirely revealable, Poiret was contributing to a very particular kind of spectacle of femininity. This sense of visual penetration gave way to a discourse of mastery; fashion secrets turn, in Poiret's work, from being a source of power for women, to a source of power for Poiret alone.

Consider first the following question. Poiret asks, '[w]hat role can a man play in such a matter [as fashion]? Do you really believe that a man can teach anything to you in matters of elegance? There is something ridiculous about attempting it, and he who comes to instruct you asks himself, to-day as he looks at you, if it is not he who is about to receive a lesson.'[39] Here again deferring to the apparently deeper knowledge of women with respect to matters of personal aesthetics, he appears to deflect the issue of his own role and establish his humility. Poiret sets himself up as a mere instrument of something greater. He is only the *servant* of *fashion*'s irrationality, he suggests numerous times throughout his lectures. Fashion, with its 'despotism', has insert the word the upper hand, as do, by association, women.

But the power this appears to attribute to women is superseded when we pay close attention to other formulations of the relationship between designer and women. For through this very articulation of his subservience to the tyranny of fashion, Poiret accomplishes the inverse; he establishes himself as master of women's desires and challenges their status as knowing agents. The 'secret' at the heart of all this, the secret knowledge that constitutes women's greater aesthetic facility, is in fact violated by the designer. Poiret thus cycles from being an instrument of fashion and women to possessing a kind of mastery that, at the very least, challenges women's capacity for knowledge and expertise in this area.

From a perspective that might value women's knowledge and agency in relation to fashion, this establishment of mastery has grave implications. Poiret tells the women of Chicago, '[a]t the moment when a woman chooses or orders a dress, she believes she is doing it in all freedom, in the full exercise of her own personality, but she is deceiving herself. It is the spirit of fashion that inspires her, that reigns over her intelligence and clouds her judgment.'[40] We see here the nature of the relationship between women and fashion that Poiret reinforces so vigorously. This relation between women and fashion is not an affiliation of equals, but a kind of *colonization* of women by fashion. Poiret's role, then, is as a benevolent medium of fashion. He is there to interpret the whimsy of this most modern force, and to *mitigate* the colonization process. He does this through, in effect, taking control of women's knowledge-making capacities. He tells them, 'you do not know yourselves, perhaps, to what degree you are at [fashion's] mercy, for you evolve unconsciously, and you come to the point of wishing the same thing as fashion wishes, but in truth you have no free will.'[41] Poiret effaces any capacity for agency that was established through women's conceptual alignment with fashion. He usurps that alignment for himself and effectively capitalizes on the power he attributes to fashion.

Cleverly, though he begins by establishing the tyrannical, despotic and above all colonial tendencies of this thing called fashion, Poiret effectively takes on its despotism, as many of his other writings show. In a 1921 interview, he is explicit about this: he asserts that modern fashion is about the 'infinite variety, caprice, individual taste' of women. But, he says, the job of the couturier is to 'colonize this disorderly whimsy: without appearing to, you impose your taste on these superficial and changeable beings.'[42] The representation of himself as a tyrant taking over from the capriciously dictatorial role of fashion itself comes out in descriptions of the women who work for him, a whole other class of women upon whom his success depends. In his second memoir, *Revenez-y*, he characterizes his role in relation to his employees as such: 'A tamer cracking his whip all the time, to keep them on edge and respectful of me, these wildcats, these loving but sly panthers, who are always ready to strike and take down their master.'[43]

Poiret's tendencies toward colonization and mastery are perhaps best revealed in his relationship with his wife, Denise (Boulet) Poiret, whom he married in 1905 and divorced in 1928. In *King of Fashion*, Poiret describes the way he was initially taken with this childhood friend when they began courting as young adults, when Poiret was at the beginning of his success: 'She was extremely simple, and all those who have admired her since I made her my wife would certainly not have chosen her in the state in which I found her. But I had a designer's eye, and I saw her hidden graces. I observed her poses and gestures, and even her faults—which might be turned to advantage.'[44] He acknowledges that most of his entourage was horrified by his choice of this woman as his wife, '[b]ut I knew where I wanted to go.'[45] Poiret is amazingly frank, in this memoir, about his reasons for choosing Denise Boulet: he wanted a living mannequin, a woman he could literally fashion to increase his social and cultural capital. He knew that if he succeeded in dressing her well, penetrating her secrets, value would accrue to him. Caroline Evans notes that she was 'her husband's best advertisement'.[46] I suggest that Poiret represents Denise as a living tableau of his capacity for mastering women. At his infamous 1911 'One Thousand and Second Night' party, Poiret placed Denise at the centre of the 'entertainment': he shut up his wife in a golden cage. Hours into the party, he 'restored her freedom', opening the cage, whereupon she 'flew out like a bird ... and was lost in the crowd'. Yet again, the anecdote of Denise's imprisonment and flight is emblematic of the instability of Poiret's representation of women. On one hand, he is secure in his ability to control them. Yet they always contain the possibility of evading his mastery, as he acknowledges in recounting the birdcage incident: 'I precipitated myself in pursuit of her, cracking my useless whip. She was lost in the crowd. Did we know, on that evening, that we were rehearsing the drama of our lives?'[47] The notion that Denise gets lost in the crowd of Poiret's own making is ambiguously suggestive. It suggests on one hand that she has failed to live up to the position that Poiret has envisioned for her; getting lost is indicative of a personal flaw of hers. Yet it also could be read to suggest that she deliberately loses herself, hinting at the ultimate failure of Poiret's control, and suggesting that she has re-appropriated her capacity for secrecy.

Though it contains such telling instances of the unsteadiness of Poiret's vision of himself, Poiret's work remains overwhelmingly characterized by the rhetoric of successful mastery through access to women's knowledge. Turning the secret inside out by accessing it makes it public. This kind of violation arrests its movement, makes it static. At the root of the representation of women's fashion secrets is a notion of a relation among women, and women alone, as they tell secrets and share their knowledge. Secrets are thus vital, fluid, evolving in time and as they circulate among people. If secrets contain a principle of uncertainty, of incompleteness and indeterminacy, then they must also contain the possibility for mobility on the part of their keepers. This is valuable when we are thinking about women. Surely unknowability in this context preserves some hope for a different kind of representation and ultimately a different kind of social relation of femininity. This is the subversive possibility of fashion, and it is what is lost when the secret is violated by Poiret. The dream of complete revelation carries with it an objectification of

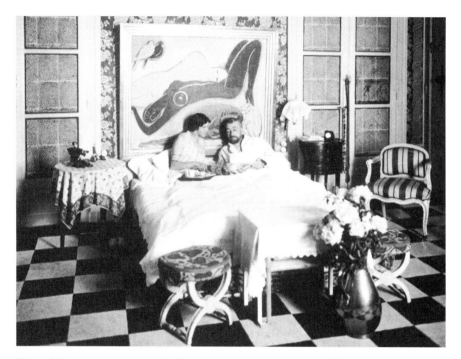

Figure 2.5   Denise Poiret and Paul Poiret at home in bed around 1925, with a Kees Van Dongen painting hanging above. Photo by Keystone-France/Gamma-Keystone via Getty Images. © Gamma-Keystone/Getty Images.

social relations, of social identities, that is decidedly damaging for women in the context of the spectacular discourses of modernity.

I want to draw this insight through to consider how it operates in Poiret's invocations of women's secrets. Recall that a significant cultural trope in Western modernity is that of the woman as static, prehistoric, outside of the modern. But fashion contained the suggestion of a non-essential feminine being in modernity—one that could act as a counter to these discourses of stasis. Poiret, by representing the secret as always revealable, intervenes in this sense of openness, change and futurity to suggest that these qualities belong to him alone, and not to the static women he dresses. Dressing them, after all, is his *profession*. Ultimately, his relentless invocation of women's secrecy emerges as a means of securing his status as a *modern*, *professional* subject. A picture of the modern couturier emerges: he is a professional revealer of secrets, a confessor. This is the status he seems to gain through his invocation of secrets, and it is a significant one, given the shift in the positioning of the arts of dress and fashion, from women's work to men's work. There is much at stake in the changing understanding of fashion creation as primarily men's work: a set of ideas about being a modern subject, about the very *nature* of being.

Figure 2.6 Denise Poiret wearing Paul Poiret's Lampshade Tunic, circa 1913. Roger Viollet Collection. © Roger Viollet/Getty Images.

GENDERING THE EPHEMERAL

Couturier mastery thus usurped the potential of women to access the future, and instead could be seen to align the designer with that future. And we certainly see this claim to the future—often figured through its threshold of the new—in Poiret's work. But the temporal rhetoric is much more complex than it might at first appear. Poiret professes allegiance to several temporal registers at once as in this aphorism, taken from an interview relatively early in his career, on the usefulness of working with the great houses Doucet and Worth before striking out on his own: 'the better we can master the past, the more power we have to tame the future.'[48] Here, he establishes what might be seen as a foundation of his own mastery: his use of the present as a vantage point from which to both situate himself in history and ensure his own future. This section explores Poiret's complex temporal positioning of himself and the women who constitute his market to reveal the ways that this particular complexity ultimately serves to deauthorize women as agents of fashion, of modernity and of history.

A survey of Poiret's self-representations reveals, at the most basic level, an oscillation between newness and tradition. Sometimes, Poiret is fashioned as cleaving to traditions. Just as often, though, he can be seen to advocate a commitment to newness for its own sake. The apparent contradictions of these positions are evident in Poiret's most famous innovation, the *Directoire* dress line. This flattening of the line, this turning away from the highly controlled and undeniably constricting shapes of Edwardian fashion, has been presented—by Poiret and by others—as a revolutionary moment in the history of fashion. It is one that is steeped, in Poiret's own self-mythologizing efforts, in the rhetoric of modernization, even of revolution: he writes, 'I waged war on the corset ... in the name of Liberty.'[49] But surely it was obvious to the observer that, as I discuss in Chapter One, the *Directoire* line was a kind of recapitulation of past styles—after all, it is so named because it refers to the fashions of the *Directoire* period, the final stage of the French Revolution, an event from which Poiret clearly draws inspiration in describing the silhouette's impact in the 1900s. These Revolutionary fashions themselves were modelled on clothing styles of Ancient Greece and Rome, which were seen to embody the democratic ideals driving the much later revolution. Of course this constant resurrection of past styles is part of fashion's overall structure. But given the importance of this stylistic moment, it is useful to think about the crystallization of past and present, tradition and newness, in Poiret's *Directoire* revival as a kind of material emblem of his conflicted relationship to time. Poiret was a master of repackaging the past. His tendency to proclaim the innovation of what were essentially historical styles holds the key to the complex figures of time that inform his self-representations.

Two major related issues emerge from a reading of Poiret's relationship to modern time: first, the concept of the ephemeral as a kind of relentless present, and second, the complex interplay of past, present and future in his work. Poiret was compelled to align himself with the rapid change embodied by an ephemeral approach. The compulsion was, of course, driven by his industry. Commercial success depended on the constant proliferation of new styles, the desire they were thought to engender in consumers and their diffusion across social spaces. His claims to newness, however, are complicated by a nostalgic vision of the past and an uncertain and pessimistic vision of the future. Ultimately, Poiret rejects the presentism that he depends on for his livelihood. In this analysis, once again the major autobiographical work, *King of Fashion*, reveals itself as the most fruitful resource. Its recounting of a whole life, including Poiret's boyhood, provides us with a sense of duration, of how Poiret represents himself in a long view, across time.

The not wholly ephemeral logic that characterizes his work has profound consequences for conceiving of women as subjects of modernity. Poiret's rhetoric is also symptomatic of broader trends in the representation of fashion; his own unstable narration of women encapsulates the confusing amalgam of roles that they take on in the fashion press more generally. Poiret evokes a curious relationship between the permanent and the ephemeral, the latter synonymous in fashion with modernity and change. He portrays himself as possessed of constancy, solidity and a certain weighty selfhood, and at the same time as unusually attuned to the feminized constructs of volatility and changeability, and gifted with a future orientation. The way this paradox plays out in the memoir makes clear its gendered dimensions. Poiret's primary memoir is a singularly self-aggrandizing work that ultimately disparages the mysteriously ephemeral feminine upon which his career and his self-representation depended. Here I focus on the differences between masculine and feminine ephemera, suggesting that Poiret's simultaneous attunement toward the permanent and the ephemeral is a novel way of writing women out of the narratives of modernity while appearing to situate them as pre-eminently modern. The story he tells compels us to ask whether consumer culture more generally relied upon a similarly conflicted femininity.

POIRET'S COMPLEX TIME

It is helpful to start at the beginning of Poiret's narration of his life, to locate the temporal dimensions of his own myth of himself. Here he establishes a progress-oriented aesthetic that underpins his philosophy of fashion. Of his parents, he writes,

> I remember watching the growth of their prosperity, and I saw the joy they took in enriching and embellishing their home. They bought, in the successive exhibitions of 1878, 1889, and 1900, everything that was in our patrimony. It was not always very suitable, but it marked an aspiration toward the best, a progression toward the beautiful. Culture cannot be improvised.[50]

A markedly *un*modern equation of goodness and beauty is notable here. This is a significant aesthetic theory, for it recurs throughout the book. It presents a certain sturdiness and permanence, an absolutism that is telling. As well, it denotes Poiret's relationship to an ancient philosophical heritage. At the same time, it manages to represent a thoroughly modern, liberal attachment to progress. But again, this temporal register is opposed to the ephemeral, which subverts the constancy that progress rests on.

Of course, an aesthetic rooted primarily in such ideals would not be lucrative for a designer in Poiret's position. That is, Poiret needed to also establish his credentials as, even in childhood, a revolutionary. He does so in describing a starry-eyed visit to the opening of the Paris Exhibition of 1889. This future-oriented exhibition left him, he writes, 'drunk with joy' in the face of the ephemerality that it represented. He writes of contingent phenomena ungoverned by logic: phantasmagoria, magic, brief luminosities. This formulation is more in keeping with the kind of persona Poiret needed to advance in order to retrospectively establish a viable connection to the impermanence, the constant change, of fashion. But note that he says, too, '[t]he Exhibition revealed to me other unforeseen wonders: the applications of electricity, the gramophone, etc. I wanted to know Edison, or to write to him to thank him and personally congratulate him on what he was giving to humanity.'[51] Even here, in positioning himself vis-à-vis these more ephemeral elements of the modern, he reveals a still quite traditional set of ethical attachments: Edison's scientific contribution will be the salvation of humanity.

This is the line that Poiret treads for the remainder of the book; in a sense he is concerned with masking himself, covering over the commitments to classicism that so clearly animate his philosophy. This is often accomplished through the invocation of an ahistorical past. Consider the chapter detailing his first employment in fashion, in the house of Jacques Doucet beginning in 1898. The chapter opens with a nostalgic invocation of the past: 'It was a blessed time, when the cares and worries of life, the vexations of tax collectors and the threats of the Socialists had not yet crushed out the pleasures of thought and all joie de vivre.'[52] But Poiret quickly papers over this nostalgic reference though the use of much stronger imagery to establish his own revolutionary sensibilities: in this same chapter, tellingly, he denigrates the other Doucet employees that he says were hostile to his modernizing appearance on the scene. These colleagues are women. He describes these saleswomen as 'the Old Guard', calling them 'aged harpies installed in the house like mites in a cheese ... ravaged by age'.[53] He refers to them as gorgons, wild beasts and felines. He is only able to escape their clutches because he befriends some of the younger saleswomen, who are described as 'pretty ... elegant'.[54] By feminizing the past as he denigrates it, Poiret is able to mark himself out as a modern subject, even an embattled and heroic one—set upon by the past's enemy representatives.

The contradictions contained in the discussions of Poiret's time at Doucet characterize the memoir: the quiet announcements made of a commitment to past values, but drowned out by brash articulations of a revolutionary sensibility. Part of what is at work here is a particular kind of class anxiety. Poiret is deeply committed to the values of the aspirational bourgeoisie in whose fold he grew up and upon which his career as a designer depended, and which was on one level threatened by any invocation of revolution, sartorial, aesthetic or otherwise.[55] But this seemingly paradoxical commitment to both past and future is also gendered. As the narrative unfolds, the invocations of youth, newness and the future become more pronounced and the depictions of Poiret's classicism and conservatism are subsumed—but certainly do not disappear. Instead, they are displaced onto complex figures of femininity. These are feminine figures that also happen to carry some of the weight of the ephemeral that Poiret himself does.

To see how this operates textually, I return to the long quotation I invoked at the beginning of this chapter to set the stage for a discussion of Poiret's relationships to women; it is so rich, so telling:

> A creative dressmaker is accustomed to foresee, and must be able to divine the trends that will inspire the day after to-morrow. He is prepared long before women themselves to accept the accidents and incidents that occur on the trajectory of evolution, and that is why we cannot believe in a resistance by women, in their clubs, or through tracts, lectures, meetings and protests of any sort, against that which to him seems logical, ineluctable, and already certain.

There is a curious temporal logic here, and it helps to explain the doubleness of Poiret's articulations of his modernity and his apparent commitment to a kind of premodern timelessness. To be successful, the designer must simultaneously occupy two different times: he must be at once attuned with newness and change that fashion represents, and also resolutely set in a static, ahistorical and permanent register. Look at the language: he foresees, but what he foresees is a kind of surely unfolding progress—'the trajectory of evolution'—that is untouchable by the knowledge and choices of women themselves. This is not, of course, the first time that Poiret invokes evolution: his discussions of progress at the beginning of the book set the stage for such rhetoric. The kind of modernity that Poiret venerates, while it appears to turn on the ephemeral,[56] is in fact simply a logic of evolutionary variation, one that retains a core essence. He writes, for instance, that '[o]ne must not suppose that each new fashion is the consecration of a definite type of garment, which will replace for ever that which is being abandoned; it is simply a variation.'[57] Elsewhere, he characterizes fashion in evolutionary terms: 'As with evolution in the natural world, changes in fashion happen according to a straight and continual line, and not in great leaps. Yesterday contains today, which presages tomorrow.'[58] Poiret's description of evolution is telling; whereas, as Elizabeth Grosz points out, Darwin's theory of evolution is characterized by chance, randomness and unpredictability, Poiret instead interprets evolution as a linear concept more in keeping with ideologies of progress.[59]

What we have here, then, is an alignment of time with knowledge. In its dependence on universal and ahistorical knowledge, the designer's orientation to the future, to the ephemeral possibility of fashion, is paradoxically predicated on his own timelessness. And note the rationality that attends to this understanding of the designer's role. He is prepared to accept 'that which to him seems logical, ineluctable, and already certain'. He simply knows—this is a kind of universal, unchanging knowing. The alignment of the designer with this kind of absolutism, and above all with rationality, is telling. It functions to position the female consumer securely in an ancient philosophical heritage that aligns women with superficiality, changeability and irrationality.

There is a temptation to read the constant invocation of the future as a kind of radical openness and ultimately an unloosing of static concepts of the women with whom fashion is associated. But in this case, the future's conceptual alignment with the *timelessness* represented by a male designer renders such a reading untenable. Since timelessness here rests on a relationship with rationality, femininity is relegated to a different future: an *unknowing* one that exists in the realm of the irrational. Indeed, the rendering of women as unknowing, and even irrational because of their ephemerality, is a theme that is borne out throughout *King of Fashion.* 'In Europe,' Poiret writes, 'we have long recognized the instability of fashion and of woman.'[60] Later, he opines in his lectures to American women, '[w]omen are always of the same opinion of fashion, which changes its mind constantly.'[61] The language of ephemerality here suggests that women are in some senses victimized or colonized by fashion, as I discuss above—not that they are active or knowledgeable consumers. The potential afforded by the juxtaposition of the feminine and the ephemeral is lost in the equation of women and fashion with triviality. The triangulation of women, fashion and irrationality speaks to the *ancient* chain of signification that associates women with artifice. It allows Poiret to set himself against them as a superior knower: he knows what is in the best interest of women, a position which bolsters his authority and guarantees—for a time, anyway—his dominance of the market.

Poiret's compromised relationship with the ephemeral is only one of the complex temporal rhythms that mark his work. The other is the relationship of tradition and newness, which is hinted at in the quotations above. Poiret's analysts—journalists, mainly—appear to be divided on the question of whether Poiret was traditional or progressive, and their views often do not accord with Poiret's own representations of himself. For instance, a 1914 article about him calls him 'singularly unmodern and untouched by the vagaries of style'.[62] This came at a time when he was still invested in the vision of himself as a revolutionary, thus suggesting his tendency to occupy and master multiple temporal registers. A 1931 *New York Times* article about the publication of *King of Fashion*, on the other hand, paints him as modern: 'alert for novelties'.[63] Yet by this late stage of his career, Poiret's own self-portrayals increasingly emphasized not his taste for novelty, but his adherence to aesthetic and fashion

Figure 2.7   Poiret on the terrasse at Salle Pleyel, in Paris, circa 1925. Photo by Lip-nitzki/Roger Viollet/Getty Images. © Roger Viollet/Getty Images.

traditions. Examining the contradictions in Poiret's invocations of present and past makes it clear that his simultaneous allegiances to tradition and innovation also elaborate a philosophy of femininity.

Poiret's self-styling as a revolutionary over his introduction of the *Directoire* line captures one of his multiple approaches to this issue. Until the last years of his career, he remained determined to present himself as a member of the *avant-garde*, as he does with a detectable hint of defensiveness here: 'The avant-garde *couturier*—no need to remind you that this describes me—must have a sturdy spirit, a sharp eye, and a strong fist. He needs to be stubborn and clairvoyant.'[64] Again, here we find a picture of the designer whose success is secured by his ability to divine the future. This is the mark of the aesthetic revolutionary, who inhabits the space of the present, but must always be on the cusp of the future.

DISTANT AND RECENT PASTS

Poiret equally often professes himself to be as turned toward the past as he is toward the present and future. In an early interview, explaining the influence of his travels on his dress design, he claims, '[popular resort towns for the elite] like Trouville, Biarritz, Baden don't interest me; my entertainments are of a higher order. I happily turn toward lands where Art finds its truest expression; it's Antiquity that inspires me.'[65] Even more tellingly, Poiret locates the source of fashion inspiration in a uniquely *French* heritage. Discussing the apparently inborn elegance and style of the Parisian woman, he argues that 'no doubt she knows this intuitively, atavistically. Her grandmother made rosettes during the Revolution, and it was her grandfather who decorated pretty medicine jars with flowers and bluebirds. For centuries, all of her ancestors were involved in industries whose wares … evidenced an artistic sense perfected over generations.'[66] The notion of 'atavism' that frames this assertion is telling, especially since Poiret is describing the essence of women's stylistic gifts. These gifts come from an unbroken (more recent) past, in which the woman is naturally located. His task, by contrast, is to draw inspiration from a more distant past and to put it to use in the service of that ultimately most modern of pursuits, dress design. We begin to see the ways that categories of past, present and future become gendered, with the past—even as it is lionized—explicitly feminized.

The feminization of the recent past reaches its peak in a piece that Poiret published in 1938 in the American fashion magazine *Harper's Bazaar*. The article is structured in the form of a conversation between Poiret—by now approaching sixty years old—and his 'young friend de Tressense, who claims that the fashions of today are more attractive than those of yesterday'.[67] The two debate this claim, with Poiret finally convincing de Tressense that twenty or more years earlier, in what is portrayed as a sort of golden age, feminine beauty and elegance were much more pronounced than they are in 1938; indeed, for Poiret the present is characterized by 'pathetic, ill-shod mannequins'.[68] The prewar period—also the period of Poiret's unchallenged dominance of fashion—'was a period of women', according to Poiret.[69] The past is not only feminized, then, but interpreted nostalgically: 'the present era has permitted many charms to vanish, without replacing them with others.'[70] As Peter Fritzsche has noted, nostalgia has its own temporal character: 'Nostalgia no longer cherishes the past for the distinctive qualities that are no longer present but also acknowledges the permanence of their absence. It thus configures periods of time as bounded in time and place and as inaccessible.'[71] This being the case, the designation of the prewar era as 'a period of women' effectively imprisons women there. If the women of today are simply 'mannequins', they lack the authenticity of women from this golden age, who stand as relics of another vision of femininity, but have no standing in the contemporary era. The potential contained in the notion of women as modern because of their close relationship with the ephemeral temporal logic of fashion thus dissolves here; today's women may be modern, but are they really women, or are they simply faceless automata? In building such a nostalgic vision of femininity, Poiret relegates 'authentic' femininity—that which matters in his aesthetic vision—to the inaccessible outside of the contemporary moment. Certainly, he celebrates this historical view of womanhood, but celebration in this case only functions to further desiccate and de-animate it.

CATALOGUING FEMININE IRRATIONALITY

It is worth considering in more detail what constitutes Poiret's vision of past feminine authenticity. The sketch that emerges reveals a great deal about the relationship of time—in the form of a time-bound femininity—to knowledge, mastery and, finally, to the all-important market. In the same nostalgic *Harper's Bazaar* article, Poiret tells de Tressense of his fondness and nostalgia for lace (replaced now, he says, by simple and therefore unfeminine fabrics): 'If you don't love lace, you don't love women. It is the very expression of their personality. Its charm springs from all that useless labor of making holes in a fabric, for no reason, for beauty, for pleasure.'[72] Here he conflates the consumer of fashion with an implicit reference to the women who make fashion, trivializing the work of production and eliding the artistry and expertise represented by lacemakers. Lacemakers' artistry and expertise is *women's* artistry, of course, which threatened and ultimately, he believes, proved fatal to his dominance of the field. Similarly, in a 1932 series of newspaper articles invoking the lost glory of Paris in the period from 1880 to 1910, Poiret constructs another material metonym for femininity. He would like to bring back the bustle, he writes, for this accessory 'made women charming because it was a defiance of sense, an assertion of their independence and their disdain for logic, an affectation'.[73] These portraits of women, which draw upon a long history of representations of women as irrational, only build on the fuller representation in *King of Fashion*, in which women emerge as endangered by their lack of reason, a lack which renders them vulnerable to the tyranny of fashion itself. As I note above, the depiction of women's vulnerability to colonization by fashion provides an opening for Poiret himself to step in and claim the territory of fashion for himself. But it is by situating the irrational woman in her temporal context that we can get a fuller picture of the role she plays in Poiret's self-representations.

First, it is important to note that rationality and time are linked, in modernity. As Genevieve Lloyd explains, and as I briefly discuss in Chapter One, the Enlightenment and immediate post-Enlightenment periods witnessed a rhetorical linking of the themes of reason and progress. This conflation of rationality and linear time characterized the unfolding of industrial modernity and undoubtedly informs Poiret's characterizations of rationality. It was the role of reason, for philosophers of this period, to facilitate humanity's emergence from immaturity and enable the progressive development of the human capacity for freedom. The linking of reason and progress excludes a figural femininity, since femininity is presumed to be mired in nature.[74] But Lloyd also locates a complexity and ambivalence in the discussion of women's relationship to reason. Describing Rousseau's understanding of reason, she notes 'a new resolution of the ambivalence of the feminine to enter western thought. The feminine was construed as an immature stage of consciousness, left behind by advancing Reason, but also as an object of adulation, as the exemplar for reason's aspirations to a future return to nature.'[75] This description of the ambivalent figuration of women as reason's Other is useful for thinking about the complex representations of irrational women in Poiret's work.

What emerges is a *succession*, over time, of irrational women. That is, the irrationality of women from the prewar era—a lack of reason which Poiret understands to have facilitated his success—gives way to a new, and peculiarly modern, kind of irrationality. It becomes clear that Poiret considers this newer form of irrationality to be at the root of his downfall. The early form was manipulatable, and was thus the guarantor of his commercial success. The danger in the new irrationality is that he cannot control it. This modern form of feminine being is impervious to the rich particularities of his style. Instead, it has let itself be colonized by others. Chanel and Patou are those he explicitly identifies in *Revenez-y*, because they are 'armed with a particular perspective, suited to adapting styles for a middling clientele and diffusing them throughout different social classes ... which denies them the title of *couturier* and *créateur*'.[76] Poiret suggests that what matters, what turns women into icons and fashion into art, is distinction, which has been lost in the 1920s. This characteristic is not always so explicitly linked to social class—indeed, Poiret sometimes lauds the innate fashion sense of, say, working-class Parisian women, who know how to individualize and distinguish themselves through their dress,[77] but Poiret generally relies on the concept of an elite class of women who embody feminine beauty through individual style. These are the women—'the beauties of my day'—whose passing he laments in the 1938 *Harper's Bazaar* article. Tracing the changing anatomy of the irrational woman in Poiret's work over the course of more than twenty years illuminates how thoroughly intertwined women are not only with his self-representational efforts, but, more importantly, with his commercial practices.

The difference between the lost 'beauties of Poiret's day', and the modern women he implicates in his downfall, lies in their individuality. For Poiret, the 'distinction' required for true style and beauty is an outgrowth of the willingness to dress according to one's 'personality', rather than according to a 'uniform' aesthetic. We first see a hint of this position in a 1910 interview, in which he condemns women for their slavish devotion to fashion and exhorts them to choose 'what suits them' rather than what their peers are wearing.[78] The article mocks fashionable women, but Poiret's attitude is ultimately positive; though women themselves have no sense of 'what suits them', he is there to guide them. This early articulation of women's incapacity for authentic expression of self acts to assure Poiret's position as a style leader. He is able to at once castigate women for not choosing styles according to their own personality *and* suggest that they are, after all, incapable of making such a choice, paving the way for him to step in as saviour. Such accounts lead, for example, to the 1921 article—cited above—in which Poiret opines that it is the job of the designer to 'colonize' women's fickle tastes, for left to themselves, they will destroy fashion.

Though it is not until the late 1920s that Poiret begins to demonstrate, in his writing and interviews, an obsession with uniformity as the death of couture, we see this sentiment beginning to grow as early as 1913, on his first trip to the United States. In a series of articles published in the *New York Times* over the course of several months in 1913 and 1914, Poiret geographically locates feminine uniformity for the first time: it resides in America. He says, '[e]ven in her dress she is imitative, but not bold … It is the struggle for uniformity. It crushes freedom, it shackles individuality, it binds all the American girls together as though they were convicts of fashion.'[79] A profile a few days later underscores the point about American women: 'She is repressed, lacking in sensibility, uninterested in art, rigid, unoriginal, bound by Puritanical conventionalities in thought and feeling.'[80] Poiret is clear that this unfortunate state of affairs is geographically particular and does not infect the French; he tells a reporter upon his arrival in the United States that 'every people makes a specialty of something, and elegance is a French thing. That is why the French mode is universal.'[81]

Locating uniformity and the lack of originality firmly in America, though, gives way in the 1920s to a more general condemnation of women—including French women. This, of course, was the postwar period, and Poiret's star had fallen slightly; he was eclipsed over the decade by others, including, most importantly, Chanel. In 1925, he lost control of his couture house. Nancy J. Troy describes the gradual loss of control over his business: 'Modern business practices modeled on American monopoly capitalism thus displaced the personalized, laissez-faire operation that had underwritten Poiret's success as the premier couturier of the postwar period.'[82] She argues that '[i]n a business context dominated by standardization, mass production, and mass consumption, his couture label became little more than a vestigial fetish deployed in protest against an inexorable process of de-individualization.'[83] By 1923, Poiret was already proclaiming the death of originality at the hand of fashion's democratization, its increasing diffusion. He implicated women in this situation: 'Today, democracy has triumphed. It is the masses who impose their tastes [upon the elite, and not the other way around]. Society women are afraid of innovation. They let themselves be led.'[84] This is a relatively gentle articulation of the problem; it gives way over the course of the decade to a more pointed indictment of women. In 1927, a journalist paraphrases Poiret: Today's couturiers

> are not the ones coming up with new ideas. Rather, it is women who impose their preferences. While we admit that some women are artists, good taste and originality are privileges of only a few and in the end, the masses make the laws and we could say that Fashion is dying, the victim of standardization and carelessness.[85]

Reason is not explicitly invoked here. Yet there is continuity between Poiret's invocations of women's fickleness and changeability, and their submission to the standardized and industrialized tendencies of postwar fashion. Recall that Poiret established a parallel between fashion and women, arguing that both were irrational, unpredictable and lacking in substance. Both were in need of his mastery, which would come in the form of a paternalistic mediation between the two. Now, it seemed, the constellation of fashion and women had spun out of control—with women's likeness to fashion flourishing under the reign of new, minimalist designers, with their simplification of women's dress. With Poiret upstaged, it is no longer the designer who controls fashion—and women. Rather, they themselves control the game.[86]

This is where we see a mutation of the concept of irrationality that is at play for Poiret. Whereas in earlier portrayals of femininity, the issue was caprice, here the issue is standardization. In apparently giving themselves over to uniformity, women have once again indulged their lack of reason: this time, by abandoning their few creative impulses. Reason is predicated upon a concept of a free and human being who uses (his) agency to make choices, creative and otherwise. Harvie Ferguson writes,

> [t]he principle of Reason was conceived as inherent in each individual, so that, when allowed freedom to express itself, the body was unfailingly directed to satisfy needs that could only be satisfied through collective life. The autonomous individual, thus, is led to choose to conduct itself in a proper manner and would inevitably choose to act in ways conducive to the maintenance and good order of the modern world.[87]

Thus the encroachment of a standardized fashion system as a deep threat to individual autonomy recasts feminine irrationality. Standardization suspends women's limited capacity to rationally choose. And this time, in Poiret's eyes, irrational women have won. As empty but somehow rapacious representatives of a consumer capitalism gone awry through its democratization, it is they and the system they represent—even more than the villainous financiers whom he writes his third memoir, *Art et phynance*, to excoriate—who have annihilated him.[88] Femininity comes to stand in for the dangerous and deadening capacities of modern industrial production.[89]

Nancy J. Troy's *Couture Culture: A Study in Modern Art and Fashion* locates Poiret at the centre of an analysis of the tense relationship between fashion's claims to the status of art and its undeniably commercial aspects. She notes that 'Poiret clung to his identity as an "artist and innovator"' while simultaneously acquiescing to the new market logic that defined fashion, which seemed at odds with the definition of fashion design as art.[90] This tension defined the end of his career. A close analysis of Poiret's own self-representational strategies extends Troy's rich reading of Poiret. Poiret's self-fashioning through writing affords an important perspective on his fight to preserve a reputation as an artist, untainted by the impurities of the market. Over and over again, he chooses to present this struggle in relational terms. He acquits himself in the dissolution of his house by establishing himself as a misunderstood and maligned artist through explicit disavowals of women. The tension between art and commerce that Troy traces is played out through the invocation of femininity. Specifically, Poiret's figuration of women and femininity draws on broader tropes of women in the modern. Over the course of his career, women move from being relegated to the outside of a vaunted modernity—the aesthetic modernity that guarantees Poiret's success and his reputation—to embodying a threatening modernity. In both cases, they bear the weight of Poiret's interest in being viewed as an innovator and as an undisputed, if deposed, king of fashion.

WOMEN AND POIRET'S LEGACY

Poiret's increasingly hostile portrayal of women from the late 1920s, if considered in this light, can also be seen as part of an ongoing attempt at self-memorialization. The path from wealth to poverty was pronounced and public for Poiret. Media in France, the United States and Britain, for instance, pounced on the story of him drawing welfare.[91] The *New York Times*'s obituary for Poiret in 1944 noted his decline from its opening line; the ultimate failure of his house, and his slow passing into obscurity, were what he was remembered for.[92] As if in part to militate against this perception, Poiret wrote prolifically after he was disassociated from his house in 1929, publishing the three autobiographical works as well as occasional pieces in major media outlets like *Paris-Soir*, Paris *Vogue* and *Harper's Bazaar*. These later writings each evince a strongly nostalgic character, and women are at the heart of them all. It is clear that

Poiret was writing, in this period, in order to secure a legacy, to try to orchestrate his own remembrance. Women, then, functioned as important figures in a memorial strategy intended to scour the dirty residue of the last years of his career. Where we see them being celebrated, it is for their prewar caprice and unreason. The homage to the bustle as representative of women's personalities appears in these later years, as does the lament for 'the beauties of my day'. Images like these are yoked to the Poiret that he would like us to remember, and they sequester women in the past. He struggles to re-emerge as a cultural player through such imagery, building a legacy upon the nostalgic appropriation of the femininity that made him as successful as he initially was. It is by accounting for *change over time* in figures of women in Poiret's self-representational archive that we can see how thoroughly women are used to sustain Poiret's mastery even after his business has been decimated.

As Bourdieu's sociology of cultural fields makes clear, the isolation of competitors in a time outside the present is a key strategy for the cultural producer. This is especially true in fashion, which depends so heavily upon its attachment to and constant renewal of the present. Only a careful scrutiny of his myriad self-representations reveals that Poiret understands his competitors to be consuming women—not Chanel or Patou or any other designer—and that he sees their chief battleground as one of knowledge. Unwittingly, he makes visible the relationship of knowledge forms to the modern marketplace. Poiret's portrayals of himself and his career are aggressively oriented to a vision of artistic genius and a repudiation of the market. On the other hand, his almost paranoid invocations of women, their withheld knowledge, and their capacity for caprice and unreason all underscore the stakes of *commercial* success for him. Poiret's conflicted and almost obsessive representations of femininity emerge as the most important and the most unstable element of the tension between art and commerce that drives his career. Their instability does not mean these images do not succeed, however. As Penelope Deutscher argues, 'contradictions and tensions do *not* mitigate [misogynist representations]. They sustain phallocentric accounts of women and femininity.'[93] Poiret's textual archive shows us that this is indeed the case: although women appear in various forms here, and they are both condescendingly indulged and bitterly berated for their 'feminine' traits, the picture that attaches to Poiret's final efforts to secure a memorial legacy for himself is the picture of women as the engineers not only of his downfall, but of the loss of an entire era. In the end, women are modern, to be sure. But the ethical and aesthetic stakes of the modern have shifted, so that the very category is called radically into question, if not disparaged. For Poiret, women only inhabit the modern when the modern is the source of his undoing. And so we begin to understand the complex role they play in his reconstructions of his life and his work: they are at once the means of his ascent and of his descent.

Figure 3.1 *Elsa Schiaparelli* by Irving Penn (1917–2009). Gelatin Silver Print, 1948. Philadelphia Museum of Art: Gift of the Artist, 2005.

–3–

Elsa Schiaparelli: Glamour, Privacy and Timelessness

Elsa Schiaparelli (1890–1973) was born in Rome and spent her adult life away from Italy, living mainly in Paris but also intermittently in the United States. Schiaparelli took up design in 1925 when, living in Paris as a divorced single mother, she was employed as a designer and stylist by a small, upstart couture house, which closed the following year. Already acquainted with members of both the fashion industry (including Poiret, whom she greatly admired) and the artistic *avant-garde*, she began designing under her own name. In 1927 Schiaparelli premiered her first collection. The debut featured the *trompe l'oeil* sweaters for which she became famous, and which led to a feature article in Paris *Vogue*. She continued to build her reputation in the late 1920s and into the 1930s, mainly with her sportswear. Though she also designed evening dress, in the early years her emphasis was on practical clothing for women—she designed women's trouser-skirts, for instance, as well as bathing suits and travel clothes. As the 1930s progressed, she remained one of the top couturiers in Paris. Though her design house persisted into the 1950s, the 1930s was the decade of her glory.

In the late 1930s, Schiaparelli began the collaborations for which she is best known, with surrealists like Salvador Dali. Though these designs represent only a small portion of her overall oeuvre, they have overshadowed her other work, and she is often remembered as a 'surrealist designer', a designation which fails to account for the variety of Schiaparelli's designs and the ways they changed over the twenty-seven years of her house's life. Still, even ostensibly simple and minimalist garments often contained small elements of construction that shared a playful or even absurd sensibility with the surrealists. She continued with *trompe l'oeil* elements, for example, in practical garments such as suits. And she earned a special reputation for her buttons, which often stood out as uncanny surprises on an otherwise sober jacket or blouse. These visual jokes included, for example, a set of buttons consisting of carrots, radishes and cabbages. *Time* magazine wrote, in 1954, 'Mme Schiaparelli persecutes the button with morbid zeal.'[1] Aside from her surrealist influences, she is well known for her perfumes, particularly *Shocking*, which was a sensation when it debuted in 1937. She also designed costumes for about sixty theatre productions and Hollywood films.

Figure 3.2 Elsa Schiaparelli (right) wearing her women's trousers in London's Hyde Park, 1931. Photo by Fox Photo/Getty Images. © Getty Images.

Schiaparelli fled Paris twice during the Second World War, and lived out most of the conflict in and around New York. Her couture house continued to run without her. When she returned to Paris after the war, she took up her place at the head of the house again, and continued to design whimsical, imaginative clothing, albeit often in styles that were quite different from the prevailing postwar style closely identified with Christian Dior. She did not, though, regain the heights of popularity that she had enjoyed before the war. Schiaparelli showed what would be her last collection in February 1954, and in December of that year, her house was declared bankrupt.

DOUBLE TIME, DOUBLE LIFE

The opening lines of Schiaparelli's 1954 autobiography, *Shocking Life*, are curious. Referring to herself in the third person, as she does intermittently

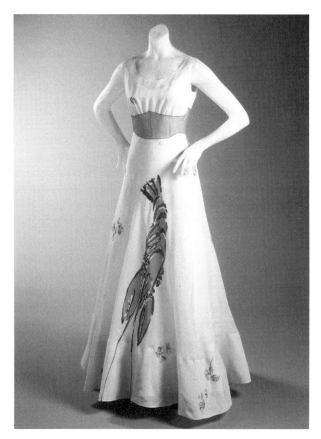

Figure 3.3 Elsa Schiaparelli's famous 'lobster dress', born of a collaboration with Salvador Dali. February 1937. Philadelphia Museum of Art, Gift of Mme Elsa Schiaparelli, 1969 (1969–232–52). © The Philadelphia Museum of Art/Art Resource.

throughout the text, Schiaparelli writes, 'I merely know Schiap by hearsay. I have only seen her in a mirror.'[2] Here, with surprising bluntness, she sets herself up as someone who is 'split', having a rich inner life characterized by multiple visions of self.[3] The rest of *Shocking Life* bears out the promise suggested by this opening, in part through Schiaparelli's repeated references to herself in the third person. The move suggests an unease with the self that runs counter to the bravado that characterizes the author's attempts to style herself as a maverick and even a revolutionary.

This overt play with a multiplicity of selves is an amplification of a feature common to life writing, as contemporary theorists of the genre note. The form was traditionally aligned with a concept of a coherent, whole self, and conventional autobiography presumes the development of a rational self over time, with the ability to clearly appraise and comment on that selfhood in writing.[4]

However, as has been pointed out by feminist and postcolonial theorists of life writing, often more experimental autobiography draws attention to the internal multiplicity of the self. This is precisely what Schiaparelli does. This is not, however, the only way in which Schiaparelli's self-representational strategy appears to contradict itself. For the reader attuned to the tempo of fashion itself, the book's time signature, as it were, also contains a significant tension. On one hand, the book describes Schiaparelli's immersion in the world of *haute couture*, with its peculiar temporality: fashion's time is rhythmic, cyclical, historical and, above all, ephemeral, fundamentally changeable: as the author herself notes, 'as soon as a dress is born it becomes a thing of the past.'[5] Schiaparelli's self-portrait in *Shocking Life* unfolds along these lines. It is a mobile, even frenetically paced narrative, a story of travel that does not alight anywhere for long, giving the impression that her identity was as ephemeral as her industry. In this sense, the temporality of the account is aligned with the narrator's complex representation of a split self. Yet the narrative refers incessantly to a 'beyond', to use Schiaparelli's words, that is home to the 'divine' elements of the self.[6] This 'beyond' has a different temporality: it is a timeless absolute. Thus an important tension in the work is between the relentless motion of time in an industry defined by such motion, and the increasingly appealing possibility of an extra-temporal dimension.

This tension in the time signature of the book is paralleled by a conflict between the biographical and autobiographical accounts of her life, one that also rests upon perceptions of the designer's orientation to time. Schiaparelli is remembered as a vanguardist, an ultra-modern. In a 2004 reflection, designer Christian Lacroix recalls: 'when, as a child or a teenager in the 1960s, I discovered her style in old fashion magazines I found at home or in flea markets, the shock of so much modernity was really cleansing.' He concludes, '[s]he is today.'[7] Thus, Lacroix positions her as (forever) related to both the present and the future.[8] This understanding of Schiaparelli as a quintessential modern is similar to press representations of her during her years in the public eye. A 1932 profile in *Harper's Bazaar*, for example, noted that '[b]eing thoroughly modern, she gives her clothes the essence of modern architecture, modern thought, and modern movement'.[9] This characterization, like others, connected Schiaparelli's distinctiveness to her innovative qualities and seized upon her connections with various artistic modernists as proof of her relevance to the now. What this approach fails to recognize is the variability of her dress design. Schiaparelli's modernism was more complex than a simple embrace of the new. For example, in the late 1930s, in the same era as she was undertaking her famous collaborations with Dali and Cocteau, she was also engaging in a more widespread neoromantic movement in fashion. Her 1939 collection included dresses with bustles, and the full-length, cinched-waist silhouette that recalled crinolined Victorian dresses and which was a feature of the months before the war (and revisited, though more exaggerat-edly, after the war by Dior and others).

Not only does her clothing design offer a counter-discourse to unfettered newness; as well, the sense of Schiaparelli as ultra-modern becomes problem-atic when read against her self-representation in *Shocking Life.* Here, she does not generally cultivate a picture of herself as an innovator, a representative of the now. The 'evidence' for her modernity that the press draws upon—her sur-realist designs, her modernist home, her relationships with artistic 'revolution-aries'—is nearly absent from this portrait. The greater emphasis lies on details of relationships, her early childhood and her adventures in the Second World War. The picture that emerges paints her as an iconoclast—just as her depic-tions in the press do—but it defines this iconoclasm merely as a personality trait and does not situate it in the context of her work, industry or relationships with artists. As I note above, the book shows her to be more oriented to time-lessness than the present. Of course, *Shocking Life* is not a complete portrait; it does not reveal the 'truth' of Schiaparelli's persona more accurately than the press reports did and do. There is no question that such a book, published the same year that she folded her design house, has a commercial aspect that complicates any such naïve reading. Nevertheless, Schiaparelli's narra-tive choices, read against the choices made by her persona as it was mediated by the press, are striking. Whatever the source of the divergence between the press record and Schiaparelli's own self-representations, this layer of tension functions as a kind of emblem: of her indefinable selfhood, to be sure, but also of the temporal complexity that pervades her work and her legacy.

Of course, the present study is about the relationship between time and femininity in the self-representations—and the press record—surrounding fashion designers. But in this case, the stakes are slightly different. The other examples in this book are men and their negotiations of femininity in relation-ship to time are about locating women, in their work and their public personae, as others in a gender system which supposes that men and women are oppo-sites. They use time to figure women as distant or as proximate, or as both at once. They thereby negotiate their own masculinity in the context of the gen-der politics of their profession and their industry. With Schiaparelli, this op-positional attribution of otherness does not work as cleanly. Because she is a woman, her use of femininity as the concept against which she establishes her professional persona is different from men's uses of femininity. Schiapa-relli, like the others, figures women as alternately close and distant, according to context. But in her case, one of the femininities she negotiates is her own. Thus the terms shift slightly in this analysis. Schiaparelli negotiates two lev-els of otherness: other women, who figure prominently though ambiguously in the text, and, most importantly, a kind of other *within.* Each of these levels of otherness is represented in overlapping, but fluctuating, time signatures. Her relationships with both tell us something about what kind of gendered position the designer is compelled to inhabit.

Of the authors in this study, none is more outwardly ambivalent about fashion as a whole, and fashion's temporality in particular, than Schiaparelli. To understand this ambivalence, it is important to recall the circumstances under which she entered fashion design. She did so out of practical necessity, as she recounts in *Shocking Life.* Divorced and living in Paris with no source of income, she began designing her famous *trompe l'oeil* sweaters as a means of making an income and establishing a vocation at what she terms a 'turning-point' in her life.[10] She was not always oriented toward fashion; '[i]t was by pure chance that she began along a path that nobody in his senses would have chosen for her.'[11] This signals a difference from the other designers in this study, and indeed from the image of the designer as someone who is vocationally driven to the work of fashion design as an art—the way an artist is imagined to be essentially drawn to their art. Schiaparelli herself thought of design as an 'art', like the others, but her short description of its artfulness is added as an afterthought, and neither expanded upon nor revisited later in the book.[12] Thus she does not feel the need to account for the growing ambivalence she describes nor for her eventual retirement. She pictures herself as always somewhat estranged from the very rhythms upon which her success and celebrity are so dependent.

Surely Caroline Evans is right to read Schiaparelli as split, following from the complex representations of self in the autobiographical work as well as her dress designs. Inspired by and extending that analysis, then, this chapter explores the temporal stakes of such a representation. What role might this interrogation of the fiction of coherent selfhood play in establishing Schiaparelli's relationship to the industry in which she worked? Here, I read Schiaparelli's *glamour* as her primary strategy for the management of multiple times. With its questioning of a number of significant opposites—surface and depth, timeless and time-bound among them—her glamour signifies, in one ambivalently feminine persona, fashion's potential to intervene in modern ways of knowing and thinking about gender and fashion.

THE SPLIT SELF AND THE GENDER POLITICS OF DESIGN

Beyond a narrowly individualist analysis, Schiaparelli's split selfhood might tell us something important about the relationship of the designer to the profession and the potential stakes of a spectacularly public career. Most notably, it tells us something about the gender politics of the profession, for a woman designer who must establish her relationship to both the tempo of the industry, and the other women for and with whom she necessarily works. There is a constant pushing and pulling at the feminine others whom

Schiaparelli represents both within and without. This instability in their rep-resentation makes it clear that for the woman designer, the process of gen-dering through time, drawing on a modality of glamour, requires an active management of her persona. Schiaparelli can best be read through a theory of glamour as a state reliant upon the quasi-magical perception of inacces-sible depth below the spectacular surface. Crucially, glamour has a particular time signature. It seems to arrest the glamorous figure, locating her outside of the modern in a timeless realm. Schiaparelli drew on glamour in order to position herself this way and also to distinguish herself from the time-bound feminine clientele upon whom her enterprise depended. The drive to situate herself outside of time, though, was always a failure: she could not escape, try as she might, the tempo that fashion imposed. The result is a highly am-bivalent self-representational strategy, in which Schiaparelli crystallizes, in her celebrity persona, the stakes of the industry for women, which included the potential to situate them both within the time of industrial modernity and beyond it.

Schiaparelli's eternal can be read as a response to the frustrating vagaries of spectacular, modern femininity. In seeking to distance herself from tropes of the modern woman, Schiaparelli effectively adds a kind of temporal den-sity to a foundational assumption in feminist studies of modernity. A host of feminist critics has outlined the ubiquity of the figure of the timeless, placid, maternal feminine in a period characterized by an intensifying everyday tempo in metropolitan life. Its pernicious effect was to sequester women in prehis-tory and disbar them from modernity. Several feminist studies of fashion have been used to demonstrate the other side of this story—to show how women's alignment with fashion actually bound them to modern time, since fashion was generally seen as an exemplar of the temporality of modern life. These accounts have tended to overlook fashion's simultaneous rhetoric of eter-nity and to arrange themselves dichotomously, such that representations of women as ultra-modern neutralize the cultural work done by representations of a timeless feminine. But in a period in which fashion was more recognizably and explicitly attuned to multiple temporal registers, including timelessness, what did it mean when a woman yearned for eternity, especially when she did so because of its apparently liberatory capacity?

There were surely multiple imperatives to present the self as invested in a temporal beyond, and the unique positioning of the fashion designer in relation to the market is one of them. It is certainly probable that the rhetoric of tran-scendence, bound up as it is conceptually with concepts of the authentic, was a necessary ingredient in any fashion designer memoir. The fashion designer needed to reassure the public of their artistry and their authenticity, since they worked in a medium that could be 'tainted' by its association with superfici-ality, inauthenticity and deceit. They laboured to be understood as artists in a sphere that was undeniably connected to commerce and that thus challenged the separation of artistry and industry. The rhetoric of timelessness, which seemed to sidestep the commerce of the industry, could help to do that. Notwithstanding this dimension of the issue, we can read Schiaparelli's rhetoric of eternity as operating on multiple levels. One of these is its offer of an implicit philosophy of femininity and eternity that, in fact, revealed a distinct ambivalence about the market.

THE TEMPO OF GLAMOUR

A review of theoretical discussions of glamour finds a remarkable consonance between the characteristics of this property and the persona of Elsa Schiaparelli as a figure related to time. There are two ways in which the emergence of glamour as a kind of social currency can be connected to time. The first is in its definition. What we find in attempting to define glamour is its link with a concept of the supernatural. Since the early nineteenth century, it has been invoked to denote some mysterious, ineffable quality. It derives from words denoting arcane knowledge, magic and the occult. As Carol S. Gould notes, '[g]lamour belongs to one inclined to bewitch or enchant.'[13] One important way in which the glamorous individual bewitches or enchants is through her or his aura of mystery, her or his ultimately enigmatic projection of self. According to Elizabeth Wilson, '[g]lamour depends on what is withheld, on secrecy, hints, and the hidden.'[14] The glamorous individual is thus distant, aloof, having a 'mysterious blend of accessibility and distance...neither transparent nor opaque...[but] translucent'.[15] Of course, there is a temporal dimension implicit in all of this: in its connections to the supernatural and the occult, glamour denotes a realm outside of time, ungoverned by the temporal logic of earthly matters. Part of the glamorous person's distance and inaccessibility, then, is due to the fact that she appears to exist in a timeless sphere. For this reason, as Wilson makes clear, she is also associated with a primal fear of death, for death is the ultimate signifier of departure from the temporal.[16] Judith Brown theorizes the cigarette as emblematic of glamour, noting that it 'seems to stop time' and points to this particular glamour as 'cold, indifferent, and deathly...curling away from earthly concerns as if on a whiff of smoke'.[17] The glamorous figure herself curls away from the earthly passage of time, arrested, static, distant. This is the individualized dimension of glamour's temporality.

The second way in which glamour responds to time is through its emergence as a result of the historically specific conditions of modernity. Historicizing the term, Stephen Gundle argues, allows us to understand its appearance as connected to democratization, urbanization, consumerism, the rise of leisure practices and the erosion of class boundaries.[18] Wilson points to its re-emergence at the beginning of the Industrial Age, with the breaking of certainties about governance and leadership in the wake of the overthrow of monarchical rule and as part of a backlash against industrialization among the Romantics.[19] For her part, Brown traces it to a more generalized industrial modernism, a broad cultural preoccupation with the threat to the sacred that was represented by mass culture. In any case, the connection of glamour to the historical condition of Western modernity is clear. Glamour emerges as a loosely aesthetic category in response to cultural change, and consequently acts as a medium of such change. It arises as an intelligible quality at the very moment when time seems to quicken, turning the everyday world into an anxious experience for metropolitan citizens.[20] Glamour might well be understood as a representation of the receding possibility of stasis in the face of the uneasily mobile experience of modern life.

Of course, glamour was usually embodied through the feminine, most notably and intelligibly through a range of iconic women and feminized objects, such as clothing and perfume.[21] Thus Gundle suggests that in addition to being a response to consumerism and democratization, glamour's popular cultural appearance during the period of the Belle Époque was an index of 'an obsession with the feminine as the cultural codifier of modernity's tensions and promise'.[22] It is a femininity which bears the weight of competing responses to the modern. Brown writes, 'Glamour appears both as commodity…and also as something distinctly modernist, formal, and tied to less material concerns than the production and packaging of goods.'[23] Here is the foundational tension of the glamorous, then, as a feminized form: it is at once situated within the rapid time of industrial modernity, with its connections to commerce, and in the timelessness of another dimension. The glamorous figure as a fashionable woman simultaneously gestures toward multiple registers of time.

This leads us to Schiaparelli, who contributes to the perception of her glamour through her constant references to some timeless dimension. Her example shows that glamour was on one hand the classic tempo of modernity, mediated through the technologies of industry and the media. It was fast, even frantic. But her portrayal reveals another aspect of that glamour, a deeply personal dimension that exceeds Schiaparelli's public availability: the timeless sphere of soul and divinity that I note above. Schiaparelli's glamour, then, challenges another binary formulation: it challenges the divide between the two concepts of time—historical and ahistorical, social and divine. Glamour, in its duality, reveals timelessness as a vital underside of the frenetic time of modernity: not its counterpoint, but its fraternal twin. It is always present, shedding light on the cracks in the modernist facade.[24]

Other characteristics of glamour emerge through Schiaparelli's self-portrait, which, in part through its portrayal of a divided identity, pictures her as remote and distant. At the same time, her accessible voice and depiction of relatively mundane episodes in her life make her approachable.[25] She bears a strong resemblance to that quintessential representation of feminine glamour, Greta Garbo, whom Brown describes as thus: 'all personality and at the same time, none: Garbo, who fascinated millions, remained a resolute mystery to her public . . . her ambition for celebrity was countered always by her resistance to it.'[26] Brown notes Garbo's 'refusals', including her silence about her personal life. She left few, if any, concrete archival traces. Of course, Schiaparelli published *Shocking Life*, and she could not refuse publicity. But she, too, was notoriously evasive about her personal life, and left no traces in the form of letters or diaries. Beyond the carefully managed public persona—necessary for the health of her business, though it flew in the face of her self-professed shyness—she remains inscrutable. Thus, in a slightly different way from Garbo, she too represents a paradoxically magnetic inaccessibility, the enigma whose mystery is ultimately the foundation of her appeal.

Since mystery and secrets suggest depth, a carefully elaborated theory of glamour does not naively reduce glamour to a surface effect. Rather, glamour can denote interiority and intellect.[27] Carol S. Gould, in fact, renders glamour as an expression of self; she argues that 'it flows from a person's own interior mode of experience.'[28] Glamour is still tied to a sort of spectacular display, and its expressions through the visual culture of modernity—film stars, fashion—show that it is, indeed, a modality of the surface. But the intuited secrets denoted by this surface complicate the relationship between surface and depth. Their relations are not oppositional, as in ancient and tired distinctions between depth as authenticity and surface as artifice. And glamour as an expression of interior life does not suggest that there is a straightforward relationship between interior and exterior, wherein the self-presentation corresponds precisely to the personality. If there were such a relationship, there could be no mystery, and the surface would lead the observer only to the truth of the self.[29] Rather, glamour is a quality that brings together surface and depth and refuses the dichotomy between them. The 'deep self' is there, but remains an enigma, and it is nothing more than this enigma that is represented through the surface relations of glamour. This is subtly but importantly different from the notion that the surface straightforwardly corresponds to or represents the truth of the interior. Here the interior remains unknowable, and the question becomes not 'what *is* the self?' but, rather, the *impossibility* of knowing that self. Not only does glamour have a profoundly interior dimension, but it is also a social mode. It sustains a relationship of active inquiry between the glamorous figure and her observers; they ask questions of her, about her. She refuses an answer.

Georg Simmel's theories of fashion and adornment are brought to mind here; he argues that fashion and adornment constitute a kind of radiant field, made up of what he calls 'human radioactivity'. The work of looking at the wearer, attempting to interpret her, links the wearer and observers in a kind of visual/material web. In this approach, adornment mediates between the individual and the social world, communicating selfhood through the visual field.[30] Glamour functions in much the same way, making connections between selves and the social world through the ongoing act of interpreting the mystery of the glamorous figure. Glamour, then, is a particularly apt concept for thinking about Schiaparelli, whose representations reveal a similar play between surface and depth. There is no question that she was perceived as a glamorous figure, and that this understanding crystallized around her visually accessible 'surface', which invited the public in, inaugurated a social relationship and maintained that relationship by refusing them further access; she kept them guessing.

With its emphasis on mystery, glamour does not collapse neatly into representations of women as outside of time. The glamorous woman is not aligned with the pace of modern life, true, but she is clearly connected to technology—film, photography and industrializing fashion. She is thus not an empty signifier of the beyond, or a utopian symbol of the possibility of escape from modern time pressures. The tempo of glamour is better understood as illegible, nonconforming to the grammar of time that moderns were accustomed to navigating. Its timelessness does not point to an essentially static feminine being. Rather, the glamorous woman resolves to a question mark. She is neither fully inside nor fully outside modernity, on the terms by which the ideologies of modernity are constituted. Glamour suggests that the rational, linear time of modernity can beget something other than its frenetically paced self, that modern time holds in reserve spaces for contemplation, for repose, for privacy. But glamour does not replicate the troubling opposition of public and private, because the glamorous figure holds the public and private together in herself: she is a figure whose inaccessibility derives from the suggestion of a private realm. As Schiaparelli's embodied glamour reveals through its dismantling of dichotomies of individual and social, private and public, interiority and surface and the modern and the timeless, the glamorous feminine figure complicates the many binary oppositions that characterize modernity. Whether this challenges conventional representations of women is the question that remains.

STRATEGIC OPACITY

To understand Schiaparelli's glamour as a quality that made her more or less enigmatic or even illegible, we must investigate her own and others' understandings of her complexity, her mastery of techniques of appearing that disrupt certainties about her. Caroline Evans has made a strong case for understanding Schiaparelli as what she calls a 'decentered subject'.[31] As Evans observes, it is Schiaparelli who represents herself in this way—certainly, *Shocking Life*'s jarring transition between the first and the third person in this narration is the clearest evidence of a kind of split self. The split functions along the lines of the 'celebrity' persona and the private self, on one level.[32] The opening lines of the book—'I merely know Schiap by hearsay. I have only seen her in a mirror. She is, for me, some kind of fifth dimension'—establish Schiaparelli's estrangement from herself, and indeed throw the self into question from the outset. She follows this with the assertion that '[h]er life has been...an everlasting question-mark'.[33] From the outset, then, the reader is confronted with a sense of uncertainty that resonates with glamour and its relations of concealment and unachieved revelation. The unfolding of the narrative, with its oscillation between first and third person narration, culminates in a short epilogue that is written, like the prologue, entirely in the third person. The book ends, then, on the note of uncertainty upon which it begins, and the purpose or message that Schiaparelli is trying to convey remains heavily obscured. This is significant for a memoir, which is presumably meant to 'shed light' upon its subject. By book-ending the volume with opaque and relatively impenetrable scenes, Schiaparelli undermines the ostensible purpose of her book.

Other writers also observe Schiaparelli's propensity for splitting and hiding elements of the self, but note its appearance as a motif of her clothing design. In a 1932 profile for *New Yorker* magazine, Janet Flanner writes, '[i]nclined to see women as something built rather than born, she uses costumes like fine veneer, the dovetailed angles, corners, and metal trim making her seem not so much merely a dressmaker as a cunning carpenter of clothes.'[34] In a recent article, Robyn Gibson turns to Schiaparelli's Desk Suit and Tea Cup Evening Coat, as well as to other, highly structured *trompe l'oeil* garments which could be confusing to the viewer but which bestowed the wearer with the power to control her own image. For instance, with the Desk Suit, '[i]n using ambiguous pockets, that is, functional and nonfunctional, only the wearer of the suit knew which was penetrable and which was closed. It rested on the wearer's discretion to reveal inner parts of herself by opening a pocket and removing something personal, intimate, perhaps shocking.'[35] Evans reads such work as a comment on 'the slippery and illusory nature of the mirror—and of representation itself—that lies at the heart of Schiaparelli's work...Whereas, say, in Vionnet's designs the masquerade of femininity is seamless, Schiaparelli tears the veil, pulls the masquerade away, and shows its workings by manipulating surface signifiers that she layers, or plays with, on the body.'[36] Thus Evans, reading these material objects against their creator's other work, her memoir, finds a continuity between her fragmented self-portrait and her designs; the latter act as a comment on femininity as a project of surfaces and concealment. She suggests that the aesthetic landscape created by Schiaparelli was an extension of an aesthetic of the self, the self that is accounted for in *Shocking Life*.

CELEBRITY AND THE MANAGEMENT OF THE PUBLIC GAZE

There *are* indeed clear parallels between Schiaparelli's disorienting designs and her self-representation. What we find in *Shocking Life* above all is a comment on celebrity as a state that hides or altogether precludes the expression of a true selfhood, just as some designs rendered the expression of self problematic. The estrangement that Schiaparelli conveys through the shifting use of the first and third person establishes the sense of unease in the relationship between these two elements. Though they are aspects of the same self, her work suggests her impression that the celebrity has taken precedence over the private self, and she watches it with some distance and incredulity, as in the following description of sitting in her studio, looking out over the comings and goings of the Place Vendôme:

> I heard all the comments and watched the innumerable photographs that were taken in front of the Boutique. Sometimes a whole family would line up in front of the windows; sometimes an enthusiastic globe-trotter without a spare cent would push the front door open, beaming under the sign of Schiaparelli, feeling momentarily like a millionaire...I could watch the arrivals and departures at the Ritz, still the most international hotel in the world, where strange people play their unconscious parts in the 'actualities'.[37]

Here she portrays her distance from her own celebrity; she watches the phenomenon that is Schiaparelli from her quiet corner of the house, which she notes is often cast in 'semi-darkness'. She is merely an observer. The final sentence is especially telling, as it reveals the parts played by the international elite who drink, dine and stay at the Ritz—a group to which she belongs—in the staging of their lives.[38] Schiaparelli here reveals an understanding of celebrity as role-playing, and the importance of performance and publicity in that play. One famous example is her very popular Newspaper Hat, made of material that was printed with newspaper headlines about her.[39] She also, famously and unlike most other designers (save for Chanel, who came out with similar statements in the 1930s), thought the moral and legal fuss raised by designers over the plagiarism of their designs was 'vain and useless', arguing that 'the moment people stop copying you, it means you are no longer any good'.[40] More than simply recognizing her celebrity as an act, then, Schiaparelli understood its potential and actual financial profitability.

Again, other commentators also note Schiaparelli's facility at exploiting her celebrity in the service of the business. Famously, she was the best publicity for her brand; she wore her garments in public and contributed to the mystique that built up around them. In this sense, we can consider her glamour as a kind of hybrid between the woman and the clothing.[41] And, though her impact and celebrity were tied in part to the audacity of her creations, Guillaume Garnier notes that she was careful to make sure this did not threaten her status: 'she knew how to gauge, and even to manage, the right proportion of eccentricity attached to her public image.'[42] Her glamour thus is to some extent a strategic production. The female designer's celebrity, in fact, placed distinctly different burdens on her from those experienced by a male designer. She was to stand out as a style icon in her own right, modelling her own designs and setting an example of chic living for the women who would be her customers. This is one of Schiaparelli's most notable characteristics. She became a living flagship of the brand in the 1930s, an emblem of the kind of modern chic her clothing line represented. This made escape, solitude and privacy next to impossible.[43] And she was a spectacle with a distinct time signature. Here, being subject to the brand meant she was subject to its resolutely historical, incessantly changeable temporal rhythms. Her own dress choices would tend to be understood as reflections of her very self by a modern public that believed in the consonance of dress and inner personality. Thus, in order to escape detection and 'capture' by the public, she needed to be fluid, changing as her dress lines changed. Her persona was flexible, ephemeral.

But, as I discuss above, with glamour, the careful construction of a surface effect does not preclude the suggestion of depth. In an interview, Schiaparelli acquaintance and art historian Gladys Favre responds to the interviewer's prompt that 'what counted for Schiaparelli was lifestyle in all its aspects' with the following telling statement: 'That's it. The neatly raked garden, well cared for on the outside, was just as important as the paintings and the furniture inside. The whole thing together expressed the values, the passions and the viewpoint of the woman of the house.'[44] This portrait of Schiaparelli's stylized home and overall aesthetic is emblematic of the approach she favoured, which does not discount the surface as an index of depth, although the content of such depth remains, for the most part, obscured. The overwhelming impression left by *Shocking Life* is of a strategically managed celebrity that is in some sense underpinned by an inaccessible self. The book hints to the reader that an authentic self exists, but does not indulge the hope of its full exposition. The reader senses that reading the memoir might ultimately yield access to the depth Schiaparelli hints at all the way through, but never makes visible. This provides the narrative force to what is in fact a rather dry account of a life; it keeps the reader engaged. When the book ends upon an enigmatic and distant note, the legacy of glamour, with its sense of mystery and timelessness, is sealed.

In a discussion of Dorothy Parker, another female celebrity active in roughly the same period as Schiaparelli, Kathleen M. Helal notes the tensions faced by a public figure aware of her own celebrity and perhaps unhappy about its effects upon her life: 'Parker emphasizes her inability to define her "self" independent of her public image. She is autobiographer and celebrity, writer and persona, private self and public image, author and authored. The ambiguity in both monologues reflects Parker's inability to identify with the role of object or agent, image or writer.'[45] Though many of the textual strategies that Schiaparelli deploys match the ostensibly autobiographical monologues by Parker—they are also ambiguous, there is some tension between private and public image—an inability to identify with either role is not a problem for Schiaparelli. In her case, precisely because the book ends on an enigmatic note, we get the sense that the author has held something in reserve in her strategic self-promotion, has rejected the identification with celebrity in favour of a return to the self.[46] Once again, the cultivation of glamour, with its suggestion of hidden depth, provides the means by which she could engage in such a rejection.

THE PLEASURE OF PRIVATE TIME

The suggestion of something held in reserve depends on the cultivation of privacy, and the appreciation of and even need for private time and space emerge as emblematic of Schiaparelli in both the press and her own narrative of her life and career. Notably, she claims in the all-important foreword to *Shocking Life* that 'the only escape is in oneself'.[47] The sentiment is borne out throughout the book, as she portrays herself as shy and in need of private space from a very young age—for instance, she uses the language of Virginia Woolf's *A Room of One's Own* to describe her creation of private space in her home for writing, as an adolescent.[48] She suggests at the end that this propensity for solitude has been carried over into adulthood: she still prefers to be alone in her house.[49] What Schiaparelli renders as her preference for aloneness, the press translates into a mysterious quality that is seen to contribute to her glamorous mystique. Janet Flanner notes Schiaparelli's penchant for isolation: 'at the age of thirty-six she still retains the tacit secrecy of a talented child, too gifted and disabused to attempt an explanation to adults.'[50] A 1934 profile in *Time* claims, '[e]ven to her intimate friends, she remains an enigma.'[51] Representations of Schiaparelli nod at her depth but fail to penetrate it. Indeed, this becomes the quintessence of her glamour: what she refuses to observers is the clearest evidence of her depth. And of course, it is this quality that is ultimately cultivated in the self-portrait in *Shocking Life*: a refusal that is of a piece with her childhood claims to private space.

A withholding of self from the public suggests that there is a second self, an other self, who is being withheld. Hers is a self-representation that is invested in the suggestion, if not the portrayal, of an authentic selfhood obscured by celebrity. The gestures toward a hidden other self seem to come as a result of an understanding of the particularly gendered stakes of celebrity and visibility

Figure 3.4   Elsa Schiaparelli at home, 1936. Photo by Lipnitzki/Roger Viollet/ Getty Images. © Roger Viollet/Getty Images.

for women. Secrecy, Schiaparelli implies, is of particular benefit to women. In the memoir, she describes screens she used to fashion makeshift dressing rooms at her first location at the Rue de la Paix. Upon making the move to the Place Vendôme, she brings the screens with her, and they function again to make dressing rooms—but also transcend their mundane usage:

> As in a confessional, the screens held their secrets. Many unknown things, sub-terfuges, and deceits were revealed in their sanctuary, but these revelations never went beyond them. They alone heard the stories of wives and mistresses, saw the maimed bodies of women considered plain. And if Schiap looks and listens with sympathy and pity, she forgets everything at six o'clock when she leaves the office—so all is safe.[52]

In this extraordinary passage, Schiaparelli invokes her relationships with other women—clients, this time—in more sensitive terms than anywhere else in the memoir. She also points toward a particularly feminine domain of secrets. The screens provide sites for the voicing of secrets about issues faced by women, specifically adultery and the feminine body image. Her construction of herself as a good keeper of secrets is notable. It is the revelation of secrets about women's intimate lives that compromises safety. Of course, women risk much greater damage than men to their sexual and professional reputations with the spotlight on their intimate lives; it is surely this knowledge that conditions Schiaparelli's decision to reveal very little, even in the apparently revelatory form of the memoir. Protecting her own secrets, her sense of an 'other self', is a means of protecting her reputation—especially as a single mother in an era and national context, interwar France, where that status would be questionable.[53] The management of her own celebrity, ostensibly all about spectacle, is shown to be as much about protecting 'the invisible' as it is about maintaining visually accessible surfaces. The evidence for such an understanding lies in her own silences about her life; very little is known of her liaisons—the lovers she had, for instance. There is no known archive of materials related to her.[54] She left few traces of her intimate life, and yet, paradoxically, *Shocking Life* is built on intimations of a rich inner world. As I have suggested, this contributes a great deal to the sense of Schiaparelli as a glamorous figure. But it is, at its root, a strategy for the maintenance of privacy.

Private time is precious because it is pleasurable. This is evident in Schiaparelli's descriptions of pleasure in the text; they are almost invariably focused on solitude and retreat. She describes a summer holiday in the Riviera early in her success, for instance: 'It was a delightful and simple summer when problems seemed smoothed out all around. I had at last some quiet hours to spend in the water and on boats, with a few simple friends.'[55] Elsewhere, she insists that quiet time in a library is one of her greatest pleasures, and she describes an attempt to steal 'an hour's relaxation' in the Prado in Madrid, even while she is desperately fleeing occupied France.[56] Notably, though most of these descriptions of privacy are linked to particular places and times, they also have a timeless dimension. Her narrations of such solitary places give the sense that she is stepping outside of the rhythms of the everyday into another time, one that permits a kind of embodied pleasure— for instance, she describes the time in the Prado as an attempt at quiet, solitary 'communion' with her 'life passions El Greco and Goya'.

This notion of embodied pleasure is critical in analyzing Schiaparelli, whose memoir is full of subtle references to the importance of passionate embodiment for women. Tellingly, she makes the following note about her first earnest lover: 'He might...have made me spiritually happy, but I was far too full of life. I was definitely aware of my body and I had a vivid imagination.'[57] She thus establishes from the outset her awareness not only of the importance of her body, but of sexual pleasure. But this subtle reference is essentially her only mention of her own sexuality; though she alludes to other lovers in *Shocking Life*, and to marriage proposals which she passionately rejected, she does

Figure 3.5   Elsa Schiaparelli and a worker dressing a client in her salon in Paris, 1935. Photo by Keystone-France/Gamma-Keystone via Getty Images. © Keystone-France/Getty Images.

so guardedly, and is rarely explicit with respect to such forms of pleasure. Sex and other forms of embodied pleasure are not repressed, then, so much as veiled, hidden, barely hinted at and seen to be experienced in the 'other time' that is foundational to the text. This is an important distinction; as I note in my discussion of Poiret, there is potential in secret-keeping, as it allows people to control the knowledge that circulates about them. Thus Schiaparelli's silences can be read not as signals of an inability to speak, but as active choices made to control her public image. In this sense, her silences speak.[58] Glamour allowed her to cultivate a third dimension—both spatial and temporal—into which what was withheld in her public persona could be fit.

That Schiaparelli might need to cultivate an 'other time' in order to experience her own potential for embodied pleasure is not surprising; as a celebrity under the scrutiny of the press, the possibility for unseen pleasure was deeply threatened. The cultivation of glamour allowed her to experience pleasure discreetly, secretly, while at the same time maintaining an appropriate public demeanour. Glamour's timelessness functioned as a kind of masking device, not in the more commonly accepted sense of masking as an artificial 'covering over' of the self, but rather as a strategic management of the elements of selfhood, a controlled ritual of appearances and veilings of the self.[59] In this account, masking is not about hiding the self, but about selectively and strategically revealing its various elements. Schiaparelli's love of masks is theorized by Caroline Evans in relation to her clothing design, but it is also evident in her own autobiographical articulations. She writes, '[a]lthough I am very shy (and nobody will believe it), so shy that the simple necessity of saying "Hallo" sometimes makes me turn icy cold, I have never been shy of appearing in public in the most fantastic and personal get-up.'[60] She then goes on to describe her love of outrageous wigs, and throughout the book, she describes her appearance in sensational garments at major events such as balls. Masking allows for both the cultivation of a glamorous exterior, and the protection of a sense of self from the scrutiny occasioned by any glamorous celebrity. Glamour emerges as a kind of strategic response, then, to the exigencies of celebrity, a way of managing the demands placed upon Schiaparelli as a public figure, while not threatening that highly necessary publicity—in fact, glamour fed that publicity. In the 'other time' of glamour, the 'other self' that is so critical to Schiaparelli remains intact, sheltered, private.

Readers might wonder, at this point, about the invocation of an 'other self', since this may appear to invoke a pure identity for Schiaparelli, untouched by celebrity and the public gaze. The notion of an 'other self', responding to an 'other time', need not imply such a reductive essence. Rather, the modality of glamour that Schiaparelli embodied allowed above all for the cultivation of an enigma at the centre of the self, an uncertainty that did not collapse into an uncritical valorization of authentic selfhood, but remained an irresolvable question, at least for the observer of this fashion celebrity. Most importantly, it is the time signature afforded by glamour—its creation of a certain stasis, its hints at the underside of modernity's tempo—that allows the glamorous figure to cultivate secrets outside of the public gaze.

TIMELESS REVOLUTION?

In withholding part of her in order to safeguard it, Schiaparelli played a pivotal role in the management of her image. This sense that she was in control of her image was part of a more general representation of her as a wilful and freedom-oriented spirit. She even links her 'revolutionary and stubborn' tendencies to being fed goat milk as a child.[61] Throughout the book, she returns to the theme of her own iconoclasm, and articulates it in temporal terms: revolution, after all, suggests the triumphant reign of the new. Of course, her 'revolutionary' character led to the collaborations for which she is so well known: with Dali, with Jean Cocteau, with Marcel Duchamp—these were vanguardists, whose reputations hinged on their embrace of the new. They are quintessential cultural modernists, allied with a vision of modernism that stresses the constant possibility of innovation. And yet even this famous allegiance to the exemplars of the new, which seemed to situate her *in time*, gave way in her self-narration to the timelessness of her glamour. Schiaparelli continued to resist her alignment with the vagaries of time. She revealed herself to be as suspicious of the ephemeral as other designers were, and this has important connections to her gendering of both herself and her clients.

The generally adoring press seized on Schiaparelli's connections to the modernists and her general stylistic audacity; this was what seemed 'available' about her in the face of her general opacity. 'Schiaparelli is the modern among the dressmakers,' London *Vogue* proclaimed in 1932, while also aligning her with those *nineteenth-century* exemplars of modernity, the dandies, in a complex temporal layering.[62] An article in the *Seattle Post-Intelligencer* gushed, '[t]he name of Schiaparelli is synonymous with a new roving spirit in fashion, undaunted by conventional circumscribed restrictions, and the degree of success she has attained attests to the fact that the world applauds her audacious interpretations of design—always in the tempo of tomorrow!'[63] Of course, press reports merely responded to the designs themselves, which were indeed often characterized by stylistic novelty, and they responded in particular to what Schiaparelli presented as her place in the field of fashion as a terrain of artistic experiment. In a 1940 lecture covered by the *New York Times*, for instance, she claimed that, unlike in New York, 'in Paris there is a central group composed of artists whose sole job is creation and design. They are not concerned with quantities, distribution, or prices. All their thoughts are devoted to the new and beautiful in cloth, patterns, and gadgets. The Paris designer is free.'[64] During the course of her career, Schiaparelli was careful to construct herself as an aesthetic maverick, certainly through her designs but also through her own verbal articulations. As noted above, though, she was equally careful not to exhaust the public's goodwill with excessive eccentric self-fashioning, and the press often notes her relatively restrained and certainly 'chic' day-to-day dress choices (as opposed to the more playful and surprising things she wore at special events).

But in the retrospective forum, the memoir, though Schiaparelli loudly and constantly proclaims her own revolutionary qualities, she does not in general relate them to aesthetic innovation or novelty. In fact, her iconoclasm figures in very different ways in *Shocking Life*; the collaborations with major artists are afforded no special place in the book. It would be tenable to claim that she merely trades on the cachet of their names—she name-drops, as she does with countless major figures—without devoting any serious attention to these relationships for which she is best remembered. In important ways, Schiaparelli flouts her audience's expectations. They read this memoir for its insights into the life of a major designer, and yet she essentially refused them

Figure 3.6 Schiaparelli in costume at couturier Jacques Fath's ball, 4 August 1952. Photo by Keystone-France/Gamma-Keystone via Getty Images. © Keystone-France/ Getty Images.

the information they sought about her working life and the fashion world. Instead, she locates her 'revolutionary' or iconoclastic qualities in straightforward assertions about her character. For instance, in an episode near the end where she calls herself 'The Indomitable', she writes: 'If ever I wished to be a man it was then. The possibility of going out alone at any time, anywhere, has always excited my envy.'[65] But even more importantly, the representation of herself as a strong-willed figure takes place in what might be considered the unexpected narrative choices in this book.

The narratives in question are organized around Schiaparelli's flight from Europe, in particular. Stories of her wartime life occupy more of the volume than do details about the establishment of her career in fashion or her aesthetic principles. On one level, this gives narrative force to the story. These are dramatic tales of wartime border crossings and flights across Europe, with the sense of the author's imminent danger exaggerated for effect. They stress Schiaparelli's quest for freedom by focusing on another kind of glamour: the kind that derives from the mystery, intrigue and danger of war. But Schiaparelli's story possesses different terms from the standard wartime narrative. Rather than focusing on national differences, part of her self-representation as revolutionary and freedom-seeking involves an implicit questioning of the nation. This is most evident in her repeated assertions that borders are deplorable to her. She describes how she was touched by Gian-Carlo Menotti's opera, *The Consul*, about the imposition of passports and related bureaucratic red tape imposed by nation-states. She characterizes such demands as 'degrading restrictions on human liberty and self-respect', and declares, '[m]y mind revolts against having to ask permission to wander on this earth which should be free and the property of all men.'[66] Near the end of the book, Schiaparelli underscores the temporal dimension of this sentiment, asking, '[w]hen will people realize that frontiers and frontier rules should be a thing of the past?'[67] This accords with her profession of a kind of internationalism, evident in descriptions of her work as a Red Cross nurse's aide in New York during the war and her desire to deploy to North Africa with her unit. (She was refused for reasons that remained unclear to her.)

Schiaparelli's location of her freedom in something other than fashion is reflected in what emerges, in narrating this same wartime period of her life, as a rejection of fashion's tendency to constrain her. She writes of getting a run in her stocking: this, she says, 'made me many friends who thought of me as a human being—not just as a fashion puppet'.[68] Then: 'all my dearest friends have never been interested in clothes, which is the best compliment they could pay me—or perhaps the best compliment I could pay myself.'[69] Here, retrospectively, Schiaparelli reveals herself to be deeply conflicted. Though fashion has enabled her fame, in her memoir she identifies it as a burden, restricting her capacity for freedom by limiting her human multi-dimensionality. National borders, then, are not the only things that contain her; so does the profession that ostensibly *enables* her.

Here she points to the stakes of celebrity in this aesthetically driven realm. It is not simply the scrutinizing gaze of the press that she finds invasive—an experience that is, of course, common to celebrities—but a set of expectations that is specific to fashion. Part of this is the same kind of ambivalence about the ephemeral that all designers experienced; fashion aligns designers with transience in a way that is unsettling for public figures who also have to build up a discursive connection to the eternal. But there is another issue at play in this case, which helps to explain why Schiaparelli implicitly denies her own intimate relationship with fashion. There is a good reason for her inclusion of another version of the split between her professional persona—universally admired for its chic—and her private self, which remains unconcerned with

Figure 3.7 Elsa Schiaparelli, accompanied by the Baron Phil-lipe de Rothschild, dresses a war orphan in Paris, 1947. Photo by Keystone-France/Gamma-Keystone via Getty Images. © Keystone-France/Getty Images.

ornament. The gendered stakes of this choice are apparent; the perception that she is a 'fashion puppet' who is inordinately interested in fashion would tend, in a cultural imaginary that feminizes and trivializes fashion, to deny Schiaparelli's rich intellectual and political life. It would reduce her to the iconic embodiment of chic that the press so often conjured. Of course, such a rejection of the conventions of the femininity that her design career nourished in other women, perpetuates the imprisoning split between surface and sub-stance, body and mind, which her clothing itself complicates.

The deep ambivalence about her own status as fashionable is also an im-plicit reference to Schiaparelli's clientele. Here we get a glimpse of one way in which feminine others figure in her self-representation. She constructs most women—understood to be interested in fashion—as unlike her. In narrating herself, she relies on a culturally available understanding of fashionable women as lacking depth. Distancing herself from these other women is a foundational act of her autobiography, because the book is written in a retrospective time. The book is published at the end of her career, and in the closing pages she narrates her disenchantment with fashion, which is revealed as a frustration with its mass scale. She asks how the cultural industries might 'find new and hitherto untried methods of progress, without losing a fraction of our creative power or our sense of beauty' and thus might respond to modern 'people who do not know the difference between meat and flesh'.[70] She left the industry, though, because of what she perceived as the triumph of a certain thoughtless industrialized fashion system and the philistines who now constituted the market. Though Schiaparelli recognized the imperative for *haute couture* to meet the demands of the apparently uncultured masses—masses that were feminized, as Andreas Huyssen argues, and never more so than in this industry—she chose this moment of their postwar triumph to retire.[71] Her dismissal of the possibilities of mass culture thus suggests as well the denigration of the conventionally feminine, which contributes in important ways to the final manipulation of her image for posterity. In an industry predicated on the new, she was concerned with 'fixing' her own image, and that involved a rejection of one form of femininity.

Here, then, Schiaparelli, in part through the invocation of a mythical feminine fashion subject, reveals the limits of her own allegiance to novelty, the very quality that the press saw as intrinsic to her. The impulse to innovate, the cultural value placed on this work, fatigues her. Though she recognizes and lauds the potential to bring rich culture to the masses without sacrificing quality, she chooses to retire rather than to carry the banner for this sort of hybrid cultural production. Instead, she reveals herself to be generally suspicious of the possibility of the new, toward the end of her career. During her wartime exile in America, she travels to Peru, and writes in retrospect that the 'sand-coloured country, broken on occasion by my beloved shocking pink, proves that there is nothing new in this world.'[72] For the development of her first clothing line upon her return to Paris after the war, she writes, '[w]ith a reminiscence of great elegance and dignity, I turned to the Regency—there is not very much new in anything.'[73] The narrative of *Shocking Life*, then, reveals a progressive disenchantment with the very terms of the fashion industry, with its insistence on constant change, and its related imperative to mass production and consumption, long associated with women.

THE OTHER TIMES OF FEMININITY

The relationship between Schiaparelli's ambivalence toward newness and her establishment of a feminine other is revealed most obviously in her complex but mostly hostile relationship toward women's independence and social emancipation. In a 1937 interview, she discusses her preference for the tailored suit for women, but notes, 'I don't mean these mannish freaks that made it difficult to distinguish between a man and a woman...They are hateful and ugly.'[74] And in *Shocking Life*, she writes mockingly of the English suffragettes who filled Piccadilly Square on her wedding day: they were 'mad masculine furies, collectively and individually hideous.'[75] She then reveals part of the reason for her ridicule: her belief that strong women are not attractive to men. But as Schiaparelli herself notes repeatedly, she is herself one of these strong women. At the end of the book, the end of her career, she muses about other possible life paths she could have taken, and wonders whether she could have made a good wife. 'My first and only experience,' she writes, 'did not give me a chance to be successful in this role. The chances of a strong-minded woman becoming a good wife to a man able and anxious to dominate her are few. And being in reality quite old-fashioned, I could never have accepted a weak man as a husband.'[76] Here she expresses a strange and contradictory sentiment of regret that often tinges her hints of love affairs. Most tellingly, this is expressed in temporal terms; she is old-fashioned, 'in reality', and thus out of step with the temporal orientation demanded by her career in fashion. The relationship of women's emancipation to time is further developed in a 1960 interview with Charles Collingwood for the CBS television program *Person to Person*. The interview took place six years after her retirement. In response to a question about whether women would be 'happier if they were more independent...individually stronger, Schiaparelli answers, 'No, I don't think so, I think really women must have been much happier when they had no responsibilities...Now [today], women have assumed all the responsibilities of men...therefore they have to be stronger and stronger, but I don't think happier.'[77]

Like Poiret, then, Schiaparelli reveals herself to be nostalgic for an earlier iteration of feminine convention (if for different reasons) and rejects the construction of the 'modern woman'. But the two others who are invoked here—'happier' women of the past, and overburdened, 'emancipated' women of today—have much closer relations with Schiaparelli herself than did Poiret's nostalgic objects. Her 'failure' to be appropriately feminine, which she suggests led to her aloneness, effectively distances her from women who embody feminine convention. But she does not sit comfortably with this status, and emerges as fundamentally ambivalent about her own independence. She would like a husband, it seems, but regrets that something—the stubborn streak that was nurtured by goat's milk, as a baby—prevents her from submitting to masculine will. Glamorous Schiaparelli holds tight to secrets about her love life. Thus 'liberated' women are as different from her as conventionally feminine women are. In a sense, all available models of womanhood are made Other, here, and part of Schiaparelli's glamour thus derives from her dissimilarity from other women. Given the over-determination of femininity in the fashion industry, which presented a host of models, all of which were peculiarly the same, the stakes of presenting oneself as an iconoclastic woman are clear. The distancing of other women was a grasp at individuality in a terrain already saturated by the iconic feminine.[78] 'There is Only One Schiaparelli', blared a 1933 headline in *Women's Wear Daily*, confirming the perception of her femininity as distinct from other models of the feminine.[79]

Of course, this ambivalence about women's independence is at odds with the tenor of her clothes. Schiaparelli first became known for her sportswear, though it is for her surrealist-inspired and generally experimental work that she is best remembered. In the memoir, Schiaparelli is clear about the importance of practical, simplified attire for modern women. She defends her introduction of the trouser skirt, which women wore for everything, including sport. And though she herself wore wigs for a time, for instance, she notes that they are not well adapted to the practical necessities of 'swimming and playing golf and running for a bus'.[80] During the Second World War, before her exile in the United States, she introduced what she called the '"cash and carry" collection', which featured 'huge pockets everywhere so that a woman, obliged to leave home in a hurry or to go on duty without a bag, could pack all that was necessary to her' and 'thus retain the freedom of her hands and yet manage to look feminine'.[81] Her clothing materialized a changing set of roles for women, one that was aligned with the widespread perception of Schiaparelli's ultra-modernity. In this sense, she created a visual language of novelty that had implications far beyond aesthetics, integrating fashion innovations with a changing gendered order.[82]

Yet this is why it becomes all the more imperative to read the language of the designer memoir alongside the visual rhetoric of the clothes themselves. Only in reading the autobiographical representations can we understand the kinds of pressures that a designer worked under, with the clothes she designed offering a cohesive counterpoint to the anxieties she crystallized as a particular kind of modern figure, a female fashion designer. For Schiaparelli as with the other designers discussed in this book, these anxieties derived in large part from the kinds of temporal contradictions sustained through fashion. Such instabilities intensified the already fragmenting experience of modern time consciousness, resulting in the drive to express mastery through the attribution of otherness to the very women upon whom the industry thrived. But for Schiaparelli, the imperative to stake a claim to self in this field did not involve a straightforward attribution of otherness to her clients. Rather, we see in the written memoir that it is read against the language of the clothing itself, a shifting relationship between the self and various feminine others who are perhaps not so very distant from herself, given Schiaparelli's femininity.

Reading the texts this way, the times that Schiaparelli uses in her constant invocation of freedom become unmistakeably gendered. The personal freedom that she so prizes has a 'time signature'—it is 'timeless'. She relates narratives that are clearly historically specific, chief among them stories of the war. But she is unsatisfied with history, with the temporal self. History is the site of the dehumanizing bureaucracy she so loathes; it is where she is subject to the will of the state. History is the site that produces constructs like the femininity that she distances herself from; almost all of Schiaparelli's more explicit meditations on femininity are attached to major historical events, such as the suffragette march on her wedding day, cited above. History also begets war; she laments what the war did to women's clothing, claiming that it masculinized them in unnecessary ways that persisted even after the war had come to an end.[83] And she expresses disappointment with the way that women 'insisted on looking like little girls' rather than elegant women, as part of the desperate effort to banish collective trauma in the aftermath of the war.[84] Ultimately history offers up unpalatable, binary alternatives to women, alternatives which Schiaparelli herself, in the cultivation of her unique glamour and allegiance to timelessness, tries to sidestep. The book's vision of women's relationship to time thus does not relegate women to the outside of modernity, but attaches them to it. In fact, in Schiaparelli's mind, femininity is altogether *too* subject to the vagaries of history, which seem to produce nothing but exaggerated visions. Schiaparelli's own temporal positioning is thus a response to the ill effects of modern history for women. Situating women in history, she seems to suggest, is by no means necessarily a remedy for the one-dimensionality of conceptions and representations of femininity. History has been as cruel to women as have perceptions that they lie outside or beyond the modern.

THE LIMITS AND POTENTIAL OF TIMELESSNESS

Schiaparelli's imperfect solution to the burdens of history is to grasp increasingly, as her self-narration unfolds, toward timelessness. She tries to cultivate a timelessness that is not *un*modern, but that sidesteps the opposition of modern and archaic. One might emblematize her career with the cosmic elements—stars, suns, starbursts—that frequently recurred in her clothing over the years. Stars have nothing to do with the earth, with the unfolding of human time. They stand entirely outside of constructs like the modern and the archaic. The narrative arc of the memoir—written, of course, in hindsight—has the designer's life unfolding toward a dawning realization that what she wants is an escape from history, into something akin to the cosmic time of these stars. This ultimately means leaving the fashion industry, for while fashion is indeed a constellation of the eternal and the relentlessly historical and changeable, the historical can never be transcended. In fact, as Schiaparelli's own descriptions show, it is history which wins, in the end—in her descriptions of her attempt to intervene in the 'little girl' fashions of the postwar period, she is shown trying in vain to introduce another, less exaggerated style. Her house never regained its prewar glory, as she was out of step with the demands of the historical moment. In other words, Schiaparelli's aesthetically challenging designs, many of them dreamlike, playful and certainly not attuned to the vagaries of history, but rather suggestive of a register outside of history, did not suit a moment in which France and the West in general were recovering from the wounds of this brutal war and either searching for ways to respond to it directly, or struggling to repress it.[85] In this case, rather than contradicting the self-constructions of the memoir, the designs were reflections of the transcendent yearnings of their creator, as these were articulated in *Shocking Life.* The postwar Schiaparelli, searching for an escape from history, articulated that desire for timelessness on multiple fronts.

Paralleling this move in her clothing, the book can be read as a classic narrative of personal growth, in which Schiaparelli's ultimate move away from her industry closes a circle and returns her to the spirit of playfulness she describes having as a child. The increasing attention to spirituality—to 'the beyond'—that she describes in the final chapters of the book reprises themes established in the earliest pages. The language is strikingly similar in the portions of the book that describe her years before fashion and those chronicling her exit from the industry. In the book's foreword, she writes, '[h]er life has been a means to something else—an everlasting question mark. Truly mystic, she believes in IT, but has not yet found out what IT is.'[86] Her choice of a figural unknowability to describe herself from the outset is telling. Not only does it establish an orientation to timelessness—the 'everlasting'—but it also entwines this timelessness with a principle of uncertainty. Mystery, of course, is a quality that governs Schiaparelli's glamour, enables her elusiveness and ultimately her self-protectiveness. It does indeed frame and contain the book's narrative; there at the beginning, it is also there at the end, when she writes of a trip to Brazil and a visit with a shaman there: 'I strongly believe in the unknown which occupies a great part of my inner self.'[87] Thus she bookends the volume with an homage to timelessness, mystery and glamour that seems to have been borne out throughout her career. She clearly wishes to transpose it, though, from the more constrained way she lived this glamour in the industry to a more personal, spiritually enriching experience.

In a commentary on the complex registers of time in autobiographical writing, Burton Pike, drawing on Freud, notes that 'the unconscious knows no concept of time'. The division of time into moments, and into structures of present, past and future, 'is a creation of the ego and the superego'.[88] He thus argues that '[w]riting autobiographically is a way of actively reintroducing time-lessness into the later, ego-determined stages of life'. Childhood, he says, offers 'models' of timelessness, 'which cannot be brought into adult life in any other way'.[89] This is why descriptions and analyses of childhood figure so prominently in life writing; they are a way of reckoning with unconscious structures that brush against the grain of modern subjectivity, of exploring modes of being that are not subject to the strictures of conventional models of selfhood. Schiaparelli's cyclical narrative can be understood in this light; in exploring models of timelessness that she says characterized her earliest years, she seeks to escape the constraints of ego and superego that are un-doubtedly maximized for celebrities and anyone living in the public eye. The knowledge that she was being scrutinized did not sit well with this shy woman. She notes her discomfort with her celebrity at various points: she was shy, she writes, so shy that she often became 'aggressive' and even 'downright rude'.[90] Later she notes, 'in moments of my greatest success I am overcome by a sense of detachment, a feeling of insecurity, a knowledge that so much is futile—and a peculiar sadness.'[91] In moments when the ego was demanded by the press and public, and the superego was vigilant in the maintenance of an appropriate demeanour for these voyeurs, Schiaparelli craved something else.

The female designer's celebrity, in fact, placed distinctly different burdens on her from those experienced by a male designer. Perhaps more than for any other species of celebrity, public visibility meant, for the modern, female fashion designer, that expressions of self were indissolubly linked to commerce. They self-fashioned strategically, after all—to sell their clothes. They embodied and brought to life a set of values represented by those material objects through the nascent concept of lifestyle, with the hope not only of selling clothes, but of selling an ethos, a sensibility that would find its logical expression in those clothes.[92] For Schiaparelli, the work of visibility meant the material embodiment of her corporate values, values which were at odds with her self-understanding. Over and over again she tells readers she is 'strongly inclined to mysticism', re-lating this spiritual emblem to an overall orientation to the world.[93] The picture of herself as otherworldly, essentially and resolutely transcendent no doubt guides the critique of materialism that she subtly develops in *Shocking Life.*[94] And yet, she remained an icon, the 'smartness' of her self-fashioning, to use the word that commentators so often used, directly linked to her sales and thus to the temporal rhythms of the fashion market. This is evident in the fol-lowing description from a 1938 article in *Women's Wear Daily*:

> Elsa Schiaparelli looked as smart as ever lunching at the Ritz with hair as up and slick as it is possible to do it, and a small, forward hat; later that same afternoon, all the *vendeuses* and mannequins in her salons had brushed up hair; new hats in the millinery department a trifle larger than last season's doll shapes.[95]

The sketch moves strikingly from Schiaparelli to the employees of her house, and finally to material things. In this description, she is itemized in a description of femininity that stretches from living woman through to inanimate items for sale, obscuring the differences between human subject and material possession. And here was the strongest incentive for Schiaparelli to distance herself from conventional femininity; conventional femininity's thing-like qualities, she saw, meant petrifaction. The consequence of her visibility was the subordination of a strongly held sense of self to the earthly demands of the market and the constraints of feminine fashionability.

Of course, this fashion iconography and these market demands were elements that she herself had created. Ultimately, her memoir reads as the narration of her refusal to meet these demands, including those of the public for her visibility. She stopped the merry-go-round and got off, she tells us pointedly. The one-page epilogue issues the final challenge to those who would continue to demand of her. But even here, her ambivalence is evident. This is clearly intended as a transcendent tableau; Schiaparelli moves to third-person narration again, and abandons narrative time. Rather, she sets a scene: of herself in her house in Hammamet, Tunisia. The theme is her sublime solitude in 'nature' ('this land of sunshine and dreams') and in 'authentic' built environments—she describes the intricate wooden latticework of her *mashrabiya* (a screened inside/outside Islamic architectural element).[96] The colonial scene is striking; as do so many metropolitan, Western subjects, Schiaparelli feels it necessary to travel to what she conceives of as the anti-modern space offered up by the colonies in order to engage in self-care. To do this, she calls upon trope of timelessness, which becomes especially pernicious when applied to the colonial situation, as it constructs 'natives' as somehow 'outside of time'. But here, still, in her attempt to situate herself outside of the time and space of fashion, she calls upon an eclectic modernist language of style, even invoking design brands to describe the space. The description of what sounds like a fashionable cosmopolitan socialite's apartment in supposedly 'anti-modern', 'anti-urban' Hammamet is by far the longest paragraph of the epilogue. It begins:

> She is lying on an orange sofa made in Paris by Jean Franck of Moroccan leather, wrapped in a vivid Scotch rug of yellow-and-black tartan, framed by narrow and low Arab cement seats with pillows made in the local bazaar, and a Hammamet straw mat on the floor. Surrounded by quantities of multicolour Italian hats bought at the Galeries Lafayette, a dispatch-case bought in New York, a cigarette-case of silver and enamelled pink rose bought in Leningrad...[etc.][97]

Thus even Schiaparelli's attempt to situate herself outside of the conventions of modern style is incomplete. The epilogue stands as a reminder of the difficulty of refuting the conventions—temporal, gendered—of the industry, to remake the designer self as an unfettered icon of timelessness.

As a story of a fashion life, this self-narration is a study in struggle. Although Schiaparelli withholds so much of herself in self-protective response to the pressures of celebrity, the temporal constraints of her industry and the limitations of feminine convention, this very withholding is rich with significance. In an industry dependent on the visible, and especially on the visibility of women, Schiaparelli's attempt to remain in the spotlight, while limiting the parts of herself that she offers to the public gaze, points to a new understanding of visibility for women in fashion. Ultimately, the construction and management of stylish but inaccessible femininity in the public eye involved a confluence of elements for Schiaparelli: the repudiation of other types of feminine visibility—chiefly those based on what were deemed feminine trivialities—and the cultivation of a timelessness that defied the tempo of fashion. The relationship between femininity and time is crucial in understanding the potential and the failures of this cultivation of limited visibility. In this case, the gesture toward a temporally unbound feminine does not *necessarily* disbar Schiaparelli from modernity, as the notion of timelessness so often does with women, but rather protects her from its spectacular excesses, mitigates the potential ravages of its fantasies of access. But of course, Schiaparelli's final assertions of herself as timeless, as her epilogue shows, are subject to the modernist economies of style from which she tries to remove herself. The female designer, expected to embody her brand and its commercial interests, is ultimately dependent on the demands of her expectant audience, and acquiesces, in her final self-representational vignette, to their demands for her capture *in time.*

Notwithstanding the ultimate failure or at least incompleteness of the move toward the eternal, Schiaparelli's memoir is an intriguing intervention into the representational politics of time. It calls into question the dichotomies on which feminist analyses of feminized timelessness have rested. Rather than being an imposition from elsewhere—social theory, literature, politics—in a bid to assuage modern anxieties, the construct of the eternal in this case has an affective dimension that links it to the psychic state of the designer herself. Nor does Schiaparelli's invocation of the concept of time overturn or neutralize the frankly experimental nature of many of her designs, which align her with the modern and which she does not reject. This is a new way of thinking about the feminine eternal, one which recognizes that the term may be strategically appropriated in ways that do not foreclose on its connection to modern time. For feminist critics, it underscores the usefulness of the frameworks and perspectives developed in fashion theory for understanding women's relationship to the modern.

Figure 4.1 Dior with a sketch, for an interview for the CBS program *Person to Person*, 7 November 1955. Photo by CBS Photo Collection/Getty Images. CBS Collection. © Getty Images.

–4–

Christian Dior: Nostalgia and the Economy of Feminine Beauty

In February 1947, Christian Dior (1905–57)—an obscure designer previously employed in the houses of Robert Piguet and Lucien Lelong, and from there quietly making a name for himself among certain elite Parisian women— showed his first dress collection. This event, which almost immediately took on a mythic gloss and remains arguably the most influential single fashion event in history, launched the collection for which Dior became best known, the *Corolle* collection, christened the 'New Look' by American fashion editor Carmel Snow of *Harper's Bazaar.* If anything is emblematic of Dior it is the exaggeratedly feminine silhouette that characterized the silhouette he introduced with this collection. It was marked by tiny waists, ample hips, and long, voluminous skirts, and explicitly conceived by its creator as a rejection of the practical, austere and apparently unfeminine styles that had characterized the Second World War and the first postwar years. Dior himself explained the context for the design in a famous quotation from his memoir: 'In December 1946, as a result of the war and uniforms, women still looked and dressed like Amazons. But I designed clothes for flower-like women.'[1]

Dior's first collection was an unqualified success, and he achieved a renown that has arguably been unmatched by any designer since. Each of his collections was named after the silhouette, or 'line', that it seemed to represent, but though his hemlines moved up and down, and skirts went from full to narrow and back again, there was a certain stylistic continuity between his collections during the decade in which he was designing under his name. As an international figure, with his celebrity buttressed by new communications technologies and the greater ease of transnational travel, he was controversial: when he went to the United States for the first time, for instance, there were demonstrations against him because he had lengthened the hemline. He was seen as having inaugurated a reactionary force in women's lives after the loosening of social strictures for women—particularly in North America— during the Second World War. The backlash against his styles, though, represented a minority view, and his garments became the epitome of fashion and remained so until his premature death from a heart attack in late 1957. His funeral reflected his fame: it was a major, well documented event—attended

Figure 4.2 Dior's 'Chérie' dinner dress, from the first collection, Spring/Summer 1947. This dress exemplifies the New Look silhouette so closely associated with Dior. The Metropolitan Museum of Art, New York. Gift of Christian Dior, 1948 (C.I.48.13a,b). Image © The Metropolitan Museum of Art. Image source: Art Resource, NY.

by celebrities and high society—and his loss was mourned by a cross-section of French society as something akin to a national tragedy.

Aside from the very particular qualities of his dress lines, Dior is today remembered as a pioneer in international branding and licensing. His was an early example of a successful, multinational fashion brand that was accessible to consumers in a variety of social strata. Women—and men—could access his brand through its licensing in affordable accessories like ties and pantyhose. Remarkably, though, he managed to retain his elite cachet and did not see his brand's cultural capital lessened during his lifetime. The 'innovative' silhouette upon which he made his reputation, and which he continued to experiment with and refine over a decade, seemed to stand out for consumers as an aesthetic intervention that somehow transcended the market that he so successfully exploited.

HISTORY AND THE COMPLEX TIME OF DIOR'S WORK

Dior's initial stylistic 'innovation', though, had a complex temporal logic. As the strong reactions to it—both favourable and unfavourable—testified, it undeniably represented a return of a much older, if not precisely historically definable, silhouette. Its temporality was captured in an apparent contradiction: embraced as 'revolutionary', the New Look's groundbreaking quality derived from its unabashed reclaiming of what might be read as a more conservative, older ideal of feminine beauty. Just as Poiret had done forty years earlier, Dior made his name on a serendipitous recurrence of a historical style. Unlike Poiret's, however, Dior's revolutionary designs traded on their *embrace* of tradition, and not their alignment with past revolutionary *breaks* with tradition.

It was, of course, wartime iterations of the feminine that Dior was reacting against with the *Corolle* collection. In Paris this included clothing designed to be practical, facilitating women's movement into bomb shelters or on bicycles in a city deprived of automobile fuel. It also reflected the scarcity of wartime, as in the cases of shoe soles made of wood, luxurious fabrics replaced by synthetics, and strictly enforced limits on the amount of fabric used for specific garments. And it included clothing that had manifold uses because bourgeois women's lives had changed drastically—they needed, apparently, garments that could carry them through the variety of social situations encountered in one day, without changing clothing.[2] The new wartime fashions of Paris, of course, were but one part of the fashion and style picture that Dior responded to. The other was quite different; rather than a 'modern', bicycling woman contributing to the war efforts, the other trends during the period of the collaborationist Vichy regime stressed the rustic simplicity and purity of a supposedly traditional feminine aesthetic. Lou Taylor, following others, notes that this 'vogue for folk styles' was connected to 'Nazi/Vichy notions of returning to the fruitful soil of Mother Earth', and the related medievalist 'revival of vernacular artisan architecture, crafts, and design'.[3] This was a part of the broader cultural politics of the Vichy regime that ruled during the years of the Nazi occupation—it was a reaction against the perceived decadence of French life since the *fin-de-siècle*, which threatened to bring about the demise of the nation.[4] Women as wearers of clothing forged in the medieval and peasant tradition would be potent symbols. Francine Muel-Dreyfus, in *Vichy and the Eternal Feminine*, notes that in 'the social philosophy of the return to "natural" communities, hierarchies, and inequalities, to "organic" solidarities, to the real ... women ... could ... become the metaphors of the return to the order of things and to purity'.[5] Indeed, both visions of femininity—the urban and the rural—were closely bound up with different visions of the French nation.

It was this context into which Dior entered with the *Corolle* collection just two and a half years after the Occupation ended in August 1944. His vision of femininity must not be divorced either from the ideological and material dimensions of the symbolic feminine of the Occupation period, nor from the national trauma brought on by this period and particularly evident in the immediate postwar years. Alexandra Palmer's analysis suggests that Dior's intervention into fashion performed two functions. First, 'Dior's exaggerated feminine perfection appealed because it helped to eradicate the memory and actions of all men and women during the war.'[6] It performed a kind of aesthetic cleansing that participated in a national repression of the atrocities enabled by the attitudes and practices that had been rampant in France during the war. This was a collective forgetting that began immediately after the Liberation in August 1944, with General Charles De Gaulle returning to Paris and delivering a famous speech which was, in Barbara Gabriel's words, 'designed to restore a certain fantasy of nationhood, one in which the glory of the French state with its mythos of being the bearer of Enlightened liberation remained intact'.[7] Clothing, of course, as a material index of cultural moods, had an important role to play in the forging of a new historical imagination for France, one which overlooked the immediate past. For Dior, this may have been a particularly acute repression, as he had worked for Lucien Lelong (a practising couturier, but also the president of the *Chambre syndicale de la couture parisienne*) during the last nearly three years of the Occupation. Lelong's legacy included negotiations with the Germans to keep the *haute couture* industry in Paris (they wanted to move it to Berlin and Vienna), always using the justification of keeping the industry afloat and preserving French jobs. Some accounts regard Lelong as a—perhaps unwilling—collaborator with the Nazi regime.[8] On the other hand, Dior's sister Catherine was an active member of the French Resistance, and was deported to a labour camp in the East in one of the last deportations from France, in June 1944. Marie-France Pochna writes that Dior housed his sister, hiding her from the authorities, every time she came to Paris. All in all, Dior's role in relation to the Occupation remains obscure. Nevertheless, his ethically uncertain involvement with Lelong must have made the drive to repress the activities of wartime all the more acute with this designer. We must bring to bear that knowledge on any analysis of Dior's constructions of femininity: these were not merely responses to war, but instruments for the management of historical trauma.

The second way that Palmer situates Dior in relation to a new national is through the precise contents of the vision of femininity that he was articulating as a kind of rejoinder to the Vichy years. Palmer reads his early creations as the forging of an image of femininity with a very particular resonance with French historical myth-making: 'Dior designed a contrived and reproducible vision of a new elite French woman that drew on hybrid aristocratic European roots. The Dior woman recalled the nobility of eighteenth-century France, the Second Empire and the Belle Époque.'[9] That is, Dior's visions of femininity crystallize not only the denial of the trauma of the Occupation, but also a related yearning for a return to past eras of apparent French glory. Remembering this historical context for the emergence of the New Look also provides some rationale for Dior's use of women as a kind of balm for the distressed modern spirit—such distress being acute and emerging from a particular, locatable trauma.

The New Look remains an important symbol. The historical work done by Dior's silhouette is emblematic of the broader temporal structure of his work and of his narration of his life over the next ten years, until his premature death in late 1957. Even more than Poiret or Schiaparelli, Dior was thinking about time. His autobiographical oeuvre consists of a memoir, *Christian Dior et moi* (*Dior by Dior*), published in 1956, and a book-length interview with two French fashion editors, which was published under the title *Je suis couturier* (*Talking about Fashion*) in 1954. Dior's published legacy also includes quite a few articles about femininity and women's fashion, and transcripts of lectures he gave or was scheduled to give at the Sorbonne near the end of his life. Of course, the sensation that the New Look created meant that Christian Dior was a major celebrity across Europe and North America from the time of his earliest collection, and so his own life writing is matched by an astonishing archive of media profiles, interviews, editorials and straightforward reportage. In all of this work, but especially in Dior's own writing about his life and career, we find an incessant rumination on the nature of time. Dior's self-representational efforts reveal a conscious grappling with a history whose complexities are captured by the simultaneously backward-looking profile and newness of the New Look. Given his blossoming as a designer during the Occupation and especially in the immediate postwar period, with its complex relationship to the trauma of wartime, the reasons for his continual interrogation of history become clear.

Dior's interest in history, though, is not revealed in a traditionally historical account. His temporal musing is more emotive, more subjective, than a historian's rendering of this period. As fashion writing often does, this is work that considers abstract, ethereal *cultural moods* as its primary object. As a catalogue of moods, many of which are mythologized with a self-conscious, melancholy yearning, the self-fashioning of Dior's memoirs can best be understood as nostalgic. Though nostalgia was first conceived as an illness, and continues to be understood as an intimate, subjective affliction, recent writing on this phenomenon reveals that it has profound implications for our modern understandings of history, politics and time itself. A close scrutiny of Dior's self-representations bears out this reading. His nostalgic stance is represented through subjective desires emerging from a particular personal history, and it is clear even in Dior's own narration that those desires were situated in his own conservative, Norman, bourgeois childhood. Arguing for their return thus meant something very specific in the postwar French context in which Dior emerged, which is generally understood as quite conservative. Indeed, Dior and others understand his success to be grounded in this historical moment. He provided what was needed in this context of postwar rebuilding and thus saw himself as responding to the establishment of a cultural mood, oriented to the restoration of a particularly French vision of 'elegance', in a generally backward-looking, nationalist era.

Marie-France Pochna, a biographer of Dior, locates the engine of Dior's class-bound nostalgia in his relationship with his mother, Marie-Madeleine (Martin) Dior. Her evidence for this repeated alignment of Dior with his mother as a time-bound emblem of femininity is unclear, but it nonetheless forms a powerful and significant theme in the biography, bookending Pochna's account of the designer's life. Pochna characterizes him at one point as a 'someone who usually looked at women from quite a different perspective, with the famous gaze which "dressed them in something else" (usually something very feminine and reminiscent, of course, of his mother)'.[10] Dior, Pochna writes, continued throughout his life to imaginatively transform his mother from a conservative, 'bourgeois, arriviste' woman into an 'ideal of sweetness, femininity, delicateness' with a profound and elegant aesthetic sense.[11] As Elissa Marder points out, we must be careful when seeking to reconcile an individual unconscious with broader social and political life: 'there may indeed be a relationship between unconscious representations of feminine figures and the place assigned to women in social and political life, but that relationship is neither transparent nor mimetic.'[12] In Dior's case, making the leap from bourgeois, Belle-Époque mother to an entire philosophy of femininity that was revealed decades later is far too simple. Nonetheless, whether or not it is *true* that Dior's approach to femininity was governed by his imaginative reconstruction of his mother, Pochna's theory introduces the notion that femininity anchored Dior's nostalgic sense. The entwinement of women and nostalgia in Dior's self-representations is thorough and complex, and is echoed in surprising ways by the press that Dior received. Altogether, what emerges is a kind of crystallization of Dior's nostalgia—and thus his operative theory of history—in a figural femininity. This occurs on a number of levels, but ultimately, it is a profoundly *material* nostalgia that Dior works through in his writing. Modern history is visible and tangible in the changing silhouette, in the lines of the dresses themselves. In effect, he materializes a nostalgic understanding of history through the woman's body. She becomes the bearer of a longed-for temporal sense, but does so in a domain—fashion—that is perpetuated through its relationship to the present and the future. In advancing an aesthetic philosophy through his representations of women, Dior makes visible the complexity of the temporal registers of the modern, and reveals their relationship to the contradiction between art and industry that both sustained and clearly troubled the designer.

NOSTALGIA AS A MODERN TEMPORAL PHENOMENON

To understand the conditions of Dior's relationship with women, one must first have an understanding of Dior as a nostalgic subject. Dior's nostalgia is most obviously revealed through the split that he invokes in *Dior by Dior* between 'Christian Dior the public figure and Christian Dior the private individual'.[13] The book is constructed on this opposition; the prologue is entitled 'The Two Christian Diors', and there Dior rather artlessly lays out what is clearly intended to be the central affective theme of the autobiography. He writes knowingly of what is at stake here: 'Perhaps I should have concentrated entirely on him, and let nothing of myself peep through ... Yet to suppress this shrinking character altogether would have seemed to me a form of cheating; it would also have deprived my story of some of its personal touches.'[14] And so—like Schiaparelli, who also bookends her memoir with portraits of herself in the third person—Dior opens the book by establishing the distance between himself and his celebrity. He sets up a tense relationship that he returns to occasionally throughout the book, stressing the learned labour of appearing as 'someone else', something which he was forced into by the pressures of publicity during the first year of his house. The book closes, predictably, with a reconciliation of the two Christians: 'Suddenly I come to view my other self with genuine respect, perhaps the wretched couturier has something to be said for him after all ... I accept the identification of myself with him.'[15] But buried between the expressions of a satisfying unity in *Dior by Dior*'s final paragraphs is this formulation: 'His role is to be a guardian of the public tastes—and that is a valuable role indeed. Meanwhile I can lurk in his brilliant shadow, and console myself that he has left me the best part of our dual personality—I can take care of the actual work, from the idea to the dress, while he maintains a dazzling worldly front for us both.'[16] Thus the self remains split—Dior's *identification* with the couturier persona must not be mistaken for an *integration* of the two selves.

This construction of his 'true' self as the 'shrinking nonentity', distinct from the celebrity who has learned to navigate the dramas of modern celebrity, inadvertently establishes Dior's nostalgia.[17] The appeal to a selfhood that is unrelated to the vicissitudes of celebrity, of publicity, of the tempo of the industry in which he worked, seems like an attempt to barricade and secure something of the self against the incursions of an inauthentic industrial apparatus. Dior's autobiographical representations are marked by both an explicit invocation of nostalgia and a related, romantic appraisal of the possibility of escape. For instance, he writes, '[w]e couturiers are like poets. A little nostalgia is necessary for us.'[18] He also privileges the concept of escape, as in this passage from *Talking about Fashion*: 'fashion comes from a dream and the dream is an escape from reality.'[19] Dior reinforces the sense that he needs

Figure 4.3   Dior reading the newspaper and drinking tea in his Paris home, 1957. Photo by Loomis Dean/Time & Life Pictures/Getty Images. © Time & Life Pictures/Getty Images.

an escape from the pace of modern life with his frequent descriptions of his country homes and his escapes to them; biographical accounts and contemporary journalism show how important these spaces were for him, and how much of his life was spent in them. In his words, '[a]lthough it is true, as is often said, that one breathes in fashion with the very air in Paris, I find that the peace and calm of the country is absolutely essential to me after a while, in order to reflect on the lessons which I have learned in the city itself.'[20] Near the end of *Dior by Dior*, too, Dior devotes a remarkable chapter to describing the homes he has lived in, arguing that it is through space that his character can be best appraised; his focus on the historical in this description cements the sense of Dior as a nostalgic subject.[21]

And so the nostalgic gaze backward is a powerful theme throughout both Dior's own self-representations and his journalistic and critical appraisals. As I have shown, there is certainly evidence for this understanding in the archives; there is no question that Dior is a nostalgic subject. But I would like to challenge the prevailing wisdom about this as a simple 'flight' response by re-reading Dior's nostalgia through contemporary theories of the condition's complexity. This forces us to nuance the received image of Dior's conservatism. He even provides us with some of the tools, in his own self-representation. He claims, for instance, '[t]emperamentally I am reactionary, not to be confused with retrograde', making a firm distinction between the tendency to respond to the present through references to the past, as he does, and the desire to banish the present.[22] In a telling reminiscence, Dior also layers times upon each other when he waxes nostalgically about growing up in the last years of the Belle Époque, a time when '[t]he future, it seemed, could only hold a greater comfort for everybody.'[23] Here he reveals himself to be nostalgic for a past time in which people believed in the future, as they do not, by inference, in the postwar present. The seeds of a more nuanced account of nostalgia thus lie in his own complicated narrations of time consciousness.

Dior's complex treatments dovetail with the recent critical turn to nostalgia. Since the late 1990s, scholarly appraisals of nostalgia have modestly blossomed. A small but important body of literature has emerged to consider the complex relationships of past, present and future that emerged in the West in the post-Revolutionary period and that bred a desire for return, spatially and temporally, to apparently lost origins. Whereas the concept of memory is relatively general, opening itself onto a myriad of affective modes, nostalgia was defined from the beginning as a longing to return, a *yearning* relationship to the past. In fact, as the literature on the condition invariably points out, the concept was developed in 1688 to describe a disease: 'historically, the word *nostalgia* was coined for the express purpose of translating a particular feeling (*Heimweh, regret, desiderium patriae*) into medical terminology.'[24] The condition was also defined as an affliction, one that could produce dire consequences. Much early attention to nostalgia, for example, was focused on its debilitating effect on soldiers, its interference with their ability to carry out their duties—and even be lethal.[25]

Marcos Piason Natali underscores the politics of the nostalgic turn in modern European history and its development into the twentieth century. The concern with nostalgia and the associated fervour for treating it were, he finds, evidence of a kind of historical imperialism. Treatments of nostalgia exercised a disciplinary function beginning in the late eighteenth century, in light of the social changes wrought by industrialization: 'In a time of increased centralization, the term was used to remove the legitimacy from heterogeneous ways of being with the past and determine the normal ways of relating to it.'[26] These 'normal' ways of being with the past are based on the dominant modern temporal regime, in which past, present and future remain discrete categories across which all moves unidirectionally, progressively. Nostalgia thus challenges this construction of normality and intervenes in the fetishization of the now, which tended to seal off groups of people as untouchable in their respective times: for instance, women in the premodern past, men in the modern present. Though there is remarkably little written on nostalgia from a feminist perspective, the politics of nostalgia make clear the potential significance of this modern concept for conceiving of the relationship between women and the time of the modern. This political history of nostalgia underscores the relevance of the concept for understanding Dior's relationship with women.

But just what kinds of relationships to past time does nostalgia reflect? Both Svetlana Boym and Peter Fritzsche have suggested that cultures of dislocation which emerged at the end of the eighteenth century are the keys to understanding the emergence of nostalgia's distinctive perspective on what is past. They note the prominence of a sense of difference, of rupture, in this period. In Fritzsche's telling, exile emerges as a distinctive condition of modern life in the immediate post-Revolutionary period: 'exile increasingly served as a remarkable signature of displacement in the modern age, "nowadays," in which a comprehensive process of destruction pushed the past away from the present.'[27] Exile—as displacement—also drives home the spatial dimension of this process, which is rendered by Boym as a new tension between the local and the global or universal that comes with developing technologies of mapping and spatial use, including travel (connected inextricably to colonization): 'nostalgia was not merely an expression of local longing, but a result of a new understanding of time and space that made the division into "local" and "universal" possible. The nostalgic creature has internalized this division, but instead of aspiring for the universal and progressive, he looks backward and yearns for the particular.'[28] Foundational for both accounts is the way that displacement—the spatial distance upon which exile was developed—becomes simultaneously a temporal quality; one becomes distant not only from a place (home), but a period. This entwinement of space and time in nostalgic consciousness is evident in Christian Dior's narration of his life; in *Dior by Dior*, for instance, Dior makes it clear that he is yearning not only for a different, prewar era, but for the architecture and interiors he associates with his childhood.

Time is mobilized, too, in unique ways by modern nostalgia. Vladimir Yankélévitch contends that in nostalgic reflection, '[t]he object of nostalgia is not a particular past, but it is rather the fact of the past, or pastness.'[29] This understanding accords with Fritzsche's later formulation—cited in Chapter One—that modernity constructed the past as problematic, and Richard Terdiman's theory of modern memory as a personal and ideological tangling with new forms of temporal experience.[30] The particularity of experience that nostalgia seems to play upon shows that nostalgia sits at the interface of personal and collective dimensions of experience, as does fashion itself. Further, as theorists of nostalgia overwhelmingly note, it is not an engagement so much with the past, which is in itself ultimately inaccessible, but with the present.[31] Nostalgia's emergence as a *response* to life in the present is the surest, most basic sign of this. As Fred Davis puts it, 'nostalgia uses the past, but is not the product of it.'[32] Rather, nostalgia develops as a reaction to events or social configurations that put the self into radical question in the now, and thus prompt reflection on the relationship between present and former identities, whether those be personal, group or even national identities. What is important here is that nostalgia undoes some very familiar dichotomous contrasts, including those between past and present, and between individual and collective experience. Perhaps, with its tendency to interrogate modes of thinking about times as drastically different from one another, nostalgia can even offer a way of making visible the conflicted relationship between women and modern time.

DIOR'S MATERIAL NOSTALGIA

Certainly, Dior's nostalgic invocations of femininity invite us to consider the complex reasons by which women get aligned with the past in fashion, and what these might mean for conceiving of women in the modern. Elissa Marder, in *Dead Time*, provides a helpful framework for thinking about the kinds of functions women fill in mediating what she calls the 'temporal disorders' of modernity, of which nostalgia surely must be considered one. Considering the poetry of Charles Baudelaire, she demonstrates that 'feminine figures regulate most expressions of temporality,' becoming 'shock absorbers' in dealing with the psychic effects of modernity's peculiar, frenetic and alienating tempo.[33] In the wake of the development of mass culture and the concomitant threat to original experience and expression that is posed by the anonymity of urban life, the tempo of modern being and the astonishing proliferation of material things, the poet (the artist) is unmoored. Femininity is the balm, the nostalgic means by which the poet can 'remove himself from the reality and temporality of the world around him'.[34] But for femininity to effectively assuage the trauma of modern temporal structures, a woman 'must become an image (preferably a dream, an illusion) or ... a lie that shields [the poet] from his own shattered perception of the world.'[35] An iconic femininity, then, emerges as an important vector of nostalgia as a response to the traumatic experience of modern life.

Here lies the connection to Dior, which is revealed through a close examination of the designer's own narrations of loss, muted and veiled though they may be. Of course, in this case, the traumatic experience of modern life is not merely industrialization, though the ongoing development of mass culture certainly threatened to destabilize Dior's self-conception as an artist. It is also the trauma of war, especially a wartime Occupation in which he was, however indirectly, implicated through his employment at Lelong. The image of femininity that Dior relies on to advance a theory of nostalgia is similar to the iconic one that Marder identifies in Baudelaire's work. In fact, in a 1959 article, Rémy G. Saisselin identifies an important set of parallels between Baudelaire and Dior, which revolve around the role of women in their respective aesthetic theories. For Baudelaire, woman transforms from a natural into an artistic thing. Dior, Saisselin writes, represents the contemporary version of Baudelaire's aesthetics: 'Dior answers Baudelaire's metaphysics of fashion: woman, abominable creature of nature, has been completely transformed by art; woman, a simple base for Dior, has become a sort of poem of curves, lines, and volumes; woman has become style. And style for Dior means form, unity, rather than detail.'[36] While Dior's closeness with individual women in his life is clear in the historical record, his attachment to iconic lines, and their attendant visions of femininity, is just as apparent. This aesthetics of femininity is yoked to a sense of historical time, one that is both personal and social. As Richard Martin and Harold Koda note, '[h]is surety in each overall silhouette and in collection signatures was the postwar antidote to the loss of fashion incurred during the war. Moreover, Dior's assertion of a strong silhouette [in 1947, with the introduction of the *Corolle* collection] came at a time and place of utmost fragility.'[37] Here is the link between postwar history, with its nostalgic turn, and the iconic woman who emerges materially through the lines of Dior's dress. Through the lines, she is imagined as a kind of agent of an alternative historical consciousness. She becomes a bearer not *of* the past, but of the possibility for a reimagined relationship to past*ness*, as Yankélévitch puts it, that compensates for the designer's temporal dislocations and yearnings.

Of course, Dior's role was that of a creator: his was an imaginative labour, however much he may have been immersed simultaneously in commerce. The production of nostalgic silhouettes and collections was seen by Dior and others as artistic work. There are some useful precedents for integrating nostalgia and the work of imagination or creation. In an influential article, Edward S. Casey theorizes nostalgia as a memorial mode that 'calls for imagination. Indeed, what could attain it other than imagination, which is the unique power by which we make present what is absent, that is, absent from perception as well as memory.'[38] The scant literature on nostalgic imagination clarifies that this imaginative work is about the forging of identity. Sean Scanlan treats it as a 'fundamentally linked to self-narrativization'.[39] *Both* Dior's fashions and his life writing can be read as means of imaginatively narrating the self, as well as of responding to history. From his self-representational strategies emerges a portrait of a self so deeply invested in feminine otherness that it becomes difficult to separate these others from himself, at times. And so, the imaginative dimension of nostalgia for Dior produces two kinds of images at once: images of femininity, and images of himself.

WOMEN AND THE RELATIONAL MASCULINE SELF

Dior's entwinement with femininity as a condition of his selfhood as a designer and celebrity can be most clearly seen in his very close working relationships with women over the course of his career. Unlike Poiret or Schiaparelli, Dior was not heavily invested in the image of the designer as a genius who both found inspiration for and executed his craft entirely alone. Dior's work contains many references to the process of dress design as collaborative, as 'passionate collective research'.[40] Tellingly, though, there is a tension in the texts between the claim to collaborative work and Dior's own need to distinguish his role in the process. Without that distinction, his celebrity—and with it, his very business—would be threatened. For example, in a chapter of *Talking about Fashion* devoted to his *premières*, the women who directed each individual workshop in the design house, he writes,

> their love of detail, of good needlecraft, of a good finish, sometimes causes them to lose sight of the balance of the line, which one has constantly to restore. Doing fine needlework and making beautiful dresses are not the same thing. The two must be linked up, of course, but linking them up is not easy. The *première,* too intent on her work, is continually absorbed in the details. The dress designer for his part must think only of essentials.[41]

Even in his generosity toward his staff, Dior reasserts the primacy of masculine artistic genius, oriented to depth, over the ultimately trivial and superficial, if indispensable, craft of dressmaking.[42] He takes on the role of master, director and visionary, whose job it is to discipline the ornamental excesses of his workers. In this portrait of the *premières*' work and in other testimony, he emerges as a benevolent, fatherly dictator. This is confirmed in testimonies by adoring workers, who note that the workers developed the custom of standing every time he entered a room.[43] As one of his most important colleagues, Carmen Colle, attested in an interview, 'Christian Dior completely shaped my life.'[44] What he instils is discipline, a submission to the 'essence' of fashion that he has privileged access to and that is crystallized in the dresses themselves. In this, he undeniably shares something of Poiret's masterly orientation, though it is considerably softened.

Nevertheless, Dior's descriptions of his work show him to be indebted to an entourage of women, some of long acquaintance, like Suzanne Luling, whom he had known since they were children in Granville, Normandy. Dior built

Figure 4.4   Dior and his colleagues fitting a dress on a model in his Paris salon, 1957. Photo by Loomis Dean/ Time & Life Pictures/Getty Images. © Time & Life Pictures/ Getty Images.

the brand with them, and these administrators, technical staff (who were intimately involved in the execution of designs), saleswomen and live models are central to the unfolding of his narratives about his company. Dior's description of Raymonde Zehnacker (referred to as Mme Raymonde or simply Raymonde) in *Dior by Dior* is particularly illuminating:

> Raymonde was to become my second self—or to be more accurate, my other half. She is my exact complement: she plays Reason to my Fantasy, Order to my Imagination, Discipline to my Freedom, Foresight to my Recklessness, and she knows how to introduce peace into an atmosphere of strife. In short, she has supplied me with all those qualities which I have never thought to acquire for myself, and has steered me successfully through the intricate world of fashion, in which I was still a novice in 1947.[45]

Of his technical director, Mme Marguerite Carré, he writes something similar: 'over the years she has become part of myself—of my "dressmaking" self, if I can so call it.'[46] Dior approaches his overwhelmingly female entourage as a kind of extension of the self. Note that in the opening sentence about Mme Raymonde, he incorporates her into himself, moving beyond the initial assertion of her otherness to him, from the more distant 'second self' to 'other half'.[47] His articulations of what is ultimately a feminine dimension of his selfhood suggest a fluidity of gender identity that is striking given his overt conservatism. These portraits of women underscore the ways that Dior's writing about women was a kind of self-portraiture.

GLAMOROUS NOSTALGIA

It is perhaps Dior's descriptions of Mitzah Bricard that are most telling, even if they do not have the same quality of incorporation that his discussions of Mmes Raymonde and Marguerite, the other members of his exalted triumvirate of women, have. Like the others, he characterizes Mme Bricard as a collaborator. But her role is never clearly specified. She functioned as a kind of muse, and certainly she has been memorialized as such.[48] Her collaboration appears, in all of his portraits of her, to simply *be*, embodying elegance outside of time: 'Mme Bricard is one of those people, increasingly rare, who make elegance their sole *raison d'être*. Gazing at life out of the windows of the Ritz, so to speak, she is superbly indifferent to such mundane concerns as politics, finance, or social change.'[49] In *Talking about Fashion*, he says, '[i]f times are hard, she will ignore them, and troubles leave her unmoved.'[50] Notably, it is Mme Bricard who inspires Dior's ideas; she catalyzes the process of creation. 'Her moods, her extremes of behaviour, her faults, her entrances, her late appearances, her theatricality, her mode of speech, her unorthodox manner of dress, her jewels, in short her presence, bring the touch of absolute elegance so necessary to the fashion house.'[51]

Unlike Dior's smooth and harmonious incorporation of Raymonde and Marguerite, the relationship with Mme Bricard (never invoked by her given name the way the others are, further distancing her) is described as tempestuous. He writes, 'I knew that her presence in my house would inspire me towards creation, as much by her reactions—and even her revolts—*against* my ideas, as by her agreements.'[52] It is a curious formulation, since what Dior values in Mme Bricard is ostensibly the same quality that is understood to be key to his success: an essential, almost inherited, understanding of the grammar of chic as something timeless, removed from the vagaries of history. And yet he describes himself as being inspired by a motto he attributes to *her*, one which he *struggled* to apply to himself: 'I will maintain.'[53] What he takes from her is her compulsion to tradition. It is a compulsion that does not come entirely naturally for him, even if that traditional orientation is the trait on which his celebrity is built. Through Mme Bricard, he *learns* to 'maintain', to steadfastly carry on the timeless French traditions of chic and couture despite the vagaries of history and commerce. In simply *being*, she fills an educative role in Dior's life, temporally reorienting him to tradition and to the French past.

As a result of this steadfastness and the repeated invocation of Mme Bricard as somehow unmoving ('Gazing at life out of the windows of the Ritz'), the portrait of her is characterized by a certain cold *hauteur*, even as she functions as a call to tradition. Whereas we are accustomed to seeing tradition as evocative of warmth, comfort and intimacy, Mme Bricard is glassy and distant. In fact, she epitomizes Judith Brown's description of transcendent glamour: 'Glamour chills ... even as it promises the impossible. Here we find another connection to the modernism that favours blankness, the polished surface, the stance of impenetrability ... the suspicion of the nothing behind it all—yet somehow, this blankness is transmuted into something that is seductive, powerful, and often simply gorgeous.'[54] Brown's discussion of glamour identifies it as a modernist signature, and she locates glamour across a range of written, visual and broadly sensual texts—such as perfume—in the first decades of the twentieth century. The aesthetic abstractions of glamour, she suggests, come as a response to the dislocation and alienation of modern life. They would at first glance seem to represent only the death of connection and of sentiment. But its emergence from alienation suggests that though it can be read as distant and cool, glamour's chill is not antithetical to emotion. Rather, that glamour, though it is 'a move away from insistent subjectivity to the impersonal style', reflects the subjective emotional experience of loss.[55] Brown clarifies the connection when she describes desire as a modality of glamour: 'Surely desire at its most excruciating in the longing for what-could-have-been but never will be, a desire that glamorizes the past. This is the tense of regret, remorse, and mourning.'[56] Here is the common ground with nostalgia, this shared territory of loss and responses to loss. Nostalgia, so often written off as overly sentimental, as an embarrassingly fussy and histrionic response to modern life, is here figured in a very different way. This icy, flinty iteration of nostalgia calls into question the demonization of nostalgia as a conservative denial of modernity. If we can see the ways that glamorous people and things function also as nostalgic vehicles, then nostalgia is clarified as a grappling with, and not an evasion of, modern life. And since the glamorous iconography of modernity is principally feminized, recognizing the connection between nostalgia and glamour re-centres femininity in discussions of modern time. It complicates and adds texture to the time that women can occupy in the modern imaginary.

In Mme Bricard as an embodiment of nostalgic glamour, we see a clear intimation of women's complex entwinement with nostalgia, and sense Dior's ambivalence toward it. Mme Bricard is a figure who responds to both the past and the present. The way Dior frames her as a gazer in the windows of the Ritz, even as she represents for him the pull of the past, is akin to the framing of that quintessentially glamorous artefact described by Brown as the bearer of the past: the photograph.[57] The stop-motion quality of this telling verbal image complicates the tendency to reduce Mme Bricard to a placid embodiment of being, for in the intimation that it captures a moment—of looking out over the relentlessly modern life of the Parisian street—it suggests rather a kind of moving threshold between the present and the past. Mme Bricard is imagined by Dior as a feminine icon that has been caught looking at the life of the now and in this sense is engaged with it. In this way, Mme Bricard crystallizes a temporal signature for Dior, one that contextualizes his career. He looks at the present, and that look defines his subsequent return to and reincorporation of historic silhouettes. That the engagement occurs via Mme Bricard as not only a muse for Dior himself, but a more general representation of postwar femininity, indicates two things: the depth of the relationship between self and feminine other that pervades Dior's work, and the intricacy of Dior's 'revolutionary conservatism', which depends on contemporary femininities for its backward-looking force.

COMPLEX INTERPLAYS OF PAST AND PRESENT

This constellation of past and present that sustains Dior's work deserves closer analysis, since it forms the basis of his invocations of femininity. He has earned a reputation for being profoundly conservative, a perception typified by Françoise Giroud in her 1987 biography: 'Conservative to the point of seeming reactionary, and sensitive to all change, which he loathed, he had a preference for walled gardens, enclosed beds, maternal women: everything that gave him a sense of protection.'[58] But a close reading of Dior's self-representations reveals that they are shot through with a profound *ambivalence* about his temporal positioning. While he claims an emotional allegiance to the past, again and again he underlines how attuned he is to the present. This tension is established in the first pages of *Dior by Dior*, when he describes his vision for the establishment of his house to his eventual backer, French cotton magnate Marcel Boussac. Boussac initially contacted Dior because he wanted to hire the designer to resurrect the couture house Gaston. Dior balked, as he was 'not meant by nature to raise corpses from the dead', an enterprise he believed was guaranteed to fail 'in a trade where novelty is so important'.[59] This key passage aids in the crucial establishment of tone and character in the autobiography. As he recounts to Boussac, Dior

> really wanted ... to create a new *couture* house under my own name, in a district of my choosing ... I wanted a house in which every single thing would be new, from the *ambiance* and the staff, down to the furniture and even the address. All around us, life was beginning anew. It was time for a new trend in fashion.[60]

Such rhetoric is familiar and expected for a designer; it is the stuff on which the fashion industry is built. But just a few sentences later, still recounting the vision, Dior claims, '[a]fter the long war years of stagnation, I believed that there was a genuine unsatisfied desire abroad for something new in fashion. In order to meet this demand, French couture would have to return to the traditions of great luxury.'[61] The means by which his couture house would realize this newness, and indeed would speak to the regenerative and apparently revolutionary quality of the postwar era, was the reconsolidation of tradition. At the end of the memoir, he again brings together the apparently twin impulses of historical change and tradition: 'It is true that we work under an ephemeral star, and only precision of design, excellence of cut, and quality of workmanship can save us.'[62] This formulation is telling: fashion's change orientation is experienced as a kind of threat, to be borne for the sake of the craft and the business but to be mitigated and guarded against through tradition. Thus the contemporary and the traditional are not opposed. Rather, the ephemeral present provides a backdrop against which to explore, revisit and reinstall the past. Dior's traditionalism emerges as a response to relentless change in fashion's time. He experiences the ephemeral present with some anxiety. Seen in this light, Mme Bricard and the stasis she represents might also be a kind of tonic for the anxious spirit that is particular to the fashion industry due to its hyper-mutability.

For elsewhere, it becomes clear that though Dior's chief propensity or instinct is to align himself with the past, he is in fact—as his need to learn from Mitzah Bricard's traditionalism suggests—immersed in the present. In a vein that is similar to Poiret, he suggests that he has a privileged relationship to the moods of contemporary life. For instance, in the first instalment of a 1952–53 series of articles for the English magazine *Modern Woman*, Dior writes, 'fashion is very logical. It is a reflection of a current reaction in the mind—almost before people are aware of it themselves. That is where the designer comes in. He must be sensitive to modern feeling—almost before it is felt!'[63] And in his memoir, he seems to reconcile to the practical necessity of rooting oneself in the present: 'We live in the times we do; and nothing is sillier than to turn one's back on them.'[64] Still, both formulations contain a tinge of regret; this is no willing or even cultivated embrace of the present, but rather one of obligation which seems, at times, to be experienced as a flaw to be overcome. As Poiret's work suggested decades earlier, the deep attunement to the present is a cross to be borne by the designer.

The contemporary and the ephemeral are twinned across Dior's work. The 'modern life' to which Dior must grudgingly accept his attunement—or enslavement?—is characterized above all else by its ephemerality. Ephemerality, he stresses, is a condition of modern life for the fashion designer *in particular*. But it is associated with a pathos connected to loss: the loss of the possibility for full and satisfying artistic expression. An integral part of Dior's self-narration is the assertion of his lack of fitness for business; he paints his father, bourgeois industrialist that he was, as an early model of all that Dior did not want to become.[65] In both the memoir and the book-length interview, he suggests that accepting his own artistic temperament was a key rite of passage.[66] If fashion design is an art, which is how Dior constantly positions it (even as he also embraces its industrial aspect), it is a forum for self-expression: 'For all its ephemerality, *couture* constitutes a mode of self-expression which can be compared to architecture or painting.'[67] But ephemerality throws the very self at its root into question; the visions that emerge in the process of creation are never allowed to flourish for long, as they must be constantly succeeded by the next thing. Dior writes regretfully of this, using the metaphors of other arts, as he frequently does: 'Imagine a manuscript perpetually erased, and indefatigably recommenced.'[68] Dior describes feeling the ephemeral keenly, as the loss of possibility for full self-expression. A major reason for the complexity of Dior's representations of time, then, is the way that the governing logic of transient time is experienced as the erasure of self.

THE MATERIAL OF FEMININITY

What also emerges in the autobiographical writing and interviews, though, is that women figure as embodiments of the temporal categories that so clearly trouble Dior, including ephemerality. To understand this attachment of the ephemeral to women's bodies, we must first understand the depth of Dior's relationship with his creations. Throughout his work, there is a striking invocation of his creations as material, even human. Fabric is a muse: 'Fabric not only expresses a designer's dreams but also stimulates his own ideas. It can be the beginning of an inspiration. Many a dress of mine is born of fabric alone.'[69] A design is a friend: 'The design seems to hail you like a friend encountering you in the street when you are on holiday. You tell yourself there can be no doubt about it at all—it *is* your friend.'[70] A dress is a child: 'Henceforth, I will follow the progress of each dress like an anxious father—proud, jealous, passionate, and tender—suffering agonies on their behalf. They have absolute power over me, and I live in perpetual dread that they will fail me.'[71] His clothing, finally, is a lover: 'The most passionate adventures in my life have therefore been with my clothes. I am obsessed with them. They pre-occupy me, they occupy me, and finally they "post-occupy" me, if I can risk the word.'[72] In these descriptions, the garments and the stuff of fashion are strikingly vital. Further, Dior's tendency to humanize his garments and even his materials indicates his profound intimacy with them. The self privileges proximity, even rejects—at least in the early stages of the design process—the conventional split between designer and their works. In narrating his relationship with his creations in these terms, Dior makes himself vulnerable to them even as he masters them. He offers up a picture of the self in impassioned relation with the object world.

With this in mind, consider the ways that Dior moves to materialize femininity through the medium of his fashions as extensions of himself. He writes, 'I think of my work as ephemeral architecture, dedicated to the beauty of the female body.'[73] The tension between ephemeral materiality and the persistence of an eternal feminine beauty is notable here. It returns us to Dior's connections with Baudelaire, who theorized the same contradictory status as the condition of modern aesthetics. But what is remarkable is that the materiality he so prizes is thus fashioned in the service of a vision of femininity. Femininity is the emblem of the troubling changeability of modern life; femininity, as drawn as he is to it, represents a trial for Dior. Further, femininity and the materiality of the garment are deeply linked with one another, and Dior's descriptions of them evoke this relationship in language that stresses their interdependence: 'The material ought to live on her shoulders, and her figure live beneath the material.'[74] Given that, as I argue above, Dior sets up his garments in a relation of mutuality and passionate material engagement with *himself*, this extension of garment to women is telling. It suggests a unique triangulation of designer, garment and woman that involves a yielding of *part* of the self to ephemeral femininity. This once again attests to the complex character of Dior's relationship to the feminine. It points to a somewhat angst-ridden production and reproduction of his gender in a profession in which gender roles are ultimately ambiguous. Is the designer feminized by his proximity to and indeed his impassioned immersion in a culture of femininity? What is more, is this feminization in part a result of the potentially contaminating changeability that women represent?

A question from interviewer Edward Murrow in a 1955 interview for the popular CBS television show *Person to Person* puts this tension into perspective. Murrow asks, 'You're about fifty years old and still a bachelor. Could this mean perhaps that you know women too well?'[75] The intimation that it is possible for men to know women 'too well' is ambiguous. What constitutes too much knowledge? And what, more importantly, is the repercussion of being

too knowledgeable? That Murrow precedes this question with an acknow-
ledgement of Dior's 'bachelorhood' is telling; it implicitly draws a link between
Dior's apparently intimate knowledge of women, his selfhood and his sexuality. Though the *Person to Person* interview is framed in worshipful terms—
throughout, Murrow appears deferential to Dior's quasi-magical knowledge
and power—this question early in the interview nevertheless can be read as
gently mocking.[76] Ellen Rosenman notes that, in Victorian England, the figure
of male milliner was 'alarming': 'A hybrid figure, he shared the fashion expertise of women but remained a respectable and successful businessman.'
Rosenman analyzes an article that, in '[v]eering between sarcasm and seri-
ousness', 'betrays the gender confusion provoked by this figure'.[77] A similar
ambivalence can be detected in Murrow's conversation with Dior. It points to
the tenuous position that Dior held even in this decade of his dominance.
Though he was not an out gay man, his constant proximity to femininity—
and the passionate incorporation of femininity that was revealed through his
material engagement with his creations—cast doubt on his sexuality.

Dior's answer to Murrow's loaded question is tellingly evasive, and suggests a displacement of this concern onto femininity. He does not reply directly. Rather, he responds: 'You know, in my house in Paris I have about
a thousand women working. And you know believe me that's quite enough
for a harem.'[78] By invoking a 'harem', Dior makes an oblique reference to
heterosexuality. But it is a sentence construction in which he himself does
not appear as the subject. Further, the word filters Dior's gender and sexuality through a colonial trope, one in which he takes charge of women, to be
sure, but which is also complicated by its establishment of him as akin to a
colonial subject. The racist conflation of 'deviant' sexualities with colonized
peoples—especially those of the 'East'—is, of course, a longstanding cultural
trope. And the first sentence of his reply is a restatement of his mastery;
he may know women well, but not 'too well', as he has not ceded any power
to them—they are, after all, his employees and clients. This construction
sheds new light on Murrow's question and the assumptions behind it. The
'excessive' knowledge of women is bound-up with power; by knowing women
'too well', a man walks a dangerously fine line between being able to master them—to turn that knowledge to his advantage—and being overtaken or
colonized by them. 'Too much' knowledge is knowledge that has gone beyond
a capacity for mastery and suggests a man's closeness with women. Dior's
reply to Murrow demonstrates his understanding of the stakes of this choice
between mastery and relationship. Though he chooses to highlight relational
incorporation of femininity at key points in his impassioned description of
his work, he is careful to redeploy his narrative of a masterful relationship
with women when his masculinity is under scrutiny. His self-representations
are skilfully managed, taking on the changeable character of the fashionable

femininities through which they are articulated, in part to deflect attention from consideration of his own masculinity and sexuality. This is a risk, given that the constant deflection from his masculinity to a femininity with which he is in passionate relation can be read as a signal of his own *intimacy* with the feminine. And the ephemeral nature of this femininity is the greatest risk of all. It hints at Dior's inability to maintain an appropriately rational and self-contained manhood. Masculine mastery, we see, has a time signature of its own: constancy.

WOMEN'S BODIES AND THE MARKET

A useful lens through which to examine Dior's relationship to femininity as ephemeral and yet embodied, is his descriptions of his models, or 'manne-quins'. These are the living women who mediate for the public both Dior's ideals of femininity and his self-concept, since he is so bound-up with the garments and the imagined femininity. In a 1957 text prepared for a lecture at the Sorbonne (apparently never delivered), Dior characterizes the premiere of a collection as the point at which the designer awaits the verdict of the most exacting jury, the public. 'Fortunately,' he writes, 'the couturier has access to the best lawyers in the world: his models. Each time he prepares to give them the floor ... he hopes that their elegance will win him the leniency of the jury.'[79] Elsewhere, he asserts, '[t]he existence of a real affinity between a couturier and his mannequins is so vital, that it is worth a few small sacrifices in order to achieve it.'[80]

The importance of the models' mediating role, standing at the intersection between Dior's psyche, his creations and the demands of clients, is reflected in the space he devotes to their loving portrayal in *Dior by Dior*. Consider the following extraordinary description of Renée:

> Of all my mannequins, Renée is probably the one who comes nearest to my ideal. Every dress she puts on seems to be a success, as though there existed an exact equivalence between her proportions and those of my imagination. She brings fabric to life so exquisitely that her face is lost. As she shows her clothes, distant, aloof, it seems as if her very life centres around the folds of the material.[81]

Here, in a description that recalls Mme Bricard's icy glamour, we see very clearly the triangulation of Dior, material garment and the embodied femininity that he passionately identifies with. But we also sense a profound ambiguity: is this woman who incarnates Dior's feminine ideal alive, or is she petrified? Note that Dior ultimately subordinates her to the clothing. She gives life to the material, but in doing so, she vanishes: 'her face is lost', she *becomes*

Figure 4.5   Dior and a model at his Sorbonne lecture, 4 August 1955. Photo by Keystone-France/Gamma-Keystone via Getty Images. © Keystone-France via Getty Images.

'distant, aloof'. The act of modelling transforms her, even drains her, transposing her vitality from her body to the garment. In a variation on the figure of the static, antimodern woman, in this instance she begins as a vital figure, and her labour within the fashion industry is precisely what arrests circulation and movement. It abstracts her body into a vehicle for the promotion of clothing. This is not a preexisting stasis, then, but one created by the specific and localized work of modelling for Dior.

The critic Saisselin, writing in 1959, recognized this abstract femininity as Dior's signature in his elaboration of the similarities between Baudelaire and Dior: 'woman, a simple base for Dior, has become a sort of poem of curves, lines, and volumes; woman has become style.'[82] 'Woman has become an abstract creature, a beautiful creature made for the contemplation of the intellect.'[83] What Saisselin is describing, of course, is akin to modernist abstraction. This might come as a surprise in relation to Dior. It is easy

Figure 4.6   Dior with one of his models on a tour of Scotland, 1955. Goodwill between the two is suggested by their expressions. Photo by Thurston Hopkins/Picture Post/Getty Images. © Getty Images.

to overlook in his work the same principles that animated some modernist avant-gardes, especially at their interwar peak. These include the subordination of representation to abstraction, and the replacement of the human body with disembodied dynamics of form. Dior argued that '*couture* was weary of catering only to painters and poets, and wanted to revert to its true function, of clothing women and enhancing their beauty.'[84] But the characteristic *hauteur* of his models meant that this 'enhancement' is more accurately read as an arresting, a subordination of the model's body to the garment, and through that, to the feminine ideal. Dior claimed to be staking out a position in opposition to what he saw as the abstractions of modernism but he in fact shared territory with the *avant-garde*, in his construction of 'ephemeral architecture, dedicated to the beauty of the female body'.[85] This 'architecture' may have been dedicated to this feminine beauty, but it had the effect of arresting that beauty in the service of various other functions. Thus this relationship with his models, affectionate and even passionate as it is, can once again be seen as a self-imaging project, a site for the elaboration and projection of fantasies about the masculine self in postwar modernity. In her reading of figurations of women in Baudelaire, Elissa Marder notes how, for the poet, 'these female figures do not and cannot exist in the world as autonomous entities or even as human beings. Instead, these female figures are the essential, necessary supplements that mediate, express, and redress the poet's experience of temporality.'[86] The way that Baudelaire achieves this use of the woman is by metaphorically cutting her body into pieces, so that a single piece (Marder examines the hair as exemplary) can become the repository of lost time.[87] Is this not similar to Dior's movement of abstracting the female body, making it into a repository of meanings related to the designer's conflicted relationship to time? Once again here, Dior's connections to Baudelaire are evident; he experiences his models as crystallizations of his nostalgia.

The odd status of these models is captured by Caroline Evans, in an article on modelling in the earlier twentieth century, in which she argues that the live couture house model was 'variously represented as both an object and a subject'.[88] In simultaneously embodying stylistic uniqueness and mute uniformity, Evans writes, the model was a bearer of a number of tensions in the modern cultural imaginary, chief among them that between art and commerce. This paradoxical status is certainly evident in Dior's treatment of his own models. He devotes pages to detailing each of the models' personalities in loving turn. But in their representation of personality and radical subordination of that personality to the logic of the garment, Dior's models are also the figures that mediate between the capricious imagination of the designer (art) and the demands of his clients (commerce). Consider this formulation in *Je suis couturier*: 'It is [the models] who bring the dresses to life and contribute to the glory of their maker.'[89] Their act of self-liquidation materializes and represents Dior's artistry to an audience, and it is not primarily an artistic audience; it is always an audience of buyers.

Dior was committed on one level to the narration of himself as an artist, and rejected the constraints of a range of modern workplaces, from the factory to the accountant's office. Yet he is well known for the ambitiousness of the business plan, for the way he revolutionized *haute couture* by facilitating transnational expansion and capitalizing on the licensing of his name for the sale of accessories and perfume. Apart from the New Look, Dior has gone down in history for his successful building of a global brand.[90] If one looks closely at Dior's own self-representations, one finds that even as he styled himself as an artist, he was remarkably accommodating of the commercial side of his operation. In *Talking about Fashion*, he admits that it is the efficient functioning of the administrative side of the house's operation that creates the conditions for the designer's freedom of expression.[91] He also characterizes the couturier as an 'idea merchant', dependent on the commercial operation to sell those ideas, which are, by virtue of the structure of fashion, 'unstable' and 'capricious'. Dior writes admiringly of the capacity of his business director, Jacques Rouet, to stabilize these ideas well enough to turn a profit from them.[92] As Joanne Entwistle argues, the fashion industry depends on the generation of 'aesthetic value', which is 'inherently unstable

Figure 4.7   Dior at work with a model in his Paris studio, 1952. Photo by Roger Wood/Getty Images. Hulton Archive. © Getty Images.

and changing; it therefore has to be stabilized and valorized by actors within the market.'[93] Dior recognized this. His models, with their remarkably static feminine qualities, were actors who were just as important to the process of value stabilization as Jacques Rouet and the administrative team. This is because, unlike Rouet and the rest, they occupied the same nebulous space as the designer himself; they *embodied* the interface between art and industry.

Consider again Dior's description of the model Renée, with her transubstantiation from woman to commodity: 'She brings fabric to life so exquisitely that her face is lost.' In this description, the static woman becomes amazingly akin to the women whom Walter Benjamin explored in his *Arcades Project* and other work. The prostitute, especially, for Benjamin represented a similar kind of stasis. She was 'seller and sold in one', as he puts it.[94] Traces of this status are also evident in his descriptions of fashionable women. In words that seem also to sum up Dior's mannequins, Esther Leslie characterizes this new type of modern woman-commodity: 'this becoming ... thing-like is the admittance into exchange, which is entry into equality, the strange equality of all who stand before the labour market ... in capitalism, an economic system of universalised exchange is socially broadcast using women as objects and enticing them as complicit subjects.'[95] Thus the abstractions of the feminine body in Dior's practice and his self-narration are closely related to the accumulation of capital. Though it might appear to be one, this Baudelairean economy of feminine beauty is no abstract aesthetic system. It is inextricable from the material relations of exchange in which Dior was unavoidably embedded.

DIOR, ART AND COMMERCE

Indeed, Dior himself reveals himself to be, alongside his models, the primary mediator of the values of these two ostensibly competing fields, art and commerce. The business-related tasks he chose are telling. Unusually, Dior wrote his own press releases, and the language he uses to describe this process is noteworthy: 'I draw up the Press release, describing the season's trend, trying to express it in as precise and unliterary language as possible. In order to think of the title, and the emblem which will crown the new fashions, I give myself over to last-minute inspiration.'[96] The process, as Dior describes it, is a *hybrid* of art and commerce. He essentially channels his artistic side, then disciplines it (by describing it in quotidian language) in order to fit the dictates of the sale. He reveals himself to be engaged in a delicate balancing act— just like the models who show these dresses—between the imperative to be the artistic personality that he is so clearly invested in, and the imperative to make his artistic work intelligible for the sake of the buyer's gaze.

What is more, just a few pages later, Dior writes,

> [i]t will perhaps come as a surprise to learn that I concern myself personally with the prices ... But the price of a dress is of fundamental importance ... But these prices, although fairly calculated, are not necessarily the right process. A dress which is fairly insignificant, may have taken far longer to make than another which is far more striking ... Yet how can we admit to our clients that 'a casual little dress' needs as much care and attention as a ball dress?[97]

Here, Dior takes on the function of the fashion industry's actors, described by Entwistle above, who negotiate aesthetic value so that it fits the dictates of the marketplace. He strategizes ways to reconcile the cost of labour, for instance, with what we might call the imaginative worth of an extravagant gown, which accrues value through its placement in a spectacular, image-based network. Thus the work that Dior does as a mediator between the aesthetic and the commercial sides of his business also demands that he bridge two registers: the material (labour costs) and the much more abstract and nebulous domain of the circulation of images. What this example makes clear is that the material and the ethereal domains of any aesthetic marketplace are in fact dependent on and help to reproduce one another. The designer, though, is not usually positioned in the uncomfortable place where Dior positions himself, potentially underlining this relationship between the commercial and the aesthetic even as he strives to preserve some conception of their difference.

Marie-France Pochna captures what is at stake here: Dior could 'fulfill his commercial vision in perfect accord with his royal master plan. Authority combined with camaraderie and extravagance to create the perfect environment for Dior to pursue the absolute truth, or, as Cecil Beaton says, a place where "fashion, the ephemeral, shares the last laugh with art, the eternal".'[98] We might dispense with the idealistic language of 'perfect harmony' and 'an absolute' and still be attentive to the major theoretical kernel here: Pochna suggests that Dior's distinct mix of artistry and mercantile interest was developed in service of a goal with temporal implications. He would use the peculiar time of fashion, contingent upon the flexibility and fickleness of the market, in order to gesture toward the absolute, to stop time. This is the temporal impulse that is crystallized in his silhouettes. It fundamentally marks Dior's self-representation. And this paradox is part of what undergirds the complexity of his temporal registers. His ambivalent and compromised turn to the past becomes a means of working through the split selfhood that follows from living the impossible tension between timeless art and time-bound commerce. If nostalgia is primarily a means of imaginatively mediating the pressures of the present day, then what are the particular present-bound circumstances that Dior faces? Many, if not most, can be traced back to the split between art and commerce whose negotiation I have just described, which is intensified by the character of modern *haute couture* as a field of aesthetic value subject to the dictates of the market. Given that his nostalgia is so thoroughly bound-up with representations of women, we are back to the question of femininity once again. Just as women function as 'tellers' of time in his work, so too is the characterization of femininity throughout the texts bound-up with the anxiously guarded boundary between art and commerce.[99] The expression of an ambiguously nostalgic femininity through the models is not related only to Dior's imaginative context. It is also related to the threats of a homogenizing commerce to Dior's status as an artist. To borrow Elissa Marder's terms again, we can see in Dior's descriptions of women how women play a double role in mediating the modern artist's temporally derived 'pain': they are at once the agents of that pain—as with the models, for example, whose life is arrested in their necessary submission to the industrial logic of fashion—and the potential remedy.[100]

THE DESIGNER AS HISTORIAN

To understand the structure of Dior's nostalgia like this—as related, through its feminizing, to the structure of commerce—allows us to redraw the meanings we attach to nostalgia, both gendering it and materializing it. Elizabeth Outka provides a helpful model in this regard. In *Consuming Traditions*, she traces the complicated relationship between past (or tradition) and present (or modernity) in several early-twentieth-century English contexts. She finds that the split between art and commerce is overlain with that between past and present. The move to commodify and sell authenticity, most often associated with tradition, involved a carefully managed blurring of the line between originality and commercially derived principles of mass reproduction. Mapped onto that were the past and the present, apparently embodying a tension between tradition and modernity, but in fact blurring it: *modern* selling techniques were used to impart a sense of *tradition* via purchased objects or experiences. The commodification of tradition as an integration of art and commerce, Outka shows, is closely related to the false temporal oppositions in modernity. She writes, '[n]ostalgic authenticity allowed an enticing manipulation of time—fracturing it, disrupting it, expanding it, condensing it.'[101] Within the apparently dichotomous structure of modern time—its pitting of past against present—material goods and other saleable things surreptitiously undermined the binary.

The presence of a body was often what made that temporal manipulation possible, Outka shows: 'A sense of time's passage might be inscribed onto objects or architectural details, suggesting a range of past moments simultaneously available in the present for a given consumer or reader. The actual or imagined body moving through these settings inverted this, bringing a mobile representation of the modern moment to an older, timeless setting.'[102] Here, we can see how the feminine embodied figures that are at the heart of Dior's self-narration function; once again, they are the mediators of time. Through their bodily proximity to the garments they wear, they act as the interface between the past-oriented aesthetic that Dior built, and the 'modern moment' that fashion relies upon. Outka's book helps us remember what is at stake here: the commercialization of this aesthetic. Not only does femininity have a role to play in navigating Dior's personal aesthetic and temporal investments, it also has a role to play in ensuring the legibility, and thus the marketability, of a traditional aesthetic in the context of a modernizing social order.

In a sense, what this analysis allows us to see is that Dior's women were used to sell time itself: its flexibility, its manipulability, in Outka's terms. They did so through their crystallization of two different times in one body. If there is any theorist who can untangle for us what is at stake here, it is Walter Benjamin. On one level, the description of the woman's body as a bearer of two different times resonates with Benjamin's theory of the dialectical image, which involves the co-existence—the 'constellation'—of two times in one object or phenomenon. Benjamin himself made fashion a preeminent concern in *The Arcades Project* because of this quality. Dior's entire aesthetic, with its material and nostalgic juxtaposition of different times, would appear to enact the very constellations that constitute the dialectical image in Benjamin's work. The dialectical image, though, contained the seeds of revolution. Does Dior's fashionable woman carry that same revolutionary potential, or does she represent the mere *facsimile* of possibility that Benjamin also identified in fashion, a form that he saw as representing the petrifaction of social relations under modern industrial capitalism? The ultimate conceit of the theory of dialectics at a standstill is that the image created in this juxtaposition of mythic past and present is itself static and iconic. It is a flash, aligned with the moment, but it brings together the fleeting and the eternal (just as Benjamin's inspiration, Baudelaire, argued that fashion and modernity did). The eternal thus takes on a complexity that belies its seeming stasis. In an exposition of Benjamin's work on fashion, Barbara Vinken writes that 'antiquity, we might say, is no longer safe. This new relation is often represented as a clash between the eternal, ideal beauty of the statue and a fashion of the moment that disfigures beauty—a clash between high and low.'[103] The dialectical image, as she makes clear in this formulation, might be said to take on the embodied quality of the statue: an arresting of circulation and movement, a transposition of life into mythical iconography ... Might this be another description of glamour?

Surely this kind of arrested circulation is captured in Dior's aesthetic. It is visible in the subordination of the woman's living body to the garment that I discuss above, and the mythic and statuesque character is also evident in the curiously still quality of photographs of Dior's work. Dior thus epitomizes Benjamin's formulation of fashion's dialectics: fashion 'couples the living body to the inorganic world'.[104] The inorganic, of course, is the material garment of fashion. But it also might be seen as the statuary that is represented by the woman of fashion in Dior's aesthetic framework. In describing the way the garment, worn by a live model, takes on or appropriates the dynamism of the woman, Dior is describing a temporally unfolding process of petrifaction; not only is this the *coupling* of the organic with the inorganic, but it is the momentary *triumph* of the inorganic—the garment itself, and the cold, monumental beauty of the statue—over the living. Women are, once again, aligned with death. This status would be supported by a reading of Benjamin: in *The Arcades Project*, images of death are commonly bound-up with feminine images, whether those be fashionable women or prostitutes.

In applying Benjamin's work to Dior, we are reminded that Dior's creations were commodities. Indeed, this is exactly what Benjamin would have us remember. After all, he envisioned the dialectical image as a means of radically interrupting the depoliticized dream state occasioned by the spectacles of commodity culture. Fashion, that commodity par excellence, can be seen as a dialectical image precisely *because* of this commodification; as Ulrich Lehmann puts it,

> the unashamedly open fetishistic character of the sartorial commodity, in both its materialist and psychoanalytic connotation, encourages a cynical view of society, as it recycles the old in order to generate new commerce. Being supremely realistic about its own limited life span, fashion continually proclaims the rift—through imminent death and rebirth—in the historical continuum.[105]

Benjamin introduces a concept of the fashion commodity as 'meta-critical', then—involved in an ongoing material critique of the very system in which it emerges. In performing its own death, fashion makes visible the stakes of obsolescence and desire that drive industrial capitalism. The recognition of this, Benjamin hopes, will spark the revolutionary awakening of the masses.

It would surely be preposterous to argue that Dior, though his work appears so clearly to constitute a series of dialectical images, mobilizes or inspires revolutionary potential in the sense of bearing a critique of capitalism. Benjamin's methodology does not, anyway, allow us to trace the historical unfolding of dissent, but rather to imagine, frame and theorize it. But although Dior's 'dialectical images' may not have inspired revolution, and have in fact been understood as figuring in an opposing way, as symptomatic of postwar conservatism, his writings surely bear the traces of his *own* recognition of his work's dialectical nature.[106] Dior emerges, I suggest, as a version of the 'materialist historian' or 'dialectician' that Benjamin repeatedly references in *The Arcades Project* and whose work he also theorizes in 'Theses on the Philosophy of History'.[107] Of course, Dior is not an historian, not a theorist—not in any conventional definition of these terms—and in this sense the comparison with Benjamin's dialectician is an unorthodox one. But Dior's writing, coupled with the visual field that he created, reveal him to be engaging in a kind of historical citation, to use Benjamin's own terms, which runs parallel to the work of the materialist historian. A look at 'Convolute N' of *The Arcades Project*, 'On the Theory of Knowledge, Theory of Progress', reveals a description of the historian's vocation that is relevant to Dior's work:

> The events surrounding the historian, in which he himself takes part, will underlie his presentation in the form of a text written in invisible ink. The history which he lays before the reader comprises, as it were, the citations occurring in this text, and it is only these citations that occur in a manner legible to all. To write history thus means to cite history. It belongs to the concept of citation, however, that the historical object in each case is torn from its context.[108]

In this understanding, the historian is particularly attentive to the present, to the 'events surrounding' her or him. Benjamin's materialist historian, as revealed in *The Arcades Project* and in 'Theses on the Philosophy of History', is not turned backward, but 'takes part' in the era in which she or he lives, allowing for the productive juxtaposition of past and present in her or his life and practice.[109] The materialist historian's method—like Benjamin's own method—consists of the nonlinear and utterly eclectic exposition of a series of historical 'facts', or ideas. Central to the non-narrative character of the doctrine of historical materialism is that 'history decays into images, not into stories'.[110]

This, of course, is precisely Dior's own method. Recall his proclamation, cited above, that '[w]e live in the times we do; and nothing is sillier than to turn one's back on them.' Dior takes pains to distinguish his own orientation to the present as the condition of his return to historical references. He turns to the past because that is what the present wants. The past is revealed, as in Benjamin's theory, as a means through which to mediate or experience the traumatic present: 'For the materialist historian, every epoch in with which he occupies himself is only prehistory for the epoch he himself must live in.'[111] In Dior's case, his citation of those historical references consists, due to the nature of the industry, of the 'decay into images' rather than narratives. Dior's historical 'writing', then, is both his actual garments and the iconic archive he created, with photographs of his models in his dresses. Certainly, as a nostalgic subject, he revels in the past, but just as Benjamin specified for the practice of the materialist historian, the material-visual field he created necessarily tore those historical references from their contexts. Indeed, that material-visual field was populated with images, in the Benjaminian sense: images are the raw data of the materialist historian. Further, like Benjamin's dialectical images, Dior's images were those 'wherein what has been comes together in a flash with the now to form a constellation'.[112] Benjamin emphasizes the arrested, the utterly still, quality of the dialectical image: 'A historical materialist cannot do without the notion of a present which is not a transition, but in which time stands still and comes to a stop.'[113] Is this not precisely what is at work in the characteristic visual language that Dior created, with its peculiarly static quality?

Of course, these images that Dior created, which qualify him as a kind of materialist historian, are inevitably feminized. They are—most of the time—images of live women, models, whose life is overcome by the garment, the object. If they are not photographs of live models, the archive of images consists of sketches of dresses abstracted from their wearers, but nevertheless feminized because they are women's garments. Benjamin asserts, '[t]o write history means giving dates their physiognomy,' and his object-oriented framework in *The Arcades Project* gives this dictum a certain literalness: this

Figure 4.8 The famous, curiously static photograph of Dior's 1947 Bar Suit, by Willy Maywald. Photo by Keystone-France/ Gamma-Keystone via Getty Images. © Gamma-Keystone via Getty Images.

physiognomy is material, it is tangible.[114] And in Dior's case, this physiognomy is still more particular; it is feminine. Again, here, we see Dior using the material bodies of women to materialize a conception of history.

Considering Dior's negotiation of his feminized dialectical images leads us back to nostalgia, and shows us once again how women function as vectors of time consciousness. Consider the dialectical image as it is embodied by the Dior model: its stopping of time distances the viewer. As Benjamin describes in 'The Work of Art in the Age of Mechanical Reproduction', the distancing of the art object from the human is a primary characteristic of what he calls the 'aura' of a work of art prior to the age of mechanical reproduction; that is, prior to the advent of techniques that allowed for the widespread diffusion of images.[115] The premodern art object, unlike the mechanically reproducible and ephemeral arts of photography and film, has an important dimension of 'permanence' that in part constitutes its 'authenticity'. It gestures to the eternal or ahistorical through its relationship to ritual and tradition—although, as Benjamin makes clear, even tradition is 'thoroughly alive and extremely changeable'.[116]

Benjamin's essay on the work of art is ambivalent about the effects of the loss of aura. As he shows elsewhere, Benjamin recognized the positive social functions of tradition.[117] On the other hand, he was tentatively optimistic about the democratizing qualities of the changes in perception that were brought about by the decline of the aura, the increasing accessibility of the visual field and the ability of mechanical reproduction to 'emancipate the work of art from its parasitical dependence on ritual'.[118] But finally, the 'Work of Art' essay famously expressed Benjamin's concern about 'the danger of a fascist appropriation of auratic art' through mobilizing the appeal of its authenticity.[119] Altogether, the piece reveals a striking scepticism about *both* aura and mass reproduction.

For this reason, the concept of the aura in decline emerges as a useful motif through which to understand Dior's feminized work. We have already seen how unsteadily and self-consciously Dior occupied his perch on the cusp of the present and an undefinable past*ness*. In his self-narration he vacillates endlessly. The autobiographical representations are marked by Dior's temporal balancing act: the clear need that he feels to establish himself as rooted in the present is countered by the pull to the past. And of course, though photographs of Dior's work have an auratic quality about them, the aura of the works in them is unavoidably compromised by their status as reproductions. The women who wear them, then, are suspended between ritual and mass reproduction, as they bear not only the weight of two different times, but also the tension between authenticity and reproduction. In a sense, in their embodiment of these two tensions, the women reveal their entwinement.

Judith Brown's discussion of glamorous celebrity, personified in Greta Garbo, is of some use here. She writes,

> Garbo's glamour—and glamour more generally—comes to stand in the place of the aura, signaling its death yet bearing its enchanted trace; glamour indeed becomes a twentieth-century response to the loss of both authenticity and spiritual belief. Glamour, emerging from the new possibilities of mass reproduction, maintains the qualities of ecstatic illumination while, at the same time, forgoes any possibility of depth or meaning.[120]

The last sentence of this description is remarkably *a propos* of Dior's models' subordination to his designs, the way they become petrified and empty in the act of modelling. In becoming glamorous, the models perform the authenticity that is linked to tradition. However, they thus become reproducible and lose the temporal depth that seems to be represented by images of the past. They are nostalgic vehicles, but in their reproducibility—their symbolic and material linking to the vicissitudes of the ephemeral fashion industry—they stand as a critique of the possibility of 'pure' nostalgia as an unfettered engagement with the present. They show that the subject, the culture, are inescapably embedded in the now.

This is precisely the paradox that Dior navigated. Pushing past their obvious roles as commercial vehicles, a careful reading of the autobiographical representations shows that they are also attempts to work through the tensions engendered by the status of the designer. He is a revered bearer of a supposedly authentic past, even as, season after fashion season, the feminized visual field that he creates drives home the impossibility of fully reproducing that past due to the industrial logic that drives fashion. In fact, I would suggest that Dior's recognition of the impracticality of that reproduction is the source of the melancholy that pervades the work. He reveals himself to be perpetually searching for a return—to an imaginative 'home', to his mother, to the period of his childhood—but to be stopped short, continually reminded by the structure of his profession and his designs that a return is not possible. Women, as the bearers of temporal complexity, are also ciphers of Dior's subjective melancholy. In this sense they are thoroughly present in the self-representations, even where they are not explicitly discussed. They are the image of the split condition of Dior's selfhood as an artist *and* an industrialist.

Of course, they are also coolly beautiful, and their beauty suggests Dior's aestheticization of his own melancholy: he belongs to a tradition that romanticizes the melancholic, often finding it singularly beautiful.[121] Consider some of the notable statements about feminine beauty that occur throughout Dior's archive: the 'true function' of couture is to 'cloth[e] women and enhanc[e] their true beauty'. And his work is 'ephemeral architecture, dedicated to the beauty of the female body'. What is clearly expressed as the *desire* for feminine beauty motivated his participation in the fashion industry. Dior's longing is to transcend the tensions that are implicit in his practice, between pastness and the present. For him, women are both highly personal expressions of the conditions of Dior's selfhood, and impersonal expressions of the yearning to leave the self behind and enter a realm of pure aesthetics. It is in this latter sense that his creations and their modelling approach the abstractions of modernist art. In this way, they claim something of the transcendent territory toward which certain forms of high modernist art gestured. Unlike the abstractions of modernist aesthetics, however, Dior's move to transcend the practicalities of an industry, and a world, which would not allow him to live in the temporal order that he yearned to, was articulated *through* women as beautiful objects.

Kathy Psomiades's work on Victorian aestheticism helps interpret this pull to transcendence, articulated through women. Psomiades analyses beauty's function in the maintenance of the belief in a rarefied sphere of aesthetic purity distinct from the realities of industry and the market. The notion of beauty, she shows, complicates the strict division of spheres into public (the market) and private (interiority and aesthetics):

> Beauty, rather than soul, is problematic, because beauty does congeal in objects, because beauty is precisely, in its sexualized appeal, the problem. Unlike soul, beauty has a material existence: straddling spiritual and material realms, it draws attention to the double nature of art, priceless and yet for sale. It is, after all, the materiality of artistic products that keeps them from complete autonomy and it is on the basis of that materiality that they are commodified.[122]

Read in this light, Dior's grasp at temporal transcendence through feminine beauty is most indissolubly linked to the structure of fashion *as a culture industry*. It is one which, like art, is deeply uncomfortable with its close relationship to the market, but which is that much more visibly dependent on the market than the artistic sphere. As Psomiades writes elsewhere, '[i]n British Aestheticism ... femininity is what permits the translation of economic into symbolic capital.'[123] Indeed, this is what I have been showing, adding that it is specifically the temporal figuration of femininity that facilitates this translation. In the fashion industry, the mediating role of feminine *beauty* is paramount, as beauty is the engine of the industry.

In a sense, then, what Dior allows us to see is the way the ambiguity of feminine figuration and the ambiguity of the industry itself collapse into one another by way of representations of time. But as Psomiades takes pains to point out, we must not necessarily give in to the seductions of ambivalence; ambivalence can be another name for the reconsolidation of traditional structures of gender, and does not necessarily point to their dismantling.[124] In the case of Dior, we see the continued shoring-up of an interlocked set of binaries—masculine and feminine, present and past, markets and art—even as these are consistently made visible through the mechanisms of the industry and through Dior's own self-representations. Ambivalence, in this case, points not much further than to an affect of private despair, and not to a liberatory ethic or aesthetic either for the women and figural femininities Dior worked with, nor for himself as a homosexual man.

Conclusion: Fashioning Self, Reflecting Ambivalence

Arguing that fashion is a series of crystallizations of cultural moods, Susan Kaiser and Karyl Ketchum comment on the relationships enabled by the odd time of this form: 'Fashion/fashionability offers perhaps the quintessential medium through which to forge...bonds of intimacy and community.'[1] These theorists are thinking through the materiality of fashion—the ways in which our clothing, and its appraisal by other people, contribute to the development of personal and collective identities. Written fashion does this, too. In the texts by Poiret, Schiaparelli and Dior, fashion enables a kind of relational articulation between designers and consumers, designers and the cultural imaginary and, finally and most importantly, designers and modern women.

Yet the self-fashioning documents of designers are overwhelmingly characterized by ambivalence. If these are depictions of relationships, they are unstable ones, and the value of such relationships to each designer is uncertain. In fact, such relationality is ultimately figured as a threat of a sort. It potentially threatens the couturier's position as a self-made genius, which is precisely the kind of myth that the fashion industry relied on. There were market-related reasons for these figures to distance themselves from the relationships that they otherwise relied on. Even where the health of a design house was not at stake (such as with Schiaparelli and Poiret), the way to transcend their cultural moment and claim a place in the fashion pantheon was to underscore their individuality. These designers' self-fashioning legacies underscore the anxious labour of denying the centrality of others to their success and even to their self-perceptions. The ambivalence detected in these works derives precisely from this: from the ways that they are profoundly marked by femininity and women and yet they retrospectively refuse that marking of the self.

The ambivalence in Poiret's work turns specifically on women's status in relation to history. Where he paints them in a positive light, it is because they bolster his image. These are times when they operate in either an ahistorical or a premodern realm. When women are portrayed in negative terms—as the cause of his demise as a couturier—it is because they are *too* modern. They are too deeply bound-up with the processes of industrial modernization that engendered mass fashion as the ultimate threat to the couturier. Poiret's ambivalence thus hinges directly on what he reads as women's knowledge, and whether it is sequestered outside history or monstrously animated within the modern moment. That knowledge, in itself, is ambivalent: it is both ancient (the domain of innate secrets) and modern (unnaturally engendered by processes of fashion's democratization and modernization). Poiret's incarnation of couturier ambivalence points to the intersection of gender, situated in time, with concepts of rationality. Fashion, as a domain that is associated, through its feminization and trivialization, with irrationality, puts the masculine couturier identity at risk.

In the case of Schiaparelli, the ambivalence rests, intriguingly, mostly with herself. Rather than displacing ambivalence onto others, her work, with its linguistically split selfhood, ground fashion's ambivalence in the designer as a feminine figure. Though this occurs through discussions of other women, these other women do not have an essentially ambivalent identity, as Schiaparelli is shown to have. They are invoked always to make a point about the designer's *own* contradictions. In her case, what is revealed is a deep cleavage between the two Schiaparellis. Ambivalence here is internalized—but it is ultimately used to portray the designer's authenticity, which provokes and authorizes her exit from the fashion industry, a field which is denigrated for its feminine superficiality. Here, then, though it is not necessarily embodied by women as clients, workers or muses, ambivalence again functions to distance the designer (though she is a woman) from femininity as other and threatening to the self.

Dior's ambivalence can be connected to this aspect of Schiaparelli's labour of selfhood. There is an intermittently visible imperative to distance the self from the feminine others upon whom he is so clearly dependent. This abjection of the feminine is in strong contrast to his articulations of relational incorporation of femininity and various women. Dior is formed in part through his *in*ability to separate women from himself, which he papers-over at key moments with a strong reassertion of his independence. The self in the major memoir, *Dior by Dior*, is split along various axes, including gender. His ambivalence derives not so much from the sense that women are a threat to his viability as a designer, but from the sense that their proximity to him will raise doubts about his claims to artistry. For women, as his accounts of his models make clear, are the vectors of business. Though he is famously friendly to commerce, his antipathy toward it suggests that he requires it be kept separate from the self, in order not to sully his artistic reputation. His ambivalence about women relates largely to his troubled relationship to art and commerce as the poles that underpin his work.

In all cases, in fact, couturier ambivalence is connected to the difficult position designers occupied on the threshold between the arts and commerce in a cultural milieu in which these two spheres were ideologically opposed. Designers displaced much of the anxiety that followed from this situation onto the women—and the figural feminine—who were patrons of their industry. As such, women bore the weight of contradiction, and became ambiguous figures themselves.[2] This book has shown that one of the means by which ambiguous meaning attached to women and femininity was the unique temporal structure of fashion. Poised between multiple constructs of time, modernist fashion was a kind of material index of the complex position of women in modernity. Attending to its time structure makes apparent the ambiguity of the very form; fashion was a site of contradiction in many ways.

This complexity aided these fashion designers in staging an implicit encounter between competing discourses of modern femininity. The ways that this played out in Poiret's, Schiaparelli's and Dior's work was a microcosm of widespread ways of representing femininity. In general, in the early twentieth century, fashion was taken seriously in contexts ranging from the popular press through social theory, and a careful reading of the writing about it—beyond the designers' self-representations—shows that it was seen to emblematize modern femininity. The transnational beauty and fashion press was a forum for both the ongoing construction and the negotiation of the anxieties and confusion provoked by the apparent modernization of femininity.[3] In this sense, the designers' use of women to represent the contradictions of their social position was simply one elaboration of a widespread tendency to use 'woman as metaphor', to invoke Eva Feder Kittay's construction once again.

The designers' attempts to conceal their entwinement with both art and commerce can also be seen as one expression of the broader ambivalent character of their industry. Fashion's role in the production of ambivalence has been theorized by many of the form's most astute analysts.[4] Most of this literature focuses on the ambiguous identity performances that clothing enables; as Anne Boultwood and Robert Jerrard write, '[t]he apparent superficiality of fashion is belied by its role in giving expression to the ambivalence derived from the internal conflict of the individual.'[5] Like Boultwood and Jerrard's work, much of the literature also views this subjective ambivalence as a product of a postmodern—not a modern—era. But the work of designers such as Poiret, Dior and Schiaparelli allows us to trace the operation of ambivalence at the height of the modern era. Indeed, these designers' self-portrayals show that the ambivalence of the identities enabled by *wearing* fashion is mirrored by the ambivalence of identities among those who negotiate it through text.

The tendency in literature about fashion is to celebrate that ambivalence, to find openness and possibility in it. Kaiser and Ketchum, for instance, write of ambivalence as 'moments of articulation that create hybrid appearances reliant on the contradictions between one identity variable and its opposite, or between one theme and its opposite'.[6] Fashion, they argue, has an ability to intervene in the overwhelmingly binary logic of the Western way of knowing: 'ambivalence can be seen as an ongoing discourse—one that incorporates the pushes and pulls of identities framed as dichotomies.'[7]

The self-representational strategies of the modern designer are characterized by precisely the kinds of ambivalence that Kaiser and Ketchum write about. The texts by Poiret, Schiaparelli and Dior are about the persistence of binary logic, and the negative consequences for those who challenge such binaries. The fluctuation between images of the self as artist and as industrialist is one component of this tension; the other is the consistent oscillation between figures of women as archaic and as modern. The location of such ambivalence about women in these designer texts, however, raises questions about whether ambivalence is, as is so often claimed, a modality of liberation. Its effects do not seem as straightforwardly positive as they are usually considered to be in fashion criticism, even as we recognize the search for openness and possibility that the term implies.

For, notwithstanding the unstable portrayals of women, the texts ultimately *uphold* some critical binaries. That is, the oscillations resolve in favour of understandings of masculinity and femininity as essentially different. All of the designers—even Dior, who is most willing to explore his subjective intimacy with femininity—are ultimately engaged in the labour of *distinction.* They push constructions of femininity away from their own identities in order to uphold the pretence of a purity of identity and singularity of purpose in the designer self. While the importance of women and femininity to designers' self-concepts suggests a relational perspective that is hopeful from a feminist point of view, the positive effect of relationality is neutralized when the relationship is deployed in order to effectively *deny* a relationship.

The major dichotomy that is upheld in this kind of rejecting relational stance is that between designer and women—most often, women as clients; this applies even to Schiaparelli, a woman herself. In general this translates, across all three designers, into either the sense that women are static and timeless or that they lack the capacity for meaningful and creative participation in fashion. These are temporal constructs, of course: the creator works in time, with the unique privilege of being either simultaneously attuned to the present and the eternal *or* being temporally transcendent. The woman, on the other hand, does not have the ability to move across time in these accounts. The dichotomy between designer and women thus folds back into the dichotomous construction of past and present that fashion seems on so many levels to challenge. While designers use fashion's complex, simultaneous allegiance to past, present and future to describe themselves, or to describe the cultural role of fashion more generally, they do not extend that temporal flexibility to women. Women do not have the suppleness that designers themselves do. Women's portrayals are unstable, to be sure, but they do not have the luxury of inhabiting multiple time signatures *at once*; where they conjure the past, they are mired in it. This is the overarching construct of femininity in these texts, taken together.

And yet it is clear that the concept of the modern woman also inhabits these texts, to varying degrees. But as I note with respect to Poiret—and it is apparent in Schiaparelli, too, with her attacks on feminists and 'mannish' modern women—where women are portrayed as up-to-the-minute through their relationship to the tempo of fashion, they are usually denigrated. In fact, the greatest distance is sought from women when they are modern, as opposed to either timeless or nostalgic. Certainly, fashion discourses often bound women to modernity, but in many cases this binding of women to the modern is symptomatic of a deep anxiety about the dissolution of the social fabric in the modern era—or, in the case of the couturier, the threat to the supremacy of the designer.[8] If she was modern, after all, then she would be dangerously close to the forces of industrialization, standardization and copying that imperilled the figure of the designer as artistic genius. Caroline Evans's excellent studies of the model as multiple show that this quintessentially modern, fashionable woman aroused desires, yes, but also fears: 'Fears about increasing mechanization and the changing role of women were projected on to the uncanny figure of the fashion mannequin who was seen as a new kind of career woman, chilly and distant, unlike the cosy actress or vampish femme fatale.'[9] This is the other side of the glamorous chill of Dior's women; her chill made her unattainable—unmasterable?—as did the potential for out-of-control production that she represented through her modernity.

Tracing designers' self-representational strategies, then, should prompt reflection on the theory that fashion simply placed women in history, in public culture—and the accompanying implicit thesis that this move toward modernization was experienced as mostly positive. It seems more accurate to posit that femininity was constructed variably, that it was not and should not be understood *either* as modern or as archaic, but as a flexible and internally multiple concept. It shifted according to local conditions and political and cultural pressures.[10] It is not helpful for feminist critics to generalize about the role of femininity in the modern period. Rather, to nuance the discussion we have been having for a couple of decades—and perhaps to revitalize it—we need to attend primarily to the contradictory character of femininity in this period, foregrounding 'the ambivalent legacy of modernity'[11] (and femininity) in our work and not supposing that the period (or women's place in it) are in any way uniform, even in Western modernity.

There is another way in which this set of designer texts puts pressure on our own binary constructs surrounding femininity and modernity. That is by calling into question the dichotomy of visibility and invisibility that has been so foundational for feminist theory of the last forty years. On one level, women are undeniably spectacular in these texts because the texts could not be separated by their readers from fashion's visual culture, saturated as it was by images of women's bodies. And yet in the construction of the feminine as the designer's other, the texts are also permeated by a discernible movement of rendering invisible. The spectacular visibility of the women is countered by the designer's eclipse of these figures. The point of the designer memoir and of other self-representational works is to aggrandize the self, and the stakes are high; the eclipse of women must be accomplished in order to secure the designer's authority. An eclipse is, indeed, an apt metaphor for the meeting of visibility and invisibility in these texts and in modernity more generally. For an eclipse, even if it is total, still transmits some trace of the eclipsed object, making the labour of eclipsing ultimately incomplete. This is a vision of women's in/visibility that can account for the varying pressures on visibility for modern women, the way they moved from visible to invisible.

Reading the pressures on the concept of femininity in these works by Schiaparelli, Dior and Poiret should not be taken as an attack on fashion. In fact, the reservations I have addressed here work to highlight what is valuable about fashion as an ally in feminist studies of modernity. It is a marvellous device precisely *because* of its ambivalence. The way it offers up a nonlinear conception of time, and casts doubt on conventional claims about gender— and surely, about social identities more generally—is indispensable for complicating our readings of women and modernity. Fashion helps our analyses become more resonant with the complex character of social life, and the competing popular discourses of femininity in the long period I am tracing here.

And so, fashion's fundamental ambiguity and multiplicity has something to teach contemporary cultural critics about how we might conceive of femininity in its relation to the modern. Recall Caroline Evans's words, quoted in Chapter One: 'Fashion is a paradigm in the way that it can carry a contradiction—this is very modern—the whole thing is a kind of "dialectical image" or "critical constellation" not just of past and present but of differing modernities, and its "now-time" can hold them together in suspension.'[12] Current modernist studies are reaching for this same paradigm—they are turning toward plural, global modernities and away from a longstanding, singular and Eurocentric definition of modernism, 'holding' different national and regional expressions of the modern 'together in suspension', to consider their articulations but not to homogenize them.[13] Studies of gender in modernity could benefit from a similar move, whereby we hold in suspension the apparently conflicting pictures of women we get from readings of texts such as these—and others, too—but do not take a position on which picture is more accurate. Rather, the focus of our critical gaze becomes the articulations themselves. And it is fashion, remarkable critical and material tool that it is, that takes us to this productive point.

Notes

INTRODUCTION: FASHION, FEMININITY AND MODERNITY IN DESIGNER SELF-FASHIONING

1. Michel Foucault, *The Order of Things: An Archaeology of the Human Sciences* (1966; Vintage, 1970), p. 310.
2. See Marshall Berman, *All that is Solid Melts into Air: The Experience of Modernity* (Simon and Schuster, 1982) for this classic formulation of modernity as a dialectic of cultural and social change, modernism and modernization. Stephen Kern's *The Culture of Time and Space 1880–1918* (Harvard University Press, 1983) provides an excellent, accessible overview of changing conceptions of space and time.
3. Harvie Ferguson, *Modernity and Subjectivity: Body, Soul, Spirit* (University Press of Virginia, 2000), p. 3.
4. 'Etre à la mode', *Vogue* (Paris), April 1930, p. 59. '[L]a Mode est indifférente comme l'oubli. Elle ignore ce qu'elle a cessé d'aimer, elle ne parait changeante que parce qu'elle est si fidèle—fidèle a son désir de plaire.'
5. See Catherine Constable, 'Making up the Truth: On Lies, Lipstick, and Friedrich Nietzsche', in Stella Bruzzi and Pamela Church Gibson, eds., *Fashion Cultures: Theories, Explorations, and Analysis* (Routledge, 2001), pp. 191–200.
6. Efrat Tseëlon, *The Masque of Femininity* (Sage, 1995), p. 14.
7. On the unique time signature of fashion, see Barbara Vinken, *Fashion Zeitgeist: Trends and Cycles in the Fashion System* (Berg, 2005); Susan Kaiser and Karyl Ketchum, 'Consuming Fashion and Flexibility: Metaphor, Cultural Mood, and Materiality', in S. Ratneshwar and David Glen Mick, eds., *Inside Consumption: Consumer Motives, Goals, and Desires* (Routledge, 2005), pp. 132–7; Patrizia Calefato, 'Time', in Lisa Adams, trans., *The Dressed Body* (Berg, 2004), pp. 123–34.
8. Elizabeth Wilson, *Adorned in Dreams: Fashion and Modernity*, rev. ed. (Rutgers University Press, 2003), p. 3.
9. Mary Louise Roberts, 'Samson and Delilah Revisited: The Politics of Women's Fashion in 1920s France', *American Historical Review* 98, no. 3 (1993), pp. 57–84; Tag Gronberg, *Designs on Modernity: Exhibiting the City in 1920s Paris* (Manchester University Press, 1998); Mary Lynn Stewart, *Dressing Modern Frenchwomen: Marketing Haute Couture, 1919–39* (Johns Hopkins University Press, 2008).
10. Charles Baudelaire, 'The Painter of Modern Life', in Jonathan Mayne, trans., *The Painter of Modern Life and Other Essays,* (Phaidon Press, 1964); Georg Simmel, 'The Philosophy of Fashion' and 'Adornment', in David Frisby and Mike Featherstone, trans., *Simmel on Culture* (Sage, 1997), pp. 187–206 and pp. 201–11; and Walter Benjamin, Convolute B, 'Fashion', in *The Arcades Project*, trans. Howard Eiland and Kevin McLaughlin (The Belknap Press, 1999).

11. Rita Felski, 'On Nostalgia: The Prehistoric Woman', in *The Gender of Modernity* (Harvard University Press, 1995), pp. 35–60. See also Anne Witz, 'Georg Simmel and the Masculinity of Modernity', *Journal of Classical Sociology* 3, no. 1 (2001), pp. 353–70; and Anne Witz and Barbara Marshall, 'The Masculinity of the Social: Toward a Politics of Interrogation', in Anne Witz and Barbara Marshall, eds., *Engendering the Social: Feminist Encounters with Social Theory* (Open University Press, 2004), pp. 19–35.

12. Rita Felski, 'Telling Time in Feminist Theory', *Tulsa Studies in Women's Literature* 21, no. 1 (2002), p. 21.

13. David Frisby, *Fragments of Modernity: Theories of Modernity in the Work of Simmel, Kracauer, and Benjamin* (MIT Press, 2004), p. 13.

14. See Ben Fine and Ellen Leopold, *The World of Consumption* (Routledge, 1993), for a discussion of the inseparability of production and consumption in fashion.

15. See Valerie Steele, 'Chanel in Context', in Juliet Ash and Elizabeth Wilson, eds., *Chic Thrills: A Fashion Reader* (University of California Press, 1992), pp. 118–26; Nancy J. Troy, *Couture Culture: A Study in Modern Fashion* (MIT Press, 2003); Yuniya Kawamura, *Fashion-ology: An Introduction to Fashion Studies* (Berg, 2005); and Christopher Breward, *The Culture of Fashion: A New History of Fashionable Dress* (Manchester University Press, 1995).

16. Penelope Deutscher, *Yielding Gender: Feminism, Deconstruction, and the History of Philosophy* (Routledge, 1997), p. 15.

17. Ibid.

18. Ibid., p. 2.

19. Eva Feder Kittay, 'Woman as Metaphor', *Hypatia* 3, no. 2 (1988), p. 63.

20. Ibid., p. 65.

21. To contextualize the ways that women are figured as the mediators of modern anxiety, see John Jervis's chapter, 'Modernity's Sphinx: Woman as Nature and Culture', in *Transgressing the Modern: Explorations in the Western Experience of Otherness* (Blackwell, 1999), pp. 107–33, and especially Elissa Marder, *Dead Time: Temporal Disorders in the Wake of Modernity* (Stanford University Press, 2001).

22. Robert Smith, 'Internal Time Consciousness of Modernism', *Critical Quarterly* 36, no. 3 (1994), p. 26.

23. Natania Meeker, '"All Times are Present to Her": Femininity, Temporality, and Libertinage in Diderot's "Sur les femmes"', *Journal for Early Modern Cultural Studies* 3, no. 2 (2003), p. 91.

24. Kathy Alexis Psomiades, 'Beauty's Body: Gender Ideology and British Aestheticism', *Victorian Studies* 36, no. 1 (1992), p. 48.

25. Ibid., pp. 46, 47.

26. See Deutscher, *Yielding Gender*; and Linda Zerilli, *Signifying Woman: Culture and Chaos in Rousseau, Burke, and Mill* (Cornell University Press, 1994).

27. Rod Rosenquist, *Modernism, the Market, and the Institution of the New* (Cambridge University Press, 2009).

28. Troy, *Couture Culture*; Steele, 'Chanel in Context'. Jacques Doucet built up an outstanding and important modern art collection. Paul Poiret designed costumes for the then-daring Ballets Russes. Elsa Schiaparelli collaborated with such modernists as Salvador Dali and Jean Cocteau; later in her career, she designed costumes for *avant-garde* theatre productions. On the close relationship

between fashion and modernist music in Paris, see Mary E. Davis, *Classic Chic: Music, Fashion and Modernism* (University of California Press, 2006).

29. See, for example, Robert Jensen, *Marketing Modernism in Fin-de-Siècle Europe* (Princeton University Press, 1993); Kevin J. H. Dettmar and Stephen Watt, eds., *Marketing Modernisms: Self-Promotion, Canonization, and Re-reading* (University of Michigan Press, 1996); Susan Burns, *Inventing the Modern Artist: Art and Culture in Gilded Age America* (Yale University Press, 1996); Lawrence Rainey, *Institutions of Modernism: Literary Elites and Popular Culture* (Yale University Press, 1998); Catherine Turner, *Marketing Modernism Between the Two World Wars* (University of Massachusetts Press, 2003); and Aaron Jaffe, *Modernism and the Culture of Celebrity* (Cambridge University Press, 2005).

30. Nancy J. Troy, 'Fashion, Art and the Marketing of Modernism', in *Couture Culture,* pp. 31–6.

31. Tiziana Ferrero-Regis, 'What is in the Name of the Fashion Designer?' (Paper presented at the Art Association of Australia and New Zealand Conference, Brisbane, Australia, 5–6 December 2008), http://eprints.qut.edu.au/18120, accessed 13 February 2011.

32. Jaffe, *Modernism,* p. 10.

33. Jean Worth, 'Harmony is the Great Secret', in *Principles of Correct Dress*, by Florence Hull Winterburn with Jean Worth and Paul Poiret (Harper and Brothers, 1914), p. 20.

34. Thomas Strychacz, *Modernism, Mass Culture, and Professionalism* (Cambridge University Press, 1993), p. 23. Italics mine.

35. Ibid., p. 24.

36. Agnès Rocamora, 'Le Monde's discours de mode: creating the créateurs', *French Cultural Studies* 13 (2002), pp. 89–90.

37. See, for instance, Sidonie Smith, 'The Universal Subject, Female Embodiment, and the Consolidation of Autobiography', in *Subjectivity, Identity, and the Body: Women's Autobiographical Practice in the Twentieth Century* (Indiana University Press, 1993); Linda Anderson, 'Autobiography and the Feminist Subject', in Ellen Rooney, ed., *The Cambridge Companion to Feminist Literary Theory* (Cambridge University Press, 2006), pp. 119–35; and Domna C. Stanton, 'Autogynography: Is the Subject Different?' in Sidonie Smith and Julia Watson, eds., *Women, Autobiography, Theory: A Reader* (University of Wisconsin Press, 1998), pp. 131–44.

38. Martin A. Danahay, *A Community of One: Masculine Autobiography and Autonomy in Nineteenth-Century Britain* (SUNY Press, 1993), p. 11.

39. Julia Watson and Sidonie Smith, 'De/Colonization and the Politics of Discourse in Women's Autobiographical Practices', in Sidonie Smith and Julia Watson, eds., *De/Colonizing the Subject: The Politics of Gender in Women's Autobiography* (University of Minnesota Press), p. xvii.

40. Pierre Bourdieu with Yvette Delsaut, 'Le couturier et sa griffe', *Actes de la recherche en science sociales* 1 (1975), p. 21. '[L]e pouvoir magique du "créateur", c'est le capital d'autorité attaché à u une position qui ne peut agir que s'il est mobilise par une personne autorisée ou mieux s'il est identifiée a une personne, a son charisme, et garanti par sa signature. Ce qui fait du Dior, ce n'est pas l'individu biologique Dior, ni la maison Dior, mais le capital de la maison Dior agissant sous les espèces d'un individu singulier qui ne peut être que Dior.'

41. Julie Rak, 'Autobiography and Production: The Case of Conrad Black', *International Journal of Canadian Studies* 25 (2002), p. 150.
42. Ibid.
43. Watson and Smith, 'De/Colonization', p. xix.
44. Nancy K. Miller, 'Representing Others: Gender and the Subject of Autobiography', *differences* 6, no. 1 (1994), p. 9.
45. Mimi Schippers, 'Recovering the Feminine Other: Masculinity, Femininity, and Gender Hegemony', *Theory and Society* 36, no. 1 (2007), p. 94.
46. Abigail Solomon-Godeau, 'The Other Side of Venus: The Visual Economy of Feminine Display', in Victoria De Grazia, ed., *The Sex of Things: Gender and Consumption in Historical Perspective* (University of California Press, 1996), p. 114.
47. Christine Buci-Glucksmann, 'Catastrophic Utopia: The Feminine as Allegory of the Modern', *Representations* 14 (Spring 1986), p. 221.
48. See Schippers, 'Recovering the Feminine Other'.
49. Harold Koda and Andrew Bolton, eds., *Poiret* (Metropolitan Museum of Art, 2007).
50. E.g. Remy G. Saisselin, 'From Baudelaire to Christian Dior: The Poetics of Fashion', *The Journal of Aesthetics and Art Criticism* 18, no. 1 (1959), pp. 109–15; Chris Brickell, 'Through the (New) Looking Glass: Gendered Bodies, Fashion and Resistance in Postwar New Zealand', *Journal of Consumer Culture* 2, no. 2 (2002), pp. 241–69. Dior is also often referenced in work about the expansion of the fashion industry and the development of new strategies of retailing, licensing, and branding, e.g. Corinne Degoutte, 'Stratégies de marques de la mode: convergence ou divergence des modèles de gestion nationaux dans l'industrie de luxe (1860–2003)?' *Entreprises et Histoire* 46 (2007), pp. 125–42.
51. Alexandra Palmer, *Dior* (V&A Publications, 2009).
52. Caroline Evans, 'Masks, Mirrors and Mannequins: Elsa Schiaparelli and the Decentered Subject', *Fashion Theory* 3, no. 1 (1999), pp. 3–32; Caroline Evans, 'Denise Poiret: Muse or Mannequin', in Harold Koda and Andrew Bolton, eds., *Poiret* (Metropolitan Museum of Art, 2007), pp. 27–9.
53. For a discussion of the rarity of analyses of fashion writing versus the visual culture of fashion, see Laird O'Shea Borrelli, 'Dressing Up and Talking about It: Fashion Writing in *Vogue* from 1968 to 1993', *Fashion Theory* 1, no. 3 (1997), pp. 247–59.
54. Roland Barthes, *The Fashion System,* trans. Matthew Ward and Richard Howard (University of California Press, 1983).
55. Ibid., p. xi.
56. Borrelli, 'Dressing Up', p. 248.
57. Pierre Bourdieu, 'But Who Created the "Creators"?' in *Sociology in Question,* trans. Richard Nice (Sage, 1993), p. 140.
58. Caroline Evans, 'Masks, Mirrors and Mannequins'.
59. Andrew Tolson, '"Being Yourself": The Pursuit of Authentic Celebrity', *Discourse Studies* 3, no. 4 (2001), pp. 443–57.
60. For a very helpful explication of the rise of the discourse of celebrity authenticity, see Kurt Curnutt, 'Inside and Outside: Gertrude Stein on Identity, Celebrity, and Authenticity', *Journal of Modern Literature* 23, no. 2 (1999–2000), pp. 291–308.
61. Richard Dyer, '*A Star is Born* and the Construction of Authenticity', in Christine Gledhill, ed., *Stardom: Industry of Desire* (Routledge, 1991), p. 136. Italics in original.
62. Curnutt, 'Inside and Outside', p. 296.

63. Ibid., p. 297.
64. Leo Braudy, *The Frenzy of Renown: Fame and its History* (Vintage, 1986), p. 469.
65. See 'Early Twentieth-Century Fashion Designer Life Writing', *CLCWeb: Comparative Literature and Culture* 13, no. 1 (2011), pp. 1–10. In this article, I offer a reading of aspects of Poiret's and Schiaparelli's memoirs that suggests that melancholy derived from the ascendancy of the industrialized American fashion industry over the French model is a primary condition of professional life for the designer. Here, I engage with the texts more broadly, suggesting that their personae indicate a larger cultural anxiety about fashion and their place in a changing industry.
66. Jens Brockmeier, 'Autobiographical Time', *Narrative Inquiry* 10, no. 1 (2000), p. 63. For more criticism which focuses on the constellation of past and present in life writing, see Susan Marson, 'The Beginning of the End: Time and Identity in the Autobiography of Violette Leduc', *Sites: Journal of Twentieth Century/Contemporary French Studies* 2, no. 1 (1998), pp. 69–87; and Burton Pike, 'Time in Autobiography', *Comparative Literature* 28, no. 4 (1976), pp. 326–43.
67. Rockwell Gray, 'Time Present and Time Past: The Ground of Autobiography', *Soundings* 64, no. 1 (1981), p. 60.
68. Ibid., p. 63.

CHAPTER 1: FASHION AND THE TIME OF MODERN FEMININITY

1. Rita Felski, *The Gender of Modernity* (Harvard University Press, 1995); Rita Felski, 'The Invention of Everyday Life', in *Doing Time: Feminist Theory and Postmodern Culture* (New York University Press, 2000); Rita Felski, 'Telling Time in Feminist Theory', *Tulsa Studies in Women's Literature* 21, no. 1 (2002), pp. 21–7; Anne Witz, 'Georg Simmel and the Masculinity of Modernity', *Journal of Classical Sociology* 3, no. 1 (2001), pp. 353–70; John Jervis, 'Modernity's Sphinx: Woman as Nature and Culture', *Transgressing the Modern: Explorations in the Western Experience of Otherness* (Blackwell, 1999), pp. 107–33.
2. Perhaps the clearest and most explicit examples of this tendency exist in the domain of aesthetics, exemplified by Adolph Loos's 1908 essay, 'Ornament and Crime', in which he aligns the decadence and indeed deathliness of modernity firmly with feminized 'ornament'. Loos, 'Ornament and Crime', in *Ornament and Crime: Selected Essays* (Ariadne Press, 1997), pp. 167–76. For more on the gendered stakes of this designation, see Llewellyn Negrin, 'Ornament and the Feminine', *Feminist Theory* 7, no. 2 (2006), pp. 219–35.
3. An excellent recent study that traces the framing of modern degeneration as feminine can be found in Elizabeth K. Menon, *Evil by Design: The Creation and Marketing of the Femme Fatale* (University of Illinois Press, 2006).
4. Peter Osborne, *The Politics of Time: Modernity and Avant-Garde* (Verso, 1995), p. xii.
5. Tony Meyers, 'Modernity, Post-Modernity, and the Future Perfect', *New Literary History* 32 (2001), p. 36.
6. One significant component of the critical conversation on the entwinement of conceptions of past and present, which I do not treat here in depth but which must be noted, is the literature on nostalgia, which will be treated more fully in Chapter 4 of this volume. As Peter Fritzsche puts it in a formulation that

underscores the mutuality of past and present, the dependence of the new upon the old, and indeed the *construction* of newness: 'nostalgia is a fundamentally modern phenomenon because it depended on the notion of historical process as the continual production of the new.' Peter Fritzsche, 'Specters of History: On Nostalgia, Exile, and Modernity', *American Historical Review* 106, no. 5 (2001), p. 1589.

7. In addition to Osborne, see Jürgen Habermas*, The Philosophical Discourse of Modernity Cambridge* (MIT Press, 1987); Reinhart Koselleck, *Futures Past: On the Semantics of Historical Time*, trans. Keith Tribe (Columbia University Press, 2004); Andrew Benjamin, *Style and Time: Essays on the Politics of Appearance* (Northeastern University Press, 2006); Susan Buck-Morss, 'Revolutionary Time: The Vanguard and the Avant-Garde', in Helga Geyer-Ryan, Paul Koopman, and Klaas Ynterna, eds., *Perception and Experience in Modernity* (Rodopi, 2002), pp. 211–25; Robert Smith, 'Internal Time-Consciousness of Modernism', *Critical Quarterly* 36, no. 3 (1994), pp. 20–9. For analyses from postcolonial studies that similarly maintain the political potential of complex relationships of past and present, see Homi Bhabha, '"Race," Time, and the Revision of Modernity', *Oxford Literary Review* 13, nos. 1–2 (1991), pp. 193–219; Dilip Gaonkar, 'On Alternative Modernities', *Public Culture* 11, no. 1 (1999), pp. 1–18; and Keya Ganguly, 'Temporality and Postcolonial Critique', in Neil Lazarus, ed., *The Cambridge Companion to Postcolonial Literary Studies* (Cambridge University Press, 2004), pp. 162–79.

8. See James Laver with Amy de la Haye, 'Early Europe', in *Costume and Fashion: A Concise History* (Thames and Hudson, 1995), pp. 50–73; and Christopher Breward, 'Medieval Period: Fashioning the Body', in *The Culture of Fashion* (Manchester University Press, 1995), pp. 7–40.

9. Gilles Lipovetsky, *The Empire of Fashion: Dressing Modern Democracy*, trans. Catherine Porter (Princeton University Press, 1994).

10. Ulrich Lehmann, *Tigersprung: Fashion and Modernity* (MIT Press, 2000); Barbara Vinken, 'Eternity: A Frill on the Dress', *Fashion Theory* 1, no. 1 (1997), pp. 59–67; Peter Wollen, 'The Concept of Fashion *in The Arcades Project*', *boundary 2* 30, no. 1 (2002), pp. 131–42; Andrew Benjamin, 'The Time of Fashion: A Commentary on Thesis XIV in Walter Benjamin's "On the Concept of History"', in *Style and Time: Essays on the Politics of Appearance* (Northwestern University Press, 2006), pp. 25–38.

11. Andrew Benjamin, 'The Time of Fashion', p. 25.

12. Though the industrialization of fashion in the early nineteenth century is generally thought to have begun with men's garments, these were military uniforms, and not fashionable clothing for sale on the commodity market. As industrialization advanced and capacity increased in the latter half of the nineteenth century, it was women's garments that came to be identified with fashion. This was due in no small part to the shift known as the Great Masculine Renunciation, in which the dark suit came to be identified as the dress standard for men, ostensibly leaving the changeability and whimsy of fashion to women's clothing. Christopher Breward, in his persuasive *The Hidden Consumer: Masculinities, Fashion, and City Life 1860–1914* (Manchester University Press, 1999), has shown that men's garments were just as subject to fashion as women's. Nevertheless, the association of fashion overwhelmingly with femininity persisted. No doubt this

was enabled by links between fashion's changeability and women's supposed fickleness and triviality.

13. Emily Apter, '"Women's Time" in Theory', *differences* 21, no. 1 (2010), p. 17.
14. Osborne, *The Politics of Time*, p. 5.
15. In discussing the time consciousness of the modern, I am privileging questions of the relationship between past, present and future. There is a different critical dialogue about the question of modernity's emergent historical consciousness as presuming continuity, homogeneity and uniformity. This is Benjamin's critique of historicism. This is not the focus of the present discussion, but is an important, and certainly related, critical conversation.
16. Koselleck, *Futures Past*, p. 14.
17. Ibid., p. 17.
18. Jürgen Habermas, 'Modernity's Consciousness of Time, and its Need for Self-Reassurance', in *The Philosophical Discourse of Modernity: Twelve Lectures* (MIT Press, 1987)*,* p. 6.
19. Meyers, p. 36. Robert Smith describes the anxiety in similar terms: 'Modernism is anxious about the loss of a solid objective, the loss of something behind temporal sequence.' Robert Smith, 'Internal Time-Consciousness', p. 26.
20. Memory became troubling in the nineteenth century—this is the argument of Richard Terdiman's important work, *Present Past: Modernity and the Memory Crisis* (Cornell University Press, 1993). He explores what he calls modernity's 'massive disruption of traditional forms of memory' (p. 5), and traces it to the way that memory insists on the presence of the past. For more on the status of memory in modernity, see Genevieve Lloyd, 'The Past: Loss or Eternal Return?' in *Being in Time: Selves and Narrators in Literature and Philosophy* (Routledge, 1993), pp. 65–82. Psychoanalysis, a thoroughly modern invention, imagines memory to be troubling. Indeed, its repression is foundational to the development of the subject.
21. Osborne, *The Politics of Time,* p. 115.
22. Christina Crosby, *The Ends of History: Victorians and 'the Woman Question'* (Routledge, 1991), p. 5.
23. Ibid., p. 2.
24. Ibid., pp. 146–8.
25. Valerie Bryson, 'Time', in Georgina Blakely and Valerie Bryson, eds., *The Impact of Feminism on Political Concepts and Debates* (Manchester University Press, 2007), p. 161.
26. Felski, 'The Prehistoric Woman', in *The Gender of Modernity* (Harvard University Press, 1995)*,* pp. 35–60; Johannes Fabian, *Time and the Other: How Anthropology Makes its Object* (Columbia University Press, 1983); also see Gaonkar, 'On Alternative Modernities'.
27. For a good discussion of the relationship between conceptions of rationality and time, see Genevieve Lloyd, 'The Public and the Private', in *The Man of Reason: 'Male' and 'Female' in Western Philosophy*, 2nd edn. (Routledge, 2003), pp. 75–86.
28. Nancy L. Green, *Ready-to-Wear and Ready-to-Work: A Century of Industry and Immigrants in Paris and New York* (Duke University Press, 1997).
29. Joanne Entwistle, *The Fashioned Body: Fashion, Dress, and Modern Social Theory* (Policy Press, 2000), p. 105.

30. Charles Baudelaire, 'The Painter of Modern Life', in Jonathan Mayne, trans., *The Painter of Modern Life and Other Essays* (Phaidon, 1965).

31. The chemise dress was the most radical of postrevolutionary styles for women. However, its simple silhouette was common for all fashionable dresses of the late 1790s and first years of the 1800s—even in formal garments such as ball gowns, which were made of more luxurious fabrics, worn with *Directoire*-styled coats and accessorized with other garments. See Laver, *Costume and Fashion*, pp. 148–53. See Valerie Steele, *Paris Fashion: A Cultural History* (Berg, 1998), pp. 48–51, for a discussion of stereotypes of *Directoire* fashion.

32. See Poiret's description of his introduction of the line in his first and most important work of autobiography, *King of Fashion*, trans. Stephen Haden Guest (1930; reprint, V&A Publications, 2009), p. 36.

33. Breward, *The Culture of Fashion*, p. 154. Breward locates the inspiration in the elaborate styles of the 1760s.

34. As Herbert Blau notes, 'the apparent logic of fashion, its undifferentiated monomania, is something of an illusion...[since] alterations in the significant features of dress, line, cut, contour, articulating the body, are still likely to take some time before inhabiting the fashion scene.' *Nothing in Itself: Complexions of Fashion* (Indiana University Press, 1999), p. 89.

35. Benjamin saw fashion as a primary example of eternal recurrence as a condition of industrial capitalism; as a revolutionary historical materialist, he thus associated fashion with petrifaction and death. Benjamin was influenced by the arguments of nineteenth-century Parisian revolutionary Louis-Auguste Blanqui in *L'Eternité par les astres.*

36. Caroline Evans, *Fashion at the Edge: Spectacle, Modernity, Deathliness* (University Press, 2003), p. 9.

37. For more on the question of fashion as a challenge to essentialized feminine identities, see Pamela Church Gibson, 'Redressing the Balance: Patriarchy, Postmodernism, and Feminism', in Pamela Church Gibson and Stella Bruzzi, eds., *Fashion Cultures: Theories, Explorations, and Analysis* (Routledge, 2001), pp. 349–62. Also on this point, see my 'Building a Feminist Theory of Fashion: Karen Barad's Agential Realism', *Australian Feminist Studies* 23, no. 58 (2008), pp. 501–15.

38. Mary Louise Roberts, 'Samson and Delilah Revisited: The Politics of Women's Fashion in 1920s France', *American Historical Review* 98, no. 6 (1993), p. 678.

39. Felski, 'Telling Time', p. 26. For a discussion of repetitive time and everyday life, also see her 'The Invention of Everyday Life'.

40. Felski, 'The Invention of Everyday Life', p. 83.

41. Ibid., p. 85.

42. Evans, *Fashion at the Edge*, pp. 306–7.

43. For more on this question of women as reminders of other temporalities in the new, see Christine Buci-Glucksmann, 'Catastrophic Utopia: The Feminine as Allegory of the Modern', *Representations* 14 (1986), pp. 220–9.

44. Evans, 'Jean Patou's American Mannequins: Early Fashion Shows and Modernism', *Modernism/Modernity* 15, no. 2 (2008), p. 260.

45. Martin Pumphrey, 'The Flapper, the Housewife, and the Making of Modernity', *Cultural Studies* 1, no. 2 (1987), p. 185.

46. Liz Conor, *The Spectacular Modern Woman: Feminine Visibility in the 1920s* (Indiana University Press, 2004).
47. Peter Stallybrass, 'Clothes, Mourning, and the Life of Things', *Yale Review* 81, no. 2 (1993), p. 35.
48. Ibid., p. 36.
49. Representative works include Anne Rosalind Jones and Peter Stallybrass, *Renaissance Clothing and the Materials of Memory* (Cambridge University Press, 2000); Justine Picardie, *My Mother's Wedding Dress* (Bloomsbury, 2005); and Marius Kwint, Christopher Breward and Jeremy Aynsley, eds., *Material Memories: Design and Evocation* (Berg, 1999). Consider, too, the encounters that are said, in that quintessentially modern form, Freudian psychoanalysis, to form the building blocks of (gendered) subjectivity: the theory of fetishism, for instance, turns on a material memory of clothing, whereby the (male) child's desire for his mother is metaphorized into a garment associated with her.
50. This is similar to the reading of modernity proposed by Christine Buci-Glucksmann in *Baroque Reason: The Aesthetics of Modernity*, trans. Patrick Camiller (Sage, 1994), in which she portrays femininity as modernity's forever-haunting counter-figure.
51. Lipovetsky, *The Empire of Fashion*, p. 4.
52. Ibid., p.149.
53. Christine Buci-Glucksmann, *Esthétique de l'éphémère* (Galilée, 2003), p. 25.
54. Ibid., p. 15.
55. Ibid., p. 24.
56. Ibid., p. 44.
57. Elsa Schiaparelli, *Shocking Life* (1954; reprint, V&A Publications, 2007), p. 42.
58. See Chapter Four of this volume for a detailed discussion of Dior's peculiar—and feminized—version of the ephemeral.
59. Pierre Bourdieu with Yvette Delsaut, 'Le couturier et sa griffe: contribution à une théorie de la magie', *Actes de la recherche en sciences sociales* 1, no. 1 (1975), p. 17. 'Le couturier participe d'un art occupant un rang inferieur dans la hiérarchie de la légitimité artistique et il ne peut pas ne pas prendre en compte dans sa pratique l'image sociale de l'avenir de son produit.'
60. Pierre Bourdieu, 'Haute Couture and Haute Culture', in Richard Nice, trans., *Sociology in Question* (Sage, 1993), p. 136.
61. Pierre Bourdieu 'But Who Created the Creators?' in Richard Nice, trans., *Sociology in Question* (Sage, 1993), p. 146.
62. Bourdieu with Delsaut, 'Le couturier et sa griffe', p. 15. 'Discréditer les principes de production et d'évaluation anciens en faisant apparaître un style qui devait une part de son autorité et de son prestige a son ancienneté ("maison de tradition", "maison en...", etc.) comme démodé, hors d'usage, dépassé.'
63. 'Fashion Becomes News', *New York Woman* 1, no. 1 (1936), p. 27.
64. Pierre Bourdieu, 'The Production of Belief: Contribution to an Economy of Symbolic Goods', in Richard Nice, trans., *Media, Culture, and Society 2* (1980), p. 289.
65. Bourdieu, 'Haute Couture and Haute Culture', p. 137.
66. Ibid., p.136.
67. Norbert Hillaire, 'Fashion and Modernity in the Light of Modern and Contemporary Art', *Institut français de la mode Research Report* no. 9 (2008), p. 8.
68. Caroline Evans and Minna Thornton, 'Fashion, Representation, Femininity', *Feminist Review* 38 (1991), p. 48.

CHAPTER 2: PAUL POIRET: CLASSIC AND NEW IN THE STRUGGLE FOR DESIGNER MASTERY

1. Jill Fields notes that '[w]omen in the United States did not toss away their corsets *en masse* after Poiret's introduction of dresses designed to be worn without corsets. Achieving the fashionable line actually still required most women to be corseted.' Jill Fields, '"Fighting the Corsetless Evil": Shaping Corsets and Culture, 1900–1930', in Philip Scranton, ed., *Beauty and Business: Commerce, Gender and Culture in Modern America* (Routledge, 2001), p. 113.
2. Cheryl Buckley and Hilary Fawcett, *Fashioning the Feminine: Representation and Women's Fashion from the Fin de Siècle to the Present* (I. B. Tauris, 2002), p. 55.
3. Harold Koda and Andrew Bolton, 'Preface: The Prophet of Simplicity', in Harold Koda and Andrew Bolton, eds., *Poiret* (Metropolitan Museum of Art, 2007), p. 13.
4. Paul Poiret, *107 Recettes Curiosités Culinaires* (Henri Jonquieres et Compagnie, 1928).
5. 'Poiret: Une silhouette parisienne', *Le miroir des modes* (June 1912), p. 242.
6. 'Etude photographique exécutée pour Vogue par le Baron de Meyer lors de sa récente visite a Paris', *Vogue* (Paris) 1, no. 12 (1 December 1923). 'La Parisienne ne peut pas ne pas aimer Poiret; elle sent en lui un des prêtres les plus convaincus de culte que l'on doit rendre à son corps.'
7. Paul Fuchs, 'Dans le royaume de la mode', *Le Crapouillot* (1 April 1921), pp. 5–6.
8. 'Le roi de la mode parle', *Le Progrès d'Athènes* (18 June 1925), n.p.
9. Paul Poiret, 'The Beauties of my Day', *Harper's Bazaar* (15 September 1938), p. 80.
10. Paul Poiret, *King of Fashion*, trans. Stephen Haden Guest (1930; reprint, V&A Publications, 2009), p. 138.
11. Pierre Bourdieu, 'The Production of Belief: Contribution to an Economy of Symbolic Goods', in Richard Nice , trans., *Media, Culture and Society 2* (1980), p. 267.
12. Ibid., p. 289. Italics in original.
13. Ibid., p. 290.
14. This is essentially a failure to account for the power—or agency—of the consumer of fashion, a tendency which is examined in Agnès Rocamora, 'Fields of Fashion: Critical Insights into Bourdieu's Sociology of Culture', *Journal of Consumer Culture* 2, no. 3 (2002), pp. 341–62.
15. Herbert Blumer offered an initial repudiation of the top-down model of fashion diffusion in 1969, in 'From Class Differentiation to Collective Selection', *The Sociological Quarterly* 10, no. 3 (1969), pp. 275–91. This perspective really took off through work in Cultural Studies, though, with Dick Hebdige's *Subculture: The Meaning of Style* (Methuen, 1979). See also Malcolm Barnard, 'Fashion, Clothing, and Social Revolution', in *Fashion as Communication* (Routledge, 2002), pp. 127–54; Angela Partington, 'Popular Fashion and Working-Class Affluence', in Juliet Ash and Elizabeth Wilson, eds., *Chic Thrills: A Fashion Reader* (Pandora, 1992), pp. 145–61.
16. Of course, Gabrielle (Coco) Chanel's work is also singled out for blame in this regard. But Poiret sees women consumers' predilections as equally, if not more, culpable. See, for example, Paul Poiret, *Revenez-y* (Gallimard, 1932), pp. 100–9; F.-A. Castellant, 'La mode est-elle en danger?' *L'Art et la Mode* (11 June 1927), p. 824; and Paul Poiret, 'The Beauties of my Day, *Harper's Bazaar* (15 September 1938).

17. Pierre Bourdieu with Yvette Delsaut, 'Le couturier et sa griffe: Contribution à une théorie de la magie', *Actes de la recherche en sciences sociales* 1, no. 1 (1975), p. 15. Italics mine. '"Faire la mode" ce n'est pas seulement démoder la mode de l'année précédente, c'est démoder les produits de ceux qui faisaient la mode l'année précédente, donc les déposséder de leur autorité sur la mode. Les stratégies des nouveaux venus...tendent à rejeter vers le passé les plus anciens.'
18. See Efrat Tseëlon, 'From Fashion to Masquerade: Toward an Ungendered Paradigm', in Joanne Entwistle and Elizabeth Wilson, eds., *Body Dressing* (Berg, 2001), pp. 103–20; Catherine Constable, 'Making up the Truth: On Lies, Lipstick, and Friedrich Nietzsche', in Stella Bruzzi and Pamela Church Gibson, eds., *Fashion Cultures: Theories, Explorations, and Analysis* (Routledge, 2000), pp. 191–200.
19. Susan Kaiser, 'Minding Appearances: Style, Truth, and Subjectivity', in Entwistle and Wilson, eds., *Body Dressing* (Berg, 2001), p. 89.
20. Jacques Derrida and Maurizio Ferraris, *A Taste for the Secret* (Polity Press, 2001), p. 31.
21. John Jervis, *Transgressing the Modern: Explorations in the Western Experience of Otherness* (Blackwell, 1999), p. 126.
22. Jeremy Gilbert, 'Public Secrets: Being-With in an Age of Perpetual Disclosure', *Cultural Studies* 21, no. 1 (2007), p. 26.
23. Luise White, 'Telling More: Secrets, Lies, and History', *History and Theory* 39 (2000), p. 22.
24. Ibid.
25. Jack Bratich describes and theorizes the condition of 'spectacular secrecy' in 'Popular Secrecy and Occultural Studies', *Cultural Studies* 21, no. 1 (2007), pp. 42–58.
26. Donna Haraway, 'Situated Knowledges: The Science Question in Feminism and the Privilege of Partial Perspective', in *Simians, Cyborgs, and Women: The Reinvention of Nature* (Routledge, 1991), p. 190.
27. Lorraine Code, 'Is the Sex of the Knower Epistemologically Significant?' in *What Can She Know? Feminist Theory and the Construction of Knowledge* (Cornell University Press, 1991), p. 5.
28. Ellen Bayuk Rosenman, 'Fear of Fashion, or, How the Coquette Got Her Bad Name', in Ilya Parkins and Elizabeth M. Sheehan, eds., *Cultures of Femininity in Modern Fashion* (University Press of New England, 2011), pp. 89–102.
29. Lorraine Code, 'Gossip, or In Praise of Chaos', in *Rhetorical Spaces: Essays on Gendered Locations* (Routledge, 1995), p. 146.
30. Poiret, *King of Fashion*, p. 8.
31. It is unclear which tour these lectures derive from. On one hand, the chapter 'My Lectures to the Americans' follows rather organically from a chapter describing in detail Poiret's first trip to the United States in 1913, and the reader is invited to assume that these lectures were indeed given during that autumn tour. But at least one lecture makes reference to the postwar era, and the lectures share thematic features with other writings from Poiret's late career. It is thus probable that they were given on his autumn 1927 lecture tour.
32. Poiret, *King of Fashion*, p. 160.
33. Ibid., p. 154.
34. Ibid., p. 156.

35. See Evelyn Fox Keller, *Secrets of Life, Secrets of Death* (Routledge, 1992); Carolyn Merchant, *The Death of Nature: Women, Ecology, and the Scientific Revolution* (Harper & Row, 1980); Monica H. Green, 'From "Diseases of Women" to "Secrets of Women": The Transformation of Gynecological Literature in the Later Middle Ages', *Journal of Medieval and Early Modern Studies* 30, no. 1 (2000), pp. 5–40.
36. Green, 'From "Diseases of Women"'', p. 7.
37. Clare Birchall, 'Cultural Studies Confidential', *Cultural Studies* 21, no. 1 (2007), p. 15.
38. Keller, *Secrets of Life*, p. 41.
39. Poiret, *King of Fashion*, p. 160.
40. Ibid., p. 158.
41. Ibid., p. 157.
42. Fuchs, 'Dans le royaume de la mode'.
43. Poiret, *Revenez-y*, pp. 103–4. 'Dompteur faisant claquer son fouet a tout instant pour tenir en haleine et en respect ces fauves, panthères câlines, mais sournoises, toujours prêtes a bondir pour faire du maitre une proie.'
44. Poiret, *King of Fashion*, p. 39.
45. Ibid.
46. Caroline Evans, 'Denise Poiret: Muse or Mannequin', in Harold Koda and Andrew Bolton, eds., *Poiret* (Metropolitan Museum of Art, 2007), p. 27.
47. Poiret, *King of Fashion*, p. 100.
48. 'Poiret: Une silhouette Parisienne', p. 242: '[P]lus on maitrise le passé, plus on a puissance pour dompter l'avenir.'
49. Poiret, *King of Fashion*, p. 36.
50. Ibid., p. 2.
51. Ibid., p. 5.
52. Ibid., p. 14.
53. Ibid.
54. Ibid., p. 15.
55. Moreover, as Bourdieu has shown in his work on fashion—and on culture more generally—the valuation of stylistic 'revolution' is not opposed to the bourgeoisie; it is intrinsic to the development of bourgeois culture. In the field of fashion, the bourgeoisie and the revolutionaries—which correspond well to the political distinction between right and left, and the Parisian Right Bank and Left Bank—occupy the same field, with revolutionaries ultimately playing the game according to the rules and bourgeoisie acceding happily to 'revolution'. '[T]he left-bank couturiers have strategies that aim to overthrow the very principles of the game—but always in the name of the game, the spirit of the game.' Pierre Bourdieu, 'Haute Couture and Haute Culture', in Richard Nice, trans., *Sociology in Question* (Sage, 1997), p. 134.
56. Poiret does, as do many contemporary theorists of fashion, define fashion as change: 'la mode, par définition c'est le changement.' 'La Mode', *La Voix professionnelle* (January 1923), n.p.
57. Poiret, *King of Fashion*, p. 138.
58. *Le Petit Parisien* (13 March 1923). 'Comme les évolutions de la nature, les transitions de la mode se font suivant une ligne continue, et non par bonds. Hier contient aujourd'hui, qui annonce demain.' 'Pourquoi les accessoires de la mode souffrent-ils d'une crise?'

59. Elizabeth Grosz, *Nick of Time: Politics, Evolution, and the Untimely* (Duke University Press, 2004); 'Thinking the New', in Elizabeth Grosz, ed., *Becomings: Explorations in Time, Memory, and Futures* (Cornell University Press, 1999); and 'Darwin and Feminism: Preliminary Investigations for a Possible Alliance', in Stacy Alaimo and Susan Hekman, eds., *Material Feminisms* (Indiana University Press, 2008).
60. Poiret, *King of Fashion*, p. 138.
61. Ibid., p. 158.
62. 'Poiret Insists on the Jupe Culotte', *New York Times* (15 March 1914).
63. Rose Lee, 'A King of Fashion Speaks from his St. Helena', *New York Times* (10 May 1931).
64. Paul Poiret, 'Quelques considérations sur la mode', *Le Figaro* (2 July 1924). 'Le couturier d'avant-garde—et je n'ai pas besoin de dire que c'est mon cas—doit avoir l'esprit bien trempé, les yeux vifs et le poing solide. Il doit être tenace et clairvoyant.'
65. 'Poiret: Une Silhouette parisienne', p. 242. '[L]es endroits comme Trouville, Biarritz, Baden ne m'amusent pas, mes distractions sont d'un ordre plus élevé. Volontiers, je dirige mes pas vers les pays ou l'Art trouve sa plus haute expression; c'est de l'antiquité que je m'inspire.'
66. Al. Terego, 'Les Opinions de Monsieur Pétrone', *La Grande Revue* (10 May 1910), pp. 157–8. 'Elle le sait par intuition, par atavisme, sans doute. Son grand-mère faisait des cocardes pendant la Révolution, et c'est son grand-père qui a décoré de fleurs et d'oiseaux bleus les jolis pots de pharmacie. D'ailleurs, tous ses aïeux, depuis des siècles…ont exercé leur activité dans des industries dont les productions…témoignent d'une adresse subtile et d'un sens artistique sans cesse perfectionné à travers les générations.'
67. Paul Poiret, 'The Beauties of my Day', p. 80.
68. Ibid., p. 81.
69. Ibid., p. 106.
70. Ibid., p. 80.
71. Peter Fritzsche, 'Specters of History: On Nostalgia, Exile, and Modernity', *American Historical Review* 106, no. 5 (2001), p. 1592.
72. Poiret, 'The Beauties of my Day', p. 106.
73. Paul Poiret, 'Paris, sans nuits, s'ennuie', *Paris-Soir* (14 July 1932). '[L]a tournure rendait les femmes charmantes parce qu'elle constituait un défi du bon sens, une affirmation de leur indépendance et de leur dédain des choses logiques.'
74. Genevieve Lloyd, 'Reason and Progress', in *The Man of Reason: 'Male' and 'Female' in Western Philosophy*, 2nd edn (Routledge, 2002), pp. 58–74.
75. Ibid., p. 58.
76. Poiret, *Revenez-y*, pp. 96–7. '[J]e les vois tous les deux armés d'un optique spéciale, habiles à adapter pour une clientèle moyenne et les diffuser dans diverses couches de la société. [Cela] leur refuse l'accès au titre de couturier et de créateur.'
77. See, for example, Terego, 'Les Opinions de Monsieur Petrone'.
78. Ibid.
79. 'Our Girls Puritans, is M. Poiret's Idea', *New York Times* (14 October 1913).
80. 'New York Has no Laughter and no Young Girls', *New York Times* (19 October 1913).

81. 'Paul Poiret Here to Tell of his Art', *New York Times* (21 September 1913). I elaborate upon Poiret's—and Schiaparelli's—geographies of fashionability across the United States and France in 'Early Twentieth-Century Fashion Designer Life Writing', *CLCWeb: Comparative Literature and Culture* 13, no. 1 (2011), pp. 1–10.

82. Troy, *Couture Culture*, p. 322.

83. Ibid., p. 323.

84. Paul Poiret, 'Comment se lance une mode—Ce qui Nous dit M. Paul Poiret', *En Attendant* (February 1923), n.p. '[A]ujourd'hui, la démocratie a pris nettement l'avantage. Etant la majorité, c'est elle qui impose ses tendances. La femme du monde a, en quelque sorte, peur d'innover. Elle se laisse conduite.'

85. Castellant, 'La mode est-elle en danger?' p. 824.

86. Poiret expresses a very real sense that a top-down model of fashion diffusion—one that preserved hierarchies, diffusing fashion from the designer down through the elite and finally to the masses—has given way to a bottom-up model, whereby the masses determine fashion. 'In the past, in the Second Empire, for instance, the light came down from on high: elegance. Fashions were launched by Empress Eugenie, or, for men, the Prince of Sagan. The aristocracy of both sexes hurried to adopt the style of a dress, the cut of a jacket or the shape of a tie. These days, it happens the other way around. The movement is from bottom to top.' Poiret, 'Comment se lance une mode', n.p. 'Autrefois, sous le second empire, par exemple, c'était d'en haut que venait la lumière, et l'occurrence: l'élégance. La mode, c'était lancée par l'Impératrice Eugénie ou, pour les hommes, par le prince de Sagan. L'aristocratie des deux sexes s'empressait aussitôt d'adopter le modèle d'une robe, la coupe d'une jaquette ou la forme d'une cravate.'

87. Harvie Ferguson, *Modernity and Subjectivity: Body, Soul, and Spirit* (University Press of Virginia, 2000), p. 40.

88. *Art et Phynance* (Lutetia, 1934) is a highly detailed and vengeful narrative of Poiret's dealings with the business interests who bankrupted him.

89. Consider the fusion of the figures of 'woman' and 'commodity' in industrial modernity, as exposed by Abigail Solomon-Godeau in 'The Other Side of Venus'. Caroline Evans brilliantly shows how standardization is embodied in feminine terms through the figure of the 'mannequin'—the live model—in the 1910s and 1920s. See Caroline Evans, 'Multiple, Movement, Model, Mode: The Fashion Parade 1900–1929', in Christopher Breward and Caroline Evans, eds., *Fashion and Modernity* (Berg, 2005); and Caroline Evans, 'Jean Patou's American Mannequins: Early Fashion Shows and Modernism', *Modernism/Modernity* 15, no. 2 (2008), pp. 243–63.

90. Troy, *Couture Culture*, p. 304. The words 'artist and innovator' are taken from a publicity brochure released by Poiret's house in 1917.

91. See 'Ex-Fashion Dictator Now Drawing the Dole', *The Glasgow Record* (13 August 1934); 'Poiret's New Start: Fashion Leader Saved from Dole', *Daily Sketch* (London) (16 August 1934); 'Paul Poiret, chômeur', *L'Ordre* (17 August 1934); 'Une conversation avec un chômeur de marque', *La Revue* (Lausanne) (2 January 1935).

92. 'Paul Poiret Dies; Dress Designer, 64', *New York Times* (3 May 1944).

93. Penelope Deutscher, *Yielding Gender: Feminism, Deconstruction, and the History of Philosophy* (Routledge, 1997), p. 7.

CHAPTER 3: ELSA SCHIAPARELLI: GLAMOUR, PRIVACY AND TIMELESSNESS

1. 'Haute Couture', *Time* (13 August 1934), p. 50.
2. Elsa Schiaparelli, *Shocking Life* (1954; reprint, V&A Publications, 2007), p. vii.
3. For a thorough discussion of Schiaparelli as a split subject, see Caroline Evans, 'Masks, Mirrors and Mannequins: Elsa Schiaparelli and the Decentered Subject', *Fashion Theory* 3, no. 1 (1999), pp. 3–32.
4. See the description of the classic subject of autobiography in Sidonie Smith, 'The Universal Subject, Female Embodiment, and the Consolidation of Autobiography', in *Subjectivity, Identity, and the Body: Women's Autobiographical Practice in the Twentieth Century* (Indiana University Press, 1993), pp. 1–23.
5. Schiaparelli, *Shocking Life*, p. 42.
6. Schiaparelli recalls feelings after a surgery near the end of her career: 'though I was in every way physically well, I lived in much closer contact with the beyond' (ibid., p. 203). In an earlier section, she states: 'the only real sin is what one does against the divine side of oneself—what is usually called the soul' (p. 11).
7. Christian Lacroix, 'Schiaparelli vue par Christian Lacroix: une mode "décapante"', *Le Monde* (28–29 March 2004). 'Mais lorsque, enfant ou adolescent, dans les années 1960, j'ai découvert son style dans les vieilles revues de l'époque trouvées dans ma famille ou aux Puces, le choc de tant de modernité était vraiment "décapant."' Elle est aujourd'hui.
8. Of course, for Lacroix to declare in 2004 that 'she is today', he in a sense imagines that she transcends time, transcends the end of her fashion career in 1954 and her death in 1974, to be present in the millennium. She remains a mobile subject, able to travel across time by way, paradoxically, of her continued existence in a timeless (spiritual) realm.
9. 'Schiaparelli', *Harper's Bazaar* (April 1932), n.p.
10. Schiaparelli, *Shocking Life*, p. 41.
11. Ibid., p. 42.
12. Ibid.
13. Carol S. Gould, 'Glamour as an Aesthetic Property of Persons', *Journal of Aesthetics and Art Criticism* 63, no. 3 (2005), p. 238. The associations of glamour with magic are also noted in Elizabeth Wilson, 'A Note on Glamour', *Fashion Theory* 11, no. 1 (2007), pp. 95–6; and its particular evocation of magical *transformation* is discussed in Judith Brown, *Glamour in Six Dimensions: Modernism and the Radiance of Form* (Cornell University Press, 2009), p. 10.
14. Wilson, 'A Note on Glamour', p. 100.
15. Virginia Postrel in Joseph Rosa, ed., *Glamour: Fashion + Industrial Design + Architecture* (Yale University Press, 2004), cited in Wilson, 'A Note on Glamour', p. 100.
16. Wilson, 'A Note on Glamour', p. 100.
17. Brown, *Glamour*, pp. 4–5.
18. Stephen Gundle, 'Mapping the Origins of Glamour: Giovanni Boldini, Paris, and the Belle Époque', *Journal of European Studies* 29 (1999), p. 270.
19. Wilson, 'A Note on Glamour', pp. 96–7.
20. The work that is invariably invoked in the glamour literature to make this case is Georg Simmel's 'The Metropolis and Modern Life', in David Frisby and Mike Featherstone, eds., *Simmel on Culture* (Sage, 1997), pp. 174–85.

21. That being said, in *Glamour in Six Dimensions*, Judith Brown makes an elegant case for the existence of forms of glamour that are masculinized or, ultimately, ungendered. But certainly the everyday grammar of glamour as it was mediated in popular culture was borne by women, and this was particularly the case in its connections with fashion.
22. Gundle, 'Mapping the Origins of Glamour', p. 270.
23. Brown, *Glamour*, p. 1.
24. In this sense, glamour strongly resembles the character of fashion, its ability to bring together the eternal and the transitory. Christine Buci-Glucksmann accounts for the relevance and potential of this ghosting of modernity for women in 'Catastrophic Utopia: The Feminine as Allegory of the Modern', *Representations* 14 (Spring 1986), pp. 220–9.
25. Joshua Gamson notes that the careful balancing of the ordinary and the extraordinary is one of the hallmarks of modern celebrity, in *Claims to Fame: Celebrity in Contemporary America* (University of California Press, 1994), p. 31.
26. Brown, *Glamour*, p. 101.
27. On glamour and the intellect, see Colbey Emmerson Reid, 'Glamour and the "Fashionable Mind"', *Soundings* 89, nos. 3–4 (2006), pp. 301–19.
28. Gould, 'Glamour as an Aesthetic Quality', p. 243.
29. Jane Gaines provides a helpful discussion of the historical emergence of an ideology of correspondence between costume and personality, in 'Costume and Narrative: How Dress Tells the Woman's Story', in Jane Gaines and Charlotte Herzog, eds., *Fabrications: Costume and the Female Body* (Routledge, 1990).
30. Georg Simmel, 'Adornment' and 'The Philosophy of Fashion', in Frisby and Featherstone, eds., *Simmel on Culture*, pp. 206–10 and pp. 187–205. In 'Notes on Glamour', cited above, Elizabeth Wilson makes a passing reference to the connection between glamour and Simmel's theory of fashion, p. 98.
31. Evans, 'Masks, Mirrors and Mannequins', pp. 4–5.
32. Of course, the professed difference between a public and private self has been revealed as a hallmark of celebrity self-narration, necessary for the viewer's sense that an authentic self rests behind the public persona. See my discussion in the Introduction.
33. Schiaparelli, *Shocking Life*, p. vii.
34. Janet Flanner, 'Profiles: Comet', *New Yorker* (18 June 1932), p. 20.
35. Robyn Gibson, 'Schiaparelli, Surrealism, and the Desk Suit', *Dress* 30 (2003), p. 51.
36. Evans, 'Masks, Mirrors, and Mannequins', p. 14.
37. Schiaparelli, *Shocking Life*, p. 187.
38. Commentators frequently note that one of the innovations that Schiaparelli represents is her comfortable positioning at the centre of the elite she clothed. As Palmer White puts it, 'the first generation couturiers, from 1860 to 1930, were considered by the *beau monde* whom they clothed to be tradespeople.' Palmer White, *Elsa Schiaparelli: Empress of Paris Fashion* (Aurum Press, 1996), p. 91. No longer was there a distinction between the *couturier* as a worker, and the wealthy and prominent clientele. Though Jacques Doucet and certainly Poiret first began to aspire to the society for whom they worked, Schiaparelli was the first to fully and unproblematically integrate these two worlds. Billy Boy suggests that Poiret became a caricature in his attempts to become part of this world. See Guillaume Garnier, 'Schiaparelli vue par', in *Hommage à Schiaparelli* (Ville

de Paris, Musée de la mode et du costume, 1984), p. 78. Evans discusses this fusion of the world of fashion and the elite in a section called 'Parties', in 'Masks, Mirrors and Mannequins', pp. 25–7.

39. The hat is described in *Shocking Life*, p. 68.
40. Ibid., p. 49.
41. 'She was the most enthusiastic and convincing model of her own creations.' Garnier, 'Schiaparelli vue par', p. 76. 'Elsa Schiaparelli est elle-même le manne-quin le plus enthousiaste et le plus convaincant de ses propres créations.' As Palmer White notes, 'she was to be seen everywhere, and she sold her clothes by wearing them in public.' White, *Elsa Schiaparelli*, p. 91.
42. Garnier, 'Schiaparelli vue par', pp. 81–2. 'Elle a su pondérer, dans l'ensemble, la juste proportion de bizarrerie que comportait son image publique.'
43. Chanel also fashioned herself as an emblem of her brand. See Valerie Steele, 'Chanel in Context', in Juliet Ash and Elizabeth Wilson, eds., *Chic Thrills: A Fashion Reader* (University of California Press, 1992), pp. 118–26.
44. 'Entretien avec Gladys C. Fabre', in *Hommage à Schiaparelli*, p. 140. Interviewer: 'On pourrait dire que ce qui comptait, pour Schiaparelli, c'était le cadre de la vie dans son ensemble.' Gladys C. Fabre: 'C'est bien ca. Le jardin ratissé, soigné à l'extérieur, était aussi important que les tableaux et les meubles à l'intérieur. L'ensemble racontait les vertus, les passions et les partis-pris de la dame du lieu.'
45. Kathleen M. Helal, 'Celebrity, Femininity, Lingerie: Dorothy Parker's Autobio-graphical Monologues', *Women's Studies* 33, no. 1 (2004), pp. 97–8.
46. These are indeed the terms by which Schiaparelli explains her decision to retire from her business; she suggests that the couture house 'by now owned and claimed me too tyrannically.' *Shocking Life*, p. 207.
47. Schiaparelli, *Shocking Life*, p. viii.
48. Ibid., pp. 12, 18.
49. Ibid., p. 155.
50. Flanner, 'Profiles: Comet', p. 23.
51. 'Haute Couture', p. 50.
52. Schiaparelli, *Shocking Life*, p. 67.
53. After the First World War and in the context of the myth of the depopulation of the country in the war, France was obsessed with rebuilding its 'national stock' through women. Pro-natalist propaganda which exhorted women to give birth to many children, but *only in the context of marriage*, was a major feature of the ideological and political landscape.
54. One may exist privately, of course, but none is publicly available or known even to the most authoritative researchers.
55. Schiaparelli, *Shocking Life*, p. 51.
56. Ibid., pp. 3, 110.
57. Ibid., p. 22.
58. For a useful discussion of silence as a form of communication, see Cheryl Glenn, *Unspoken: The Rhetoric of Silence* (Southern Illinois University Press, 2004), especially 'Defining Silence', pp. 2–19.
59. Efrat Tseëlon, 'From Fashion to Masquerade: Toward an Ungendered Paradigm', in Joanne Entwistle and Elizabeth Wilson, eds., *Body Dressing* (Berg, 2001), pp. 103–20.
60. Schiaparelli, *Shocking Life*, p. 55.

61. Ibid., p. 3

62. 'The Paris Dress Parade: As seen by a man', *Vogue* (London) (14 September 1932), p. 33.

63. Dorothy Brassington, 'Noted Designer's Sparkling Styles', *Seattle Post-Intelligencer* (21 February 1935).

64. 'Schiaparelli Sees Paris Style Mecca', *New York Times* (11 December 1940).

65. Schiaparelli, *Shocking Life*, p. 41.

66. Ibid., p. 192.

67. Ibid., p. 182.

68. Ibid., p. 147.

69. Ibid., p. 148.

70. Ibid., p. 207.

71. In his classic essay, Huyssen argues that high cultural modernists figured mass culture as feminine and engaged in a spirited defence of an implicitly masculinized high culture. Andreas Huyssen, 'Mass Culture as Woman: Modernism's Other', in *After the Great Divide: Modernism, Mass Culture, Postmodernism* (Indiana University Press, 1986), pp. 44–63. For a related argument, see Ann Douglas, *Terrible Honesty: Mongrel Manhattan in the 1920s* (Farrar, Straus and Giroux, 1996), in which she argues that the modernist impulse is 'matricidal' in response to the feminized culture of the nineteenth century.

72. Schiaparelli, *Shocking Life*, p. 129.

73. Ibid., p. 159.

74. 'Schiaparelli on Shopping Trip', *Lowell Sun* (Massachusetts) (4 January 1937).

75. Schiaparelli, *Shocking Life*, p. 26.

76. Ibid., p. 206.

77. Interview with Charles Collingwood, *Person to Person* (CBS) (18 March 1960).

78. On serialization and interchangeability of women in the fashion industry, see Caroline Evans's work on models in 'Multiple, Movement, Model, Mode: The Mannequin Parade 1900–1929', in Christopher Breward and Caroline Evans, eds., *Fashion and Modernity* (Berg, 2005), pp. 125–46; and 'Jean Patou's American Mannequins: Early Fashion Shows and Modernism', *Modernism/Modernity* 15, no. 2 (2008), pp. 242–63.

79. 'There is Only One Schiaparelli', *Women's Wear Daily* (26 May 1933), p. 4.

80. Schiaparelli, *Shocking Life*, p. 55.

81. Ibid., p. 104.

82. Mary Louise Roberts outlines the way that fashion materialized a changing gender order for women, arguing that '[t]he fantasy of liberation [that new fashions created] then became a cultural reality in itself that was not without importance'. 'Samson and Delilah Revisited: The Politics of Women's Fashion in 1920s France', *American Historical Review* 98, no. 3 (1993), p. 682.

83. Schiaparelli, *Shocking Life*, pp. 158–9.

84. Ibid., p. 159.

85. Direct response to war does not necessarily mean sobriety. As Schiaparelli notes, and as the popularity of Dior's creations attest, the aftermath of this World War brought with it a certain stylistic levity.

86. Schiaparelli, *Shocking Life*, p. vii.

87. Ibid., p. 198.

88. Burton Pike, 'Time in Autobiography', *Comparative Literature* 28, no. 4 (1976), p. 333.

89. Ibid., p. 335.
90. Schiaparelli, *Shocking Life*, p. 12.
91. Ibid., p. 55.
92. For more on the emergence of a concept of lifestyle in women's lives, see Martin Pumphrey, 'The Flapper, the Housewife, and the Making of Modernity', *Cultural Studies* 1, no. 2 (1987), pp. 179–94.
93. Schiaparelli, *Shocking Life*, p. 9.
94. For example, she is critical of the way that in America, 'the commercial sense would take advantage of death' (ibid., p. 57). Schiaparelli is also careful to note that '[u]nlike many women I have never received any important gifts of jewels, money, or material possessions' (p. 179).
95. 'The Case of "Hair Up Versus Hair Down" is Reopened in Paris', *Women's Wear Daily* (11 February 1938).
96. Schiaparelli, *Shocking Life*, p. 209.
97. Ibid.

CHAPTER 4: CHRISTIAN DIOR: NOSTALGIA AND THE ECONOMY OF FEMININE BEAUTY

1. Christian Dior, *Dior by Dior*, trans. Antonia Fraser (1957; V&A Publications, 2007), pp. 22–3.
2. For a comprehensive discussion of the changes in fashion during the Occupation, see Dominique Veillon, *Fashion Under the Occupation*, trans. Miriam Kochan (Berg, 2002). Also see Lou Taylor, 'The Work and Function of the Paris Couture Industry during the German Occupation of 1940–1944', *Dress* 22 (2005), pp. 34–44.
3. Taylor, 'The Work and Function of the Paris Couture Industry', p. 38. Also see Sarah Wilson, 'Collaboration in the Fine Arts', in Gerhard Hirschfeld and Patrick Marsh, eds., *Collaboration in France: Politics and Culture during the Nazi Occupation, 1940–1944* (Berg, 1989), pp. 103–25.
4. On Vichy's war against 'decadence', see Robert Paxton, *Vichy France: Old Guard and New Order 1940–44*, revised edn (Columbia University Press, 2001), pp. 146–8. For specific applications of this perception in the visual arts and design, see Michele Cone, *Artists under Vichy: A Case of Prejudice and Persecution* (Princeton University Press, 1992), especially pp. 65–82.
5. Francine Muel-Dreyfus, *Vichy and the Eternal Feminine: A Contribution to the Political Sociology of Gender*, trans. Kathleen A. Johnson (Duke University Press, 2001), p. 5.
6. Alexandra Palmer, *Dior* (V&A Publications, 2009), p. 32.
7. Barbara Gabriel, 'The Wounds of Memory: Mavis Gallant's "Baum, Gabriel (1935–)," National Trauma, and Postwar French Cinema', *Essays on Canadian Writing* 80 (2003), p. 199.
8. See, for instance, Rhonda Garelick, 'High Fascism', *New York Times* (6 March 2011). In the wake of Dior designer John Galliano's dismissal for a vitriolic anti-Semitic outburst in early 2011, claims circulated on the Internet and in some press reports that, presumably because of his employment at Lelong, Dior 'dressed the wives of Nazi officers'. This account suggests an active collaboration. Dominique Veillon shows that the number of fashion ration cards issued to

German women during the war never exceeded 200—about 1 per cent of the total number issued (pp. 116–17); certainly, the primary activity of *haute couture* during this period remained clothing French women. Veillon does, however, identify a 1941 agreement between Lelong and German-financed newspaper *Paris-Soir*, in which the paper would give Lelong free publicity in exchange for his supplying gowns to four women; this certainly implicates Lelong in a variety of accommodation of the German regime (p. 118). As well, Sarah Wilson notes that Lelong was photographed with Hitler's sculptor, Arno Breker, at the private viewing of Breker's Paris exhibition in May 1942. Wilson, 'Collaboration in the Fine Arts', p. 119. This narrative is complicated, however, by the fact that Lelong suggested in the immediate aftermath of the Liberation that 'the minister of industrial production...create a commission to purge couture' (Veillon, p. 142) of wartime collaborators. Lelong himself was tried under these auspices for his 1942 negotiations with a German administrator but he was acquitted. Veillon, *Fashion under the Occupation*, pp. 92–3. All in all, Lelong's is a complex case, and so ascertaining Dior's role vis-à-vis the Occupation is difficult.

9. Palmer, *Dior*, p. 32.
10. Marie-France Pochna, *Christian Dior: The Man Who Made the World Look New*, trans. Joanna Savill (Arcade Publishing, 1996), p. 166.
11. This quotation is from the original French biography by Pochna—certain passages were omitted in the English translation. Marie-France Pochna, *Christian Dior* (Flammarion, 1994), p. 30. 'D'une femme bourgeoise et arriviste, le fils fabrique un idéal de douceur, de féminité, de délicatesse.'
12. Elissa Marder, 'The Sex of Death and the Maternal Crypt', *Parallax* 15, no. 1 (2009), p. 7.
13. *Dior by Dior*, p. viii.
14. Ibid.
15. Ibid., p. 194.
16. Ibid.
17. Ibid.
18. Ibid., p. 61.
19. Christian Dior, *Talking about Fashion*, as told to Élie Rabourdin and Alice Chavane, trans. Eugenia Shepherd (Putnam, 1954), p. 36.
20. *Dior by Dior*, p. 22.
21. Dior writes: 'Probably the simplest way to give an idea of my own character is to take you with me into various different houses where I have lived from childhood onwards.' Ibid., p. 167. For a detailed exposition of Dior's anchoring of his nostalgic selfhood in particular spaces, see Ilya Parkins and Lara Haworth, 'The Public Time of Private Space in *Dior by Dior*', *Biography* 35, no. 3 (2012).
22. Ibid., p. 122.
23. Ibid., p. 171.
24. Jean Starobinski, 'The Idea of Nostalgia', trans. William Kemp, *Diogenes* 14 (1966), p. 84.
25. For the early history of the concept, see Starobinski, 'The Idea of Nostalgia', and Svetlana Boym, 'From Cured Soldiers to Incurable Romantics: Nostalgia and Progress', in *The Future of Nostalgia* (Basic Books, 2001), pp. 3–18.
26. Marcos Piason Natali, 'The Politics of Nostalgia: An Essay on Ways of Relating to the Past' (PhD diss., University of Chicago, 2000), p. 20.

27. Peter Fritzsche, 'Specters of History: On Nostalgia, Exile, and Modernity', *American Historical Review* 106, no. 5 (2001), p. 1588.

28. Boym, *The Future of Nostalgia*, p. 11.

29. Vladimir Yankélévitch, *L'irréversible et la nostalgie* (Flammarion, 1974), p. 290. 'L'objet de la nostalgie ce n'est pas tel ou tel passé, mais c'est bien plutôt le fait du passé, autrement dit la passéité.'

30. Fritzsche, 'Specters of History', p. 1588; Terdiman, *Present Past: Modernity and the Memory Crisis* (Cornell University Press, 1993), chapters 1 and 2.

31. See Boym, *The Future of Nostalgia;* Natali, 'The Politics of Nostalgia'; Fritzsche, 'Specters of History'; Michael Pickering and Emily Keightley, 'Modalities of Nostalgia', *Current Sociology* 54, no. 6 (2006), pp. 919–41; Fred Davis, *Yearning for Yesterday: A Sociology of Nostalgia* (The Free Press, 1979).

32. Davis, *Yearning for Yesterday*, pp. 10–11.

33. Elissa Marder, *Dead Time: Temporal Disorders in the Wake of Modernity* (Stanford University Press, 2001), p. 8.

34. Ibid., p. 52.

35. Ibid., p. 35.

36. Rémy G. Saisselin, 'From Baudelaire to Christian Dior: The Poetics of Fashion', *The Journal of Aesthetics and Art Criticism* 18, no. 1 (1959), p. 114.

37. Richard Martin and Harold Koda, 'Introduction', in *Christian Dior* (Metropolitan Museum of Art, 1996), n.p.

38. Edward S. Casey, 'The World of Nostalgia', *Man and World* 20, no. 4 (1987), p. 367.

39. Sean Scanlan, 'Narrating Nostalgia: Modern Literary Homesickness in New York Narratives, 1809–1925' (PhD diss., University of Iowa, 2008), p. 26.

40. *Dior by Dior*, p. 74. Dior's detailed descriptions of the design process in both *Dior by Dior* and *Talking about Fashion* make central the women involved in it. See the chapter 'From the "Toile" to the Dress' in *Dior by Dior* and 'The Collection is Born' in *Talking about Fashion*, pp. 31–75. It is telling that Dior decided to devote so much of this space, ostensibly intended for him to tell his own story, to the women with whom he worked. Biographer Pochna notes that 'Dior always showed the greatest respect and concern for his workrooms and apprentices and the spiritual importance of their craft.' Pochna, *Christian Dior* (English translation), p. 236.

41. Dior, *Talking about Fashion*, pp. 24–5.

42. For a useful overview of feminist approaches to the gendered distinction between art as masculine and craft as feminine, see Llewellyn Negrin, 'Ornament and the Feminine', *Feminist Theory* 7, no. 2 (2006), pp. 219–35.

43. Esmeralda de Réthy and Jean-Louis Perreau, *Monsieur Dior et nous* (Anthèse, 1999), p. 110. The fatherly attitude is further revealed in the book's anecdotes from former workers.

44. Pochna, *Christian Dior*, p. 222.

45. *Dior by Dior*, p. 12.

46. Ibid., p. 13.

47. In *Monsieur Dior et nous*, Réthy and Perreau call Raymonde Dior's 'alter ego', p. 32.

48. For example, see Katya Foreman, 'The Muse: Mitzah Bricard', *WWD* (27 February 2007). In 2009, John Galliano—then the house of Christian Dior's designer—designed a collection inspired by Mme Bricard.

49. *Dior by Dior*, p. 12.
50. Dior, *Talking about Fashion*, p. 48.
51. Ibid.
52. *Dior by Dior*, p. 13.
53. Ibid.
54. Judith Brown, *Glamour in Six Dimensions: Modernism and the Radiance of Form* (Cornell University Press, 2009), p. 5.
55. Ibid., p. 7.
56. Ibid., p. 86.
57. Ibid., p. 87.
58. Françoise Giroud, *Christian Dior*, trans. Sascha Van Dorssen (Rizzoli, 1987), p. 17.
59. *Dior by Dior*, p. 7.
60. Ibid, p. 8.
61. Ibid.
62. Ibid., p. 193.
63. Christian Dior, 'Dior', *Modern Woman* (April 1952), p. 31.
64. *Dior by Dior*, p. 52.
65. 'As for the few visits I made to my father's factories, they have left appalling memories: I am sure my horror of machines and my firm resolve never to work in an office or anything like it date from then.' *Dior by Dior*, pp. 168–9.
66. 'Banking? A government job? An ordered life with regular hours? All that was out of the question.' Dior, *Talking about Fashion*, p. 4.
67. *Dior by Dior*, p. 64.
68. Ibid., p. 79.
69. Dior, *Talking about Fashion*, p. 34.
70. *Dior by Dior*, p. 62.
71. Ibid., p. 79. Later Dior stresses that he is 'a very unnatural father, because once the opening of the collection is over, I lose interest in my children, and practically never see them again' (p. 114).
72. Ibid., pp. 57–8.
73. Ibid., p. 189.
74. Ibid., p. 147.
75. Christian Dior, interview with Edward Murrow, *Person to Person* on CBS (11 April 1955).
76. Indeed, the whole interview can be analyzed as an ironic text, with Murrow's apparent admiration for Dior undercut by the interviewer's subtle attempts to distance himself from any knowledge of the fashion industry.
77. Ellen Bayuk Rosenman, 'Fear of Fashion; or, How the Coquette Got Her Bad name', in Ilya Parkins and Elizabeth M. Sheehan, eds., *Cultures of Femininity in Modern Fashion* (University Press of New England, 2011), p. 95.
78. Interview with Edward Murrow, *Person to Person*.
79. Christian Dior, 'Texte de 1957', in *Conférences écrites par Christian Dior* (Institut français de la mode/Editions du regard, 2003), pp. 33–4. 'Heureusement—je vous avais dit dès le début—le couturier dispose, de sa part, des meilleurs avocats du monde: ses mannequins. Chaque fois qu'il s'apprête à leur donner la parole—comme je le fais maintenant—il espère que leur élégance lui vaudra l'indulgence du jury.'
80. *Dior by Dior*, p. 136.
81. Ibid., p. 132.

82. Saisselin, 'From Baudelaire to Christian Dior', p.114.
83. Ibid., p. 115.
84. *Dior by Dior*, p. 27.
85. Ibid., p. 189.
86. Marder, *Dead Time*, p. 34.
87. '[I]n order to "chop up time", Baudelaire must first redefine space as enclosure and the female body as something that has no "openings": no mouth, no eyes, no hands, no fingers, sex or breasts.' Ibid., p. 40.
88. Caroline Evans, 'Jean Patou's American Mannequins: Early Fashion Shows and Modernism', *Modernism/Modernity* 15, no. 2 (2008), p. 261.
89. Dior, *Talking about Fashion*, p. 78.
90. For early analyses of this capacity, see Lucien Francois, 'Christian Dior', in *Comment un nom deviant une griffe* (Gallimard, 1961), pp. 221–9; and Catherine Perreau, *Christian Dior* (Helpé, 1953). For a recent, historicized critical reading, see Alexandra Palmer, *Dior*, especially 'Chapter Five: Global Expansion and Licences'.
91. Dior, *Talking About Fashion*, p. 101.
92. Ibid., p. 104.
93. Joanne Entwistle, *The Aesthetic Economy of Fashion: Markets and Values in Clothing and Modelling* (Berg, 2009), p. 6.
94. Walter Benjamin, 'Paris, the Capital of the Nineteenth Century <Exposé of 1935>', in Howard Eiland and Kevin McLaughlin, trans., *The Arcades Project* (Belknap Press of Harvard University Press, 1999), p. 40.
95. Esther Leslie, 'On Making-Up and Breaking-Up: *Woman* and *Ware, Craving* and *Corpse* in Walter Benjamin's Arcades Project', *Historical Materialism* 1, no. 1 (1997), pp. 76, 77.
96. *Dior by Dior*, p. 95.
97. Ibid., p. 99.
98. Pochna, *Christian Dior* (English translation), p. 236.
99. I borrow the term 'tellers' of time from Elissa Marder in *Dead Time*.
100. Marder, *Dead Time*, p. 17.
101. Elizabeth Outka, *Consuming Traditions: Modernity, Modernism, and the Commodified Authentic* (Oxford University Press, 2009), p. 9.
102. Ibid.
103. Barbara Vinken, 'Eternity: A Frill on the Dress', *Fashion Theory* 1, no. 1 (1997), p. 61.
104. Benjamin, 'Paris, the Capital of the Nineteenth Century <Exposé of 1935>', p. 8.
105. Ulrich Lehmann, *Tigersprung: Fashion and Modernity* (MIT Press, 2000), p. 230.
106. Though it is legitimate to claim that Dior was a conservative, it is important not to let the years of his fame obscure evidence that he was sympathetically aware, at points in his life, of socialist critiques. Dior flirted with Bolshevism in the 1920s, and revealed his openness when he took a 1931 trip to the USSR. Pochna analyzes his overall political 'dilettantism', suggesting that Dior was more interested in 'participating in history' and 'being one of the crowd' than aligning himself with any specific political ideology. Pochna, *Christian Dior*, original French edition, p. 76. 'L'envie de se trouver la où se passé quelque chose, de marcher parmi la foule, de participer à l'histoire de son temps, d'une façon qui reflète plus le dilettantisme et la curiosité qu'un désir d'engagement.'

107. Benjamin, 'Theses on the Philosophy of History', in Hannah Arendt, ed., *Illuminations* (Schocken, 1968).
108. Benjamin, 'Convolute N: On the Theory of Knowledge, Theory of Progress' (N11, 3), in *The Arcades Project*, p. 476.
109. The grave dangers of working with the gaze turned toward the past are articulated in 'Theses on the Philosophy of History', through Benjamin's famous image of the angel of history, imaged after Paul Klee's *Angelus Novus.*
110. Benjamin, 'Convolute N' (N11, 4), p. 476.
111. Ibid. (N9a, 8), p. 474.
112. Ibid. (N2a, 3), p. 462.
113. Benjamin, 'Theses on the Philosophy of History', p. 262.
114. Benjamin, 'Convolute N' (N11, 2), p. 476.
115. Walter Benjamin, 'The Work of Art in the Age of Mechanical Reproduction', in *Illuminations*, pp. 222–3.
116. Ibid., p. 223.
117. Benjamin, 'The Storyteller: Reflections on the Work of Nikolai Leskov', in *Illuminations*, pp. 83–110.
118. Benjamin, 'The Work of Art', p. 224.
119. Michael P. Steinberg, 'The Collector as Allegorist', in Michael P. Steinberg, ed., *Walter Benjamin and the Demands of History* (Cornell University Press, 1996), p. 96.
120. Brown, *Glamour*, p. 105.
121. Here again, we find a connection to Baudelaire, whose aestheticization of his experience of the fractured subjectivity of modernity is at the root of his best known poetry.
122. Kathy Psomiades, 'Beauty's Body: Gender Ideology and British Aestheticism', *Victorian Studies* 36, no. 1 (1992), p. 45.
123. Ibid., p. 48.
124. Following Psomiades in this argument in terms confined to the modernist period and Walter Benjamin is Eva Geulen, 'Toward a Genealogy of Gender in Walter Benjamin's Writing', *The German Quarterly* 69, no. 2 (1996), pp. 161–80.

CONCLUSION: FASHIONING SELF, REFLECTING AMBIVALENCE

1. Susan B. Kaiser and Karyl Ketchum, 'Consuming Fashion and Flexibility: Metaphor, Cultural Mood, and Materiality', in S. Ratneshwar and David Glen Mick, eds., *Inside Consumption: Consumer Motives, Goals, and Desires* (Routledge, 2005), p. 131.
2. Although ambiguity (which denotes variable meaning) and ambivalence (which denotes a state of being) have different meanings, I follow Fred Davis in stressing their fundamental interrelation. He writes, 'while the multiple meanings of ambiguity may arise from any of a variety of sources—phonemic resemblances, shifting contexts, cultural variability, evasive intent, or euphemism—ambiguity is so regularly the by-product of ambivalence as to be subjectively indistinguishable from it ... Because of ambivalence's "natural" ties to the multiple

meanings that are ambiguity, the opposing pulls one feels over how to dress translate, at the level of perception, into mixed, contradictory, conflicting, or, at the very least, inchoate identity messages.' Fred Davis, *Fashion, Culture, and Identity* (University of Chicago Press, 1992), pp. 21–2.

3. A perfect illustration of the semiotic complexity of the relationship between modernity and femininity is the varied, transnational set of essays contained in *The Modern Girl Around the World: Consumption, Modernity, and Globalization,* edited by the The Modern Girl Around the World Research Group (Duke University Press, 2008). Each of the many essays in this volume foregrounds the tensions and contradictions embodied in the figure of the modern girl, illustrating the global ubiquity of the tendency to embody anxieties about modernity in female figures in the press and popular discourses of various kinds.

4. These include Elizabeth Wilson, *Adorned in Dreams: Fashion and Modernity*, revised edn (Rutgers University Press, 2003), ch. 11; Alexandra Warwick and Dani Cavallero, *Fashioning the Frame: Boundaries, Dress, and the Body* (Berg, 1998); Davis, *Fashion, Culture, and Identity*, pp. 21–99; Anne Boultwood and Robert Jerrard, 'Ambivalence, and the Relation to Fashion and the Body', *Fashion Theory* 4, no. 3 (2000), pp. 301–22; Kaiser and Ketchum, 'Consuming Fashion'; and Caroline Evans, *Fashion at the Edge: Spectacle, Modernity, and Deathliness* (MIT Press, 2003).

5. Boultwood and Jerrard, 'Ambivalence', p. 302.

6. Kaiser and Ketchum, 'Consuming Fashion', p. 135.

7. Ibid., p. 137.

8. The best formulated evidence for the claim that twentieth-century fashion modernized women but produced an attendant conservative impulse born from anxiety, remains Mary Louise Roberts's 'Samson and Delilah Revisited: The Politics of Women's Fashion in 1920s France', *American Historical Review* 98, no. 3 (1993), pp. 657–84. Roberts's careful analysis is useful because it reminds us of the duality or even multiplicity of the effects of modernizing fashion on women's social status.

9. Caroline Evans, 'Jean Patou's American Mannequins: Early Fashion Shows and Modernism', *Modernism/Modernity* 15, no. 2 (2008), p. 261. Also see Evans's article 'Multiple, Movement, Model, Mode: The Mannequin Parade 1900–1929', in Christopher Breward and Caroline Evans, eds., *Fashion and Modernity* (Berg, 2005), pp. 125–45.

10. I am here influenced by The Modern Girl Around the World Research Group, whose formulation of their methodology in the introduction to their edited volume about modern girlhood and globalization includes a discussion of what they call connective comparison. 'Connective comparison,' they write, 'avoids recourse to abstract types and instead focuses on how specific local processes condition each other. It scrutinizes the idea of discrete temporal and geographic locations by positing specific local developments in conversation with those occurring elsewhere in the world . . . Connective comparison is, thus, a method that neither reads peculiar phenomena as deviations from an abstracted "norm" nor one that measures such developments against those postulated by theories of inevitable modernization. Rather, it puts into practice Johannes Fabian's insight that the time of modernity is lateral and simultaneous, not evolutionary or

stagist. Connective comparison avoids establishing temporal priority in a man- ner that privileges linear causality'. *The Modern Girl Around the World*, p. 3–4.

11. Rita Felski, *The Gender of Modernity* (Harvard University Press, 1995), p. 208.

12. Evans, *Fashion at the Edge*, pp. 306–7.

13. See Douglas Mao and Rebecca L. Walkowitz, 'The New Modernist Studies', *PMLA* 123, no. 3 (2008), pp. 737–48.

Bibliography

Alaimo, S. and S. Hekman, eds. (2008), 'Darwin and Feminism: Preliminary Investigations for a Possible Alliance', in *Material Feminisms*, Bloomington: Indiana University Press.

Anderson, L. (2006), 'Autobiography and the Feminist Subject', in E. Rooney, ed., *The Cambridge Companion to Feminist Literary Theory*, Cambridge: Cambridge University Press.

Apter, E. (2010), '"Women's Time" in Theory', *differences*, 21/1, pp. 1–18

Barnard, M. (2002), 'Fashion, Clothing, and Social Revolution', in *Fashion as Communication*, New York: Routledge.

Barthes, R. (1983), *The Fashion System*, Berkeley: University of California Press.

Baudelaire, C. (1965), 'The Painter of Modern Life', in *The Painter of Modern Life and Other Essays*, London: Phaedon.

Benjamin, A. (2006), *Style and Time: Essays on the Politics of Appearance,* Chicago: Northeastern University Press.

Benjamin, W. (1968a), 'Theses on the Philosophy of History', in H. Arendt, ed., *Illuminations*, New York: Schocken.

Benjamin, W. (1968b), 'The Work of Art in the Age of Mechanical Reproduction', in H. Arendt, ed., *Illuminations*, New York: Schocken.

Benjamin, W. (1968c), 'The Storyteller: Reflections on the Work of Nikolai Leskov', in H. Arendt, ed., *Illuminations*, New York: Schocken.

Benjamin, W. (1999), *The Arcades Project*, Cambridge, MA: Belknap Press of Harvard University Press.

Berman, M. (1982), *All that is Solid Melts into Air: The Experience of Modernity*, New York: Simon and Schuster.

Bhabha, H. (1991), '"Race," Time, and the Revision of Modernity', *Oxford Literary Review*, 13/1–2, pp. 193–219.

Birchall, C. (2007), 'Cultural Studies Confidential', *Cultural Studies*, 21/1, pp. 5–21.

Blau, H. (1999), *Nothing in Itself: Complexions of Fashion*, Bloomington: Indiana University Press.

Blumer, H. (1969), 'From Class Differentiation to Collective Selection', *The Sociological Quarterly*, 10/3, pp. 275–91.

Borrelli, L. B. (1997), 'Dressing Up and Talking about It: Fashion Writing in Vogue from 1968 to 1993', *Fashion Theory*, 1/3, pp. 247–59.

Boultwood, A. and R. Jerrard (2000), 'Ambivalence, and the Relation to Fashion and the Body', *Fashion Theory*, 4/3, pp. 301–22.

Bourdieu, P. (1980), 'The Production of Belief: Contribution to an Economy of Symbolic Goods', *Media, Culture, and Society*, 2, pp. 267–89.

Bourdieu, P. (1993a), 'Haute Couture and Haute Culture', in R. Nice, trans., *Sociology in Question*, London: Sage.

Bourdieu, P. (1993b), 'But Who Created the "Creators"?' in R. Nice, trans., *Sociology in Question*, London: Sage.

Bourdieu, P. and Y. Delsaut (1975), 'Le couturier et sa griffe: Contribution à une théorie de la magie', *Actes de la recherche en sciences sociales*, 1/1, pp. 15–21.

Boym, S. (2001), 'From Cured Soldiers to Incurable Romantics: Nostalgia and Progress', in *The Future of Nostalgia*, New York: Basic Book.

Braudy, L. (1986), *The Frenzy of Renown: Fame and its History*, New York: Vintage.

Brassington, D. (1935), 'Noted Designer's Sparkling Styles', *Seattle Post-Intelligencer*, 21 February.

Bratich, J. (2007), 'Popular Secrecy and Occultural Studies', *Cultural Studies*, 21/1, pp. 42–58.

Breward, C. (1995), 'Medieval Period: Fashioning the Body', in *The Culture of Fashion*, Manchester: Manchester University Press.

Breward, C. (1995b), *The Culture of Fashion: A New History of Fashionable Dress*, Manchester: Manchester University Press.

Breward, C. (1999), *The Hidden Consumer: Masculinities, Fashion, and City Life 1860–1914*, Manchester: Manchester University Press.

Brockmeier, J. (2000), 'Autobiographical Time', *Narrative Inquiry*, 10/1, pp. 51–73.

Brickell, C. (2002), 'Through the (New) Looking Glass: Gendered Bodies, Fashion and Resistance in Postwar New Zealand', *Journal of Consumer Culture*, 2/2, pp. 241–69.

Brown, J. (2009), *Glamour in Six Dimensions: Modernism and the Radiance of Form*, Ithaca: Cornell University Press.

Bryson, V. (2007), 'Time', in G. Blakely and V. Bryson, eds., *The Impact of Feminism on Political Concepts and Debates*, Manchester: Manchester University Press.

Buckley, C. and H. Fawcett (2002), *Fashioning the Feminine: Representation and Women's Fashion from the Fin de Siècle to the Present,* London: I. B. Taurus.

Buci-Glucksmann, C. (1986), 'Catastrophic Utopia: The Feminine as Allegory of the Modern', *Representations,* 14, pp. 220–9.

Buci-Glucksmann, C. (1994), *Baroque Reason: The Aesthetics of Modernity,* London: Sage.

Buci-Glucksmann, C. (2003), *Esthétique de l'éphémère,* Paris: Galilée.

Buck-Morss, S. (2002), 'Revolutionary Time: The Vanguard and the Avant-Garde', in H. Geyer-Ryan, P. Koopman and K. Internee, eds., *Perception and Experience in Modernity*, Amsterdam: Rodopi.

Burns, S. (1996), *Inventing the Modern Artist: Art and Culture in Gilded Age America*, New Haven: Yale University Press.

Calefato, P. (2004), *The Dressed Body*, Oxford: Berg.

Casey, E. (1987), 'The World of Nostalgia', *Man and World,* 20/4, pp. 361–84.

Castellant, F. A. (1927), 'La mode est-elle en danger?', *L'Art et la Mode*, 11 June.

Code, L. (1991), *What Can She Know? Feminist Theory and the Construction of Knowledge*, Ithaca: Cornell University Press.

Code, L. (1995), *Rhetorical Spaces: Essays on Gendered Locations*, New York: Routledge.

Cone, M. (1992), *Artists under Vichy: A Case of Prejudice and Persecution*, Princeton, NJ: Princeton University Press.

Conor, L. (2004), *The Spectacular Modern Woman: Feminine Visibility in the 1920s*, Bloomington: Indiana University Press.

Constable, C. (2000), 'Making up the Truth: On Lies, Lipstick, and Friedrich Nietzsche', in S. Bruzzi and P. C. Gibson, eds., *Fashion Cultures: Theories, Explorations, and Analysis*, London: Routledge.

Crosby, C. (1991), *The Ends of History: Victorians and 'the Woman Question'*, New York and London: Routledge.

Curnutt, K. (1999–2000), 'Inside and Outside: Gertrude Stein on Identity, celebrity, and Authenticity', *Journal of Modern Literature, 23/2*, pp. 291–308.

Danahay, M. A. (1993), *A Community of One: Masculine Autobiography and Autonomy in Nineteenth-Century Britain*, Albany: SUNY Press.

Davis, F. (1979), *Yearning for Yesterday: A Sociology of Nostalgia,* New York and London: The Free Press.

Davis, F. (1992), *Fashion, Culture, and Identity*, Chicago: University of Chicago Press.

Davis, M. E. (2006), *Classic Chic: Music, Fashion and Modernism*, Berkeley: University of California Press.

Degoutte, C. (2007), 'Stratégies de marques de la mode: convergence ou divergence des modèles de gestion nationaux dans l'industrie de luxe (1860–2003)?', *Entreprises et Histoire*, 46, pp. 125–42.

de Réthy, E. and J.-L. Perreau (1999), *Monsieur Dior et nous*, Paris: Anthèse.

Derrida, J. and M. Ferraris (2001), *A Taste for the Secret*, Cambridge: Polity Press.

Dettmar, K. J. H. and S. Watts, eds. (2003), *Marketing Modernisms: Self-Promotion, Canonization, and Re-reading*, Ann Arbor: University of Michigan Press.

Deutscher, P. (1997), *Yielding Gender: Feminism, Deconstruction, and the History of Philosophy*, London: Routledge.

Dior, C. (1952), 'Dior', *Modern Woman*, April.

Dior, C. (1954), *Talking about Fashion*, New York: Putnam.

Dior, C. (2003), 'Texte de 1957', *Conférences écrites par Christian Dior*, Paris: Institut français de la mode/Editions du regard.

Dior, C. (2007), *Dior by Dior*, London: V&A Publications.

Douglas, A. (1996), *Terrible Honesty: Mongrel Manhattan in the 1920s*, New York: Farrar, Straus and Giroux.

Dyer, R. (1991), 'A Star is Born and the Construction of Authenticity', in C. Gledhill, ed., *Stardom: Industry of Desire*, London: Routledge.

Entwistle, J. (2000), *The Fashioned Body: Fashion, Dress, and Modern Social Theory*, Cambridge: Policy Press.

Entwistle, J. (2009), *The Aesthetic Economy of Fashion: Markets and Values in Clothing and Modeling*, Oxford: Berg.

'Etre à la mode' (1930), *Vogue*, Paris, April.

'Etude photographique exécutée pour Vogue par le Baron de Meyer lors de sa récente visite a Paris' (1923), *Vogue,* Paris, 12 December.

Evans, C. (1999), 'Masks, Mirrors and Mannequins: Elsa Schiaparelli and the Decentered Subject', *Fashion Theory*, 3/1, pp. 3–32.

Evans, C. (2003), *Fashion at the Edge: Spectacle, Modernity, Deathliness*, New Haven and London: Yale University Press.

Evans, C. (2005), 'Multiple, Movement, Model, Mode: The Fashion Parade 1900–1929', in C. Breward and C. Evans, eds., *Fashion and Modernity*, Oxford: Berg.

Evans, C. (2007), 'Denise Poiret: Muse or Mannequin', in H. Koda and A. Bolton, eds., *Poiret*, New York: Metropolitan Museum of Art.

Evans, C. (2008), 'Jean Patou's American Mannequins: Early Fashion Shows and Modernism', *Modernism/Modernity*, 15/2, pp. 242–63.

Evans, C. and M. Thornton (1991), 'Fashion, Representation, Femininity', *Feminist Review,* 38, pp. 48–66.

'Ex-Fashion Dictator Now Drawing the Dole' (1934), *The Glasgow Record*, 13 August.

Fabian, J. (1983), *Time and the Other: How Anthropology Makes its Object*, New York: Columbia University Press.

'Fashion Becomes News' (1936), *New York Woman*, 1/1, p. 27.

Felski, R. (1995), *The Gender of Modernity*, Cambridge, MA: Harvard University Press.

Felski, R. (2000), *Doing Time: Feminist Theory and Postmodern Culture*, New York: New York University Press.

Felski, R. (2002), 'Telling Time in Feminist Theory', *Tulsa Studies in Women's Literature*, 21/1, pp. 21–7.

Ferguson, H. (2000), *Modernity and Subjectivity: Body, Soul, and Spirit*, Charlottesville: University Press of Virginia.

Ferrero-Regis, T. (2008), "What is in the Name of the Fashion Designer?" (Paper presented at the Art Association of Australia and New Zealand Conference, Brisbane, Australia, 5–6 December), http://eprints.qut.edu.au/18120, accessed 13 February 2011.

Fields, J. (2001), '"Fighting the Corsetless Evil": Shaping Corsets and Culture, 1900–1930', in P. Scranton, ed., *Beauty and Business: Commerce, Gender and Culture in Modern America*, New York: Routledge.

Fine, B. and E. Leopold. (1993), *The World of Consumption*, London: Routledge.

Flanner, J. (1932), 'Profiles: Comet', *The New Yorker*, 18 June.

Foreman, K. (2007), 'The Muse: Mitzah Bricard', *WWD*, 27 February.

Foucault, M. (1970), *The Order of Things: An Archaeology of the Human Sciences*, New York: New York.

Francois, L. (1961), 'Christian Dior', in *Comment un nom devient une griffe,* Paris: Gallimard.

Frisby, D. (1988), *Fragments of Modernity: Theories of Modernity in the Work of Simmel, Kracauer, and Benjamin*, Cambridge: MIT Press.

Fritzsche, P. (2001), 'Specters of History: On Nostalgia, Exile, and Modernity', *American Historical Review*, 106/5, pp. 1588–92.

Fuchs, P. (1921), 'Dans le royaume de la mode', *Le Crapouillot,* 1 April.

Gabriel, B. (2003), 'The Wounds of Memory: Mavis Gallant's "Baum, Gabriel (1935-)" National Trauma, and Postwar French Cinema', *Essays on Canadian Writing*, 80, pp. 189–216.

Gaines, J. (1990), 'Costume and Narrative: How Dress Tells the Woman's Story', in J. Gaines and C. Herzog, eds., *Fabrications: Costume and the Female Body*, London: Routledge.

Gamson, J. (1994), *Claims to Fame: Celebrity in Contemporary America*, Berkeley: University of California Press.

Ganguly, K. (2004), 'Temporality and Postcolonial Critique', in N. Lazarus, ed., *The Cambridge Companion to Postcolonial Literary Studies*, Cambridge: Cambridge University Press.

Gaonkar, D. (1999), 'On Alternative Modernities', *Public Culture*, 11/1, pp. 1–18.

Garelick, R. (2011), 'High Fascism', *New York Times,* 6 March.

Garnier, G. (1984), 'Schiaparelli vue par . . .', in *Hommage à Schiaparelli,* Paris: Ville de Paris, Musée de la mode et du costume.

Geulen, E. (1996), 'Toward a Genealogy of Gender in Walter Benjamin's Writing', *The German Quarterly*, 69/2, pp. 161–80.

Glenn, C. (2004), *Unspoken: The Rhetoric of Silence*, Carbondale: Southern Illinois University Press.

Glucksmann-Buci, C. (1986), 'Catastrophic Utopia: The Feminine as Allegory of the Modern', *Representations*, 14/2, pp. 220–9.

Gibson, P. C. (2001), 'Redressing the Balance: Patriarchy, Postmodernism, and Feminism', in P. C. Gibson and S. Bruzzi, eds., *Fashion Cultures: Theories, Explorations, and Analysis,* London: Routledge.

Gibson, R. (2003), 'Schiaparelli, Surrealism, and the Desk Suit', *Dress,* 30, pp. 48–59.

Gilbert, J. (2007), 'Public Secrets: Being-With in an Age of Perpetual Disclosure', *Cultural Studies*, 21/1, pp. 22–41.

Giroud, F. (1987), *Christian Dior*, New York: Rizzoli.

Gould, C. S. (2005), 'Glamour as an Aesthetic Property of Persons', *Journal of Aesthetics and Art Criticism*, 63/3, p. 237–47.

Gray, R. (1981), 'Time Present and Time Past: The Ground of Autobiography', *Soundings*, 64/1, pp. 52–74.

Green, M. H. (2000), 'From "Diseases of Women" to "Secrets of Women": The Transformation of Gynecological Literature in the Later Middle Ages', *Journal of Medieval and Early Modern Studies*, 30/1, pp. 5–40.

Green, N. L. (2007), *Ready-to-Wear and Ready-to-Work: A Century of Industry and Immigrants in Paris and New York*, Durham, NC: Duke University Press.

Gronberg, T. (1998), *Designs on Modernity: Exhibiting the City in 1920s Paris,* Manchester: Manchester University Press.

Grosz, E. (2004), *Nick of Time: Politics, Evolution, and the Untimely*, Durham, NC: Duke University Press.

Grosz, E., ed. (1999), 'Thinking the New', in *Becomings: Explorations in Time, Memory, and Futures,* Ithaca, NY: Cornell University Press.

Gundle, S. (1999), 'Mapping the Origins of Glamour: Giovanni Boldini, Paris, and the Belle Époque', *Journal of European Studies*, 29, pp. 269–95.

Habermas, J. (1987), *The Philosophical Discourse of Modernity*, Cambridge, MA: MIT Press.

Haraway, D. (1991), 'Situated Knowledges: The Science Question in Feminism and the Privilege of Partial Perspective', in *Simians, Cyborgs, and Women: The Reinvention of Nature*, New York: Routledge.

'Haute Couture' (1934), *Time*, 13 August.

Hayseed, A. (1986), 'Mass Culture as Woman: Modernism's Other', in *After the Great Divide: Modernism, Mass Culture, Postmodernism*, Bloomington: Indiana University Press.

Hebdige, D. (1979), *Subculture: The Meaning of Style*, New York: Methuen.

Helal, K. M. (2004), 'Celebrity, Femininity, Lingerie: Dorothy Parker's Autobiographical Monologues', *Women's Studies*, 33/1, pp. 77–102.

Hillaire, N. (2008), 'Fashion and Modernity in the Light of Modern and Contemporary Art', *Institut français de la mode Research Report*, 9, pp. 8–11.

Jaffe, A. (2005), *Modernism and the Culture of Celebrity*, Cambridge: Cambridge University Press.

Jensen, R. (1993), *Marketing Modernism in Fin-de-Siècle Europe*, Princeton: Princeton University Press.

Jervis, J. (1999), *Transgressing the Modern: Explorations in the Western Experience of Otherness*, Oxford: Blackwell.

Jones, A. R. and P. Stallybrass (2000), *Renaissance Clothing and the Materials of Memory,* Cambridge: Cambridge University Press.

Kaiser, S. (2001), 'Minding Appearances: Style, Truth, and Subjectivity', in J. Entwistle and E. Wilson, eds., *Body Dressing*, Oxford: Berg.

Kaiser, S. and K. Ketchum (2005), 'Consuming Fashion and Flexibility: Metaphor, Cultural Mood, and Materiality', in S. Ratneshwar and D. G. Mick, eds., *Inside Consumption: Consumer Motives, Goals, and Desires*, London: Routledge.

Kawamura, Y. (2005), *Fashion-ology: An Introduction to Fashion Studies*, Oxford: Berg.

Keller, E. F. (1992), *Secrets of Life, Secrets of Death*, New York, Routledge.

Kern, S. (1983), *The Culture of Time and Space 1880–1918*, Cambridge, MA: Harvard University Press.

Kittay, E. F. (1988), 'Woman as Metaphor', *Hypatia*, 3/2, pp. 63–86.

Koda, H. and A. Bolton, eds. (2007), *Poiret*, New York: Metropolitan Museum of Art.

Koselleck, R. (2004), *Futures Past: On the Semantics of Historical Time*, New York: Columbia University Press.

Kwint, M., C. Breward and J. Aynsley, eds. (1999), *Material Memories: Design and Evocation*, Oxford: Berg.

Lacroix, C. (2004), 'Schiaparelli vue par Christian Lacroix: une mode "décapante"', *Le Monde*, March 28–29.

'La Mode' (1923), *La Voix professionnelle*, January.

Laver J. and A de la Haye (1995), 'Early Europe', in *Costume and Fashion: A Concise History*, London: Thames and Hudson.

Lee, R. (1931), 'A King of Fashion Speaks from his St. Helena', *New York Times*, 10 May.

Lehmann, U. (2000), *Tigersprung: Fashion and Modernity*, Cambridge, MA: MIT Press.

'Le roi de la mode parle' (1925), *Le Progrès d'Athènes*, 18 June.

Leslie, E. (1997), 'On Making-Up and Breaking-Up: Woman and Ware, Craving and Corpse in Walter Benjamin's Arcades Project', *Historical Materialism*, 1/1, pp. 66–89.

Lipovetsky, G. (1994), *The Empire of Fashion: Dressing Modern Democracy*, Princeton, NJ: Princeton University Press.

Lloyd, G. (1993), 'The Past: Loss or Eternal Return?' in *Being in Time: Selves and Narrators in Literature and Philosophy*, New York: Routledge.

Lloyd, G. (2002), 'Reason and Progress', in *The Man of Reason: 'Male' and 'Female' in Western Philosophy*, 2nd edn, New York: Routledge.

Loos, A. (1997), 'Ornament and Crime', in *Ornament and Crime: Selected Essays*, California: Ariadne Press.

Mao, D. and R. L. Walkowitz (2008), 'The New Modernist Studies', *PMLA*, 123/3, pp. 737–48.

Marder, E. (2001), *Dead Time: Temporal Disorders in the Wake of Modernity*, Stanford: Stanford University Press.

Marder, E. (2009), 'The Sex of Death and the Maternal Crypt', Parallax, 15/1, p. 5–20.

Marson, S. (1998), 'The Beginning of the End: Time and Identity in the Autobiography of Violette Leduc', *Sites: Journal of Twentieth Century/Contemporary French Studies*, 2/1, pp. 69–87.

Martin, R. and H. Koda (1996), 'Introduction', in *Christian Dior*, New York: Metropolitan Museum of Art.

Meeker, N. (2003), '"All Times are Present to Her": Femininity, Temporality, and Libertinage in Diderot's "Sur les femmes"', *Journal for Early Modern Cultural Studies*, 3/2, pp. 68–100.

Menon, E. K. (2006), *Evil by Design: The Creation and Marketing of the Femme Fatale*, Urbana and Chicago: University of Illinois Press.

Merchant, C. (1980), *The Death of Nature: Women, Ecology, and the Scientific Revolution*, San Francisco: Harper & Row.

Meyers, T. (2001), 'Modernity, Post-Modernity, and the Future Perfect', *New Literary History*, 32, pp. 33–45.

Miller, N. K. (1994), 'Representing Others: Gender and the Subject of Autobiography', *differences*, 6/1, pp. 1–27.

Mule-Dreyfus, F. (2001), *Vichy and the Eternal Feminine: A Contribution to the Political Sociology of Gender*, Durham, NC: Duke University Press.

Murrow, E. (1955), 'Interview with Christian Dior', *Person to Person*, CBS, 11 April.

Natali, M. P. (2000), 'The Politics of Nostalgia: An Essay on Ways of Relating to the Past', PhD diss., University of Chicago.

Negrin, L. (2006), 'Ornament and the Feminine', *Feminist Theory*, 7/2, pp. 219–35.

Osborne, P. (1995), *The Politics of Time: Modernity and Avant-Garde*, London: Verso.

Outka, E. (2009), *Consuming Traditions: Modernity, Modernism, and the Commodified Authentic*, Oxford and New York: Oxford University Press.

Palmer, A. (2009), *Dior,* London: V&A Publications.

'Paul Poiret Dies; Dress Designer, 64' (1944), *New York Times*, 3 May.

Parkins, I. (2008), 'Building a Feminist Theory of Fashion: Karen Barad's Agential Realism', *Australian Feminist Studies*, 23/58, pp. 501–15.

Parkins, I. (2011), 'Early Twentieth-Century Fashion Designer Life Writing', *CLCWeb: Comparative Literature and Culture*, 13/1, pp. 1–10.

Parkins, I. and L. Haworth (2012), 'The Public Time of Private Space in *Dior by Dior*', *Biography*, 35/3.

Partington, A. (1992), 'Popular Fashion and Working-Class Affluence', in J. Ash and E. Wilson, eds., *Chic Thrills: A Fashion Reader*, London: Pandora.

'Paul Poiret, chômeur' (1934), *L' Ordre*, 17 August.

'Paul Poiret Here to Tell of his Art' (1913), *New York Times,* 21 September.

Paxton, R. (2001), *Vichy France: Old Guard and New Order 1940–44*, revised edn, New York: Columbia University Press.

Perreau, C. (1953), *Christian Dior,* Paris: Helpé.

Picardie, J. (2005), *My Mother's Wedding Dress*, New York: Bloomsbury.

Pickering, M. and E. Keightley (2006), 'Modalities of Nostalgia', *Current Sociology*, 54/6, pp. 919–41.

Pike, B. (1976), 'Time in Autobiography', *Comparative Literature*, 28/4, pp. 326–42.

Pike, B. (1976), 'Time in Autobiography', *Comparative Literature*, 28/4, pp. 326–43.

Pochna, M.-F. (1994), *Christian Dior*, Paris: Flammarion.

'Poiret Insists on the Jupe Culotte' (1914), *New York Times*, 15 March.

Poiret, M. (1913), 'Our Girls Puritans, is M. Poiret's Idea', *New York Times*, 14 October.

Poiret, P. (1923), 'Comment se lance une mode—Ce qui Nous dit M. Paul Poiret', *En Attendant*, February.

Poiret, P. (1924), 'Quelques considérations sur la mode', *Le Figaro*, 2 July.

Poiret, P. (1928), *107 Recettes Curiosités Culinaires*, Paris: Henri Jonquieres et Compagnie.

Poiret, P. (1932), 'Paris, sans nuits, s'ennuie', *Paris-Soir*, 14 July.

Poiret, P. (1934), *Art et Phynance*, Paris: Lutetia.

Poiret, P. (1938), 'The Beauties of my Day', *Harper's Bazaar*, 15 September.

Poiret, P. (2009), *King of Fashion*, London: V&A Publications.

'Poiret's New Start: Fashion Leader Saved from Dole' (1934), *Daily Sketch*, London, 16 August.

'Poiret: Une silhouette parisienne' (1912), *Le miroir des modes*, June 1912.

Pochna, M.-F. (1996), *Christian Dior: The Man Who Made the World Look New*, in J. Savvily, trans, New York: Arcade Publishing.

'Pourquoi les accessoires de la mode souffrent-ils d'une crise?' (1923), *Le Petit Parisian*, 13 March.

Psomiades, K. A. (1992), 'Beauty's Body: Gender Ideology and British Aestheticism', *Victorian Studies*, 36/1, pp. 31–52.

Pumphrey, M. (1987), 'The Flapper, the Housewife, and the Making of Modernity', *Cultural Studies*, 1/2, pp. 179–94.

Rainey, L. (1998), *Institutions of Modernism: Literary Elites and Popular Culture*, New Haven: Yale University Press.

Rak, J. (2002), 'Autobiography and Production: The Case of Conrad Black', *International Journal of Canadian Studies*, 25, pp. 149–68.

Reid, C. E. (2006), 'Glamour and the "Fashionable Mind"', *Soundings*, 89/3–4, pp. 301–19.

Roberts, M. L. (1993), 'Samson and Delilah Revisited: The Politics of Women's Fashion in 1920s France', *American Historical Review*, 98/3, pp. 657–84.

Rocamora, A. (2002), 'Le Monde's discours de mode: creating the créateurs', *French Cultural Studies*, 13, pp. 83–98.

Rocamora, A. (2002), 'Fields of Fashion: Critical Insights into Bourdieu's Sociology of Culture', *Journal of Consumer Culture*, 2/3, pp. 341–62.

Rosenman, E. B. (2011), 'Fear of Fashion, or, How the Coquette Got Her Bad Name', in I. Parkins and E. M. Sheehan, eds., *Cultures of Femininity in Modern Fashion*, Lebanon, NH: University Press of New England.

Rosenquist, R. (2009), *Modernism, the Market, and the Institution of the New*, Cambridge: Cambridge University Press.

Saisselin, R. G. (1959), 'From Baudelaire to Christian Dior: The Poetics of Fashion', *The Journal of Aesthetics and Art Criticism*, 18/1, pp. 109–15.

Scanlan, S. (2008), 'Narrating Nostalgia: Modern Literary Homesickness in New York Narratives, 1809–1925', PhD diss., University of Iowa.

'Schiaparelli' (1932), *Harper's Bazaar*, April.

Schiaparelli, E. (2007), *Shocking Life*, London: V&A Publications.

'Schiaparelli Sees Paris Style Mecca' (1940), *New York Times*, 11 December.

Schippers, M. (2007), 'Recovering the Feminine Other: Masculinity, Femininity, and Gender Hegemony', *Theory and Society*, 36/1, pp. 85–102.

Simmel, G. (1997), 'The Metropolis and Modern Life', in D. Frisby and M. Featherstone, eds., *Simmel on Culture*, London: Sage.

Smith, R. (1994), 'Internal Time-Consciousness of Modernism', *Critical Quarterly*, 36/3, pp. 20–9.

Smith, S. (1993). 'The Universal Subject, Female Embodiment, and the Consolidation of Autobiography', in *Subjectivity, Identity, and the Body: Women's Autobiographical Practice in the Twentieth Century*, Bloomington: Indiana University Press.

Smith, S. and J. Watson (1992), 'De/Colonization and the Politics of Discourse in Women's Autobiographical Practices', in S. Smith and J. Watson, eds., *De/Colonizing the Subject: The Politics of Gender in Women's Autobiography*, Minneapolis: University of Minnesota Press.

Solomon-Godeau, A. (1996), 'The Other Side of Venus: The Visual Economy of Feminine Display', in V. De Grazia, ed., *The Sex of Things: Gender and Consumption in Historical Perspective*, Berkeley: University of California Press.

Stallybrass, P. (1993), 'Clothes, Mourning, and the Life of Things', *Yale Review*, 81/2, pp. 183–207.

Stanton, D.C. (1998), 'Autogynography: Is the Subject Different?', in S. Smith and J. Watson, eds., *Women, Autobiography, Theory: A Reader*, Madison: University of Wisconsin Press.

Starobinski, J. (1966), 'The Idea of Nostalgia', *Diogenes*, 14, pp. 81–103.

Steele, V. (1992), 'Chanel in Context', in J. Ash and E. Wilson, eds., *Chic Thrills: A Fashion Reader*, Berkeley: University of California Press.

Steele, V. (1998), *Paris Fashion: A Cultural History*, Oxford: Berg.

Steinberg, M. P. (1996), 'The Collector as Allegorist', in M. P. Steinberg, ed., *Walter Benjamin and the Demands of History*, Ithaca: Cornell University Press.

Stewart, M. L. (2008), *Dressing Modern Frenchwomen: Marketing Haute Couture, 1919–39*, Baltimore: Johns Hopkins University Press.

Strychacz, T. (1993), *Modernism, Mass Culture, and Professionalism*, Cambridge: Cambridge University Press.

Taylor, L. (2005), 'The Work and Function of the Paris Couture Industry during the German Occupation of 1940–1944', *Dress*, 22, pp. 34–44.

Terdiman, R. (1993), *Present Past: Modernity and the Memory Crisis*, Ithaca, NY: Cornell University Press.

Terego, A. (1910), 'Les Opinions de Monsieur Pétrole', *La Grande Revue*, 10 May.

'The Case of "Hair Up Versus Hair Down" is Reopened in Paris' (1938), *Women's Wear Daily*, 11 February.

The Modern Girl Around the World Research Group (2008), *The Modern Girl Around the World: Consumption, Modernity, and Globalization*, Durham, NC: Duke University Press.

'The Paris Dress Parade: As seen by a man' (1932), *Vogue*, London, 14 September.

Tolson, A. (2001), '"Being Yourself": The Pursuit of Authentic Celebrity', *Discourse Studies*, 3/4, pp. 443–57.

Turner, C. (2003), *Marketing Modernism Between the Two World Wars*, Amherst: University of Massachusetts Press.

Troy, N. J. (2003), *Couture Culture: A Study in Modern Fashion*, Cambridge: MIT Press.

Tseëlon, E. (1995), *The Masque of Femininity,* London: Sage.

Tseëlon, E. (2001), 'From Fashion to Masquerade: Toward an Ungendered Paradigm', in J. Entwistle and E. Wilson, eds., *Body Dressing*, Oxford: Berg.

'Une conversation avec un chômeur de marque' (1935), *La Revue, Lausanne*, 2 January.

Veillon, D. (2002), *Fashion Under the Occupation*, trans. M. Kochan, Oxford: Berg.

Vinken, B. (1997), 'Eternity: A Frill on the Dress', *Fashion Theory*, 1/1, pp. 59–67.

Vinken, B. (2005), *Fashion Zeitgeist: Trends and Cycles in the Fashion System*, Oxford: Berg.

Warwick, A. and D. Cavallero (1998), *Fashioning the Frame: Boundaries, Dress, and the Body*, Oxford: Berg.

White, L. (2000), 'Telling More: Secrets, Lies, and History', *History and Theory*, 39, pp. 11–22.

White, P. (1996), *Elsa Schiaparelli: Empress of Paris Fashion*, London: Aurum Press.

Wilson, E. (2003), *Adorned in Dreams: Fashion and Modernity*, revised edn, New Brunswick, NJ: Rutgers University Press.

Wilson, E. (2007), 'A Note on Glamour', *Fashion Theory*, 11/1, pp. 95–107.

Wilson, S. (1989), 'Collaboration in the Fine Arts', in G. Hirschfield and P. Marsh, eds., *Collaboration in France: Politics and Culture during the Nazi Occupation, 1940–1944*, Oxford: Berg.

Witz, A. (2001), 'Georg Simmel and the Masculinity of Modernity', *Journal of Classical Sociology*, 3/1, pp. 353–70.

Witz, A. and B. Marshall (2004), 'The Masculinity of the Social: Toward a Politics of Interrogation', in A. Witz and B. Marshall, eds., *Engendering the Social: Feminist Encounters with Social Theory*, Berkshire: Open University Press.

Wollen, P. (2002), 'The Concept of Fashion in The Arcades Project', *boundary 2*, 30/1, pp. 131–42.

Worth, J. (1914), 'Harmony is the Great Secret', in F. Winterburn, J. Worth and P. Poiret, *Principles of Correct Dress*, New York: Harper and Brothers.

Yankélévitch, V. (1974), *L'irréversible et la nostalgie*, Paris: Flammarion.

Zerilli, L. (1994), *Signifying Woman: Culture and Chaos in Rousseau, Burke, and Mill*, Ithaca: Cornell University Press.

Index